Life of Rev. A. Crooks

*A Wesleyan Methodist Minister who Campaigned
for Temperance and the Abolition of Slavery*

By E. W. Crooks

"Servant of God, well done;
Rest from thy loved employ;
The battle fought, the victory won;
Enter thy Master's joy."

PANTIANOS
CLASSICS

Published by Pantianos Classics

ISBN-13: 978-1-78987-093-0

First published in 1875

Contents

Introductory

The present work is issued to perpetuate the precious memory of Adam Crooks, as well as respond to the general demand of a stricken people. Thrown upon the stage of action when the world of morals was being shaken in Church and State by priests and politicians, who held that the right of American Slavery was not to be questioned, the subject of this memoir, though still in his youth, withstood the baseless claims of this vaunting Goliah.

This early stand for God and humanity started him upon the pathway of independence of thought and action, which characterized all his afterlife.

His sense of honor, his dignified manhood, his fidelity to the truth, his faith in God, his deep piety, his practical common sense, his unflinching fortitude, his tender sympathies, his breadth of thought, his care for the common weal, and his philanthropic spirit made him a natural leader. Men felt like trusting him, and no man ever felt that trust betrayed.

This memoir has been prepared, for the most part, by her whose journey for nearly twenty-two years has been at his side. That her deepest interest has entwined around the objects of his toils and fortunes, it is eminently fitting that to these pages should be given that careful and truthful expression of the facts of history, which her intimacy with him will warrant.

And now that his dust so quietly rests in his hillside home, no one will wonder that she feels deeply bereaved as she still takes up the burden of life, and walks the rough ways of the world all alone. Still anxious for the dear people whom he loved so much and left so soon, with his companions in arms, we know she still prays that each may be loyal to duty, until one by one all may join him again in the Paradise of God.

L. N. S.

TO THE

FAITHFUL SOLDIERS IN THE MORAL CONFLICT; —

HIS ASSOCIATES IN

THIS HOLY WAR: —

TO THOSE

WHO FELL AROUND HIM, AND TO THOSE

WHO SURVIVE, AND UNTO

HIM

TO WHOM WE DEDICATE OUR SABBATHS,

OUR SANCTUARIES, AND OURSELVES, THIS VOLUME IS

FAITHFULLY AND LOVINGLY INSCRIBED.

Life of Rev. Adam Crooks, A. M.

Early History

Adam Crooks was born in Leesville, Carroll County, Ohio, on the 3rd of May, A. D., 1824. He was the son of William and Elizabeth Crooks, and the fourth child of a family of thirteen. His father was a man of the world, but taught his family the strictest honesty and truthfulness. But that blessed gift of Heaven, a godly mother, by her uniform piety and the agency of the Holy Spirit, often awakened in him the most pungent convictions of sin, and led to secret prayer and solemn promises of reformation, but nothing further.

When some fourteen years of age, a singular incident occurred, which was destined, under Divine Providence, to shape his future course. His brother William, some four years his senior, was somewhat skeptical as to the divine origin of Christianity, remarked, in a careless manner, "I do not believe in religion. I believe those who profess it are hypocrites; but if I should ever go to the altar for prayers, I should never leave it until I knew for certain." Although not a Christian himself, yet Adam secretly prayed with all the fervor of his heart that William might be constrained to go to the altar. For he thought his brother's conversion a thing very desirable, it was not an hour until William was most deeply convicted, and at the altar the next evening he found salvation. He became an exemplary Christian, and a devoted minister of the Gospel; and on February 14th, 1847, went up to glory.

From the hour of his brother's conversion, Adam became a secret seeker of personal salvation, frequently praying twenty times a day, but seemingly to no effect; for he thus wandered in darkness for months. But the blessed hour of deliverance came. It was one Spring morning, he was returning from his place of secret prayer, across his father's farm. Just as the sun spread his golden mantle over field and forest, and saluted his eyes, his faith took hold on G-od, and the Sun of righteousness poured in His rays upon the new-born soul. Nor was this light evanescent. It was the incessant dawn of an eternal day. Prayer was almost momentary; spiritual communion was constant; stated hours of prayer were observed, and with his brother William he fasted every Friday. The genuineness of early piety and the conversion of children is illustrated in his conversion, which occurred at the age of fourteen years, and might have been earlier; his convictions and knowledge being equal to it.

The early educational advantages of this prominent Christian worker, like that of many before him, were only medium. Attending school during the

Winters, and working hard on his father's farm, of which he had principal charge from unusually early years, he became inured to hard-handed toil. But he had an insatiable thirst for knowledge; seldom in the house, if only for a few minutes, with hands empty of a book, and often arising before day to master some difficult lesson. When about twenty years of age he spent two Summers at an academy under the auspices of the Presbyterians, some two miles from home.

Among his papers is found a report of his standing while at this school.

"STUDIES.

Arithmetic, English Grammar, Geography, 'Watts on the Mind' and Ancient History.

Absent from Prayers — ...Never.
"" Recitation — ...Never.
Application — ...Excellent.
Improvement — ...Excellent.

REMARKS.

Anything that may he said by us of Mr. Crooks, must be of a commendatory character. His course, while with us, has been that of a gentleman and of a Christian. His talents are good, and his promises of usefulness are flattering.

Jas. Mathews,
A. Swaney, - Instructors

But having been a student through life, he has mastered a thousand lessons to which many a collegian has failed to give his attention. The "divine desire to know" will convert field, or forest, or lake, or landscape, or island, or ocean, or continent into a university.

He united with the Methodist Protestant Church, of which his parents were members, while his brother William joined the Methodist Episcopal Church. He was much the youngest of any in the Church, yet willing thus early to walk alone, so long as it appeared to be the path of duty. Always generous toward other denominations, and willing to point sinners to the Cross at any altar where Christ appeared, he attended religious meetings, far and near, irrespective of denominations. He deeply deplored the want of spirituality among his own people.

When about sixteen years of age, he deeply felt the need of a more thorough Christian experience. He was greatly profited by reading the "Life of William Carvosso," and sought, with ceaseless anxiety, the blessing of entire sanctification. He sought it as distinctly as justification. He trusted fully in Jesus as a Savior from all taint of, and tendency to sin, and realized the speechless joy of complete salvation. This, like conversion, was effected when alone, and free from the pressure of external excitement.

Convinced of the complicity of the Methodist Protestant Church with chattel slavery, it ceased to be a congenial home to one who had nothing in view but God and his glory, and man's well-being. The heart longed for an opportunity to free itself by change of church-relationship. This opportunity was presented when the venerated Edward Smith organized a Wesleyan Methodist Church in his native village, July 25th, 1843. That day Brother Crooks was elected class-leader. This change of church-home, and open antagonism to slavery, no perils nor privations ever caused him to regret.

Early Ministry

His call to the Gospel ministry was an ever-living and ineffaceable conviction. Yet it greatly distressed his mind: First, by fears that it was a fire of his own kindling. Second, by an oppressive sense of his own incapacity; hence, for years) it was the subject of earnest solicitude and prayer. These embarrassments were held in abeyance by the firm purpose to do every duty at whatever cost, and the assurance that God would call to no duty in which he would not, in some way, supply all deficiencies. But his soul found complete rest only in the settled purpose to await and cheerfully conform to the opening of God's providence. And this became the key to his entire subsequent life: to, in all things follow the united leadings of God's providence, Spirit and Word.

The 4th of May, 1844, being just twenty years of age, he accepted license to exhort. Under this, however, he always took a text and preached, as systematized thought was more natural and easy to his type of mind.

August, 1845, he joined the Allegheny Conference, and went as junior preacher to the Erie circuit. Here came a trial to his Christian fidelity. The headquarters of the Erie circuit was Erie city. There was not a white member in the Church, and this feeble colored Church was the only one on this circuit of two preachers. The prospect was forbidding, indeed. The first Sabbath morning in Erie made a deep impression. Thoughts of "Sweet home," and pleasant social position there, and of the intense prejudice against any white man, whose motives, however Christ-like, showed practical sympathy for the then hated colored race. A painful sense of isolation caused tears unbidden to flow - But thoughts of Jesus — the mockings, scourging and cast-off purple, and forsaken in that dreadful "hour of the powers of darkness," dried them all away.

He found them very poor — many of them fugitives from slavery, and very ignorant. He consented to become one of them, to lift them up.. He established a night-school, for their instruction — was earnest in arousing their ambition to become intelligent as well as good. They were very grateful, and thought they never before had found such a friend. His stay among them was brief, as at the expiration of six weeks he was called to Allegheny City, to labor in concert with his brother William, then in the second year of his ministry, boarding with Rev. B. Loughead, who long has been a member of the Allegheny Conference. This became a pleasant and profitable year.

On the following year he went as junior preacher to the Zanesville circuit, in company with Rev. G. Richey, preacher in charge, and now President of the Central Ohio Conference.

Brother Richey, in a funeral discourse preached at Leesville, the home of his boyhood and youth, says: "He was my co-laborer on the Zanesville circuit. My house, during that year, was his principal home. I knew him well and loved him much. Indeed, it was only necessary to know him well in order to love him. He was not only an amiable Christian, but an affable gentleman. He seemed to possess the 'wisdom of the serpent, and harmlessness of the dove.' In morals he had the innocence of the lamb, and the courage of the lion. This year his brother in the flesh, in the Lord, and in the ministry — William — loved more than life itself, was called from earth to heaven.

Call to The South.

"The Allegheny Conference, held at Mesopotamia, Ohio, September, 1847, received an urgent letter from North Carolina, asking for a minister. Every eye seemed to turn to Brother Crooks as the man for that place. After a season of devout, earnest, silent prayer, in which the entire Conference engaged, Brother Crooks arose—his cheeks pale as marble — and said, '*I will go*, sustained by your prayers. *In the name of my Savior I will go* to North Carolina.'"

He has often said, "The question presented itself to me, can you give your life for the cause? I felt that I could, and went." He gave his life when he consented to go.

He was ordained Elder at that Conference, September 21st, one year in advance of the rules, in order to fit him for the work on his mission. His parchment is signed, "T. Guy, President of Conference."

Four years of toil, self-sacrifice, peril and success ensued. By the close of the first year, an opening in Grayson County, Virginia, called for another man. Jarvis C. Bacon responded. The work extended both in Virginia and North Carolina. New doors opened, calls to "Come over and help us," multiplied, and at the expiration of the second year, Jesse McBride took the field already opened, leaving Brother Crooks to go more deeply "into the regions beyond." The history of these years will be given in extracts from letters to the *Wesleyan*, written on that moral battle-field.

More fitting than anything we can present are the following pen pictures drawn by himself, of his journey south, and his labors amid the scenes of slavery with its Bibles and whips and slave-pens.

Circumstances not unfrequently contribute largely in rendering recorded events interesting. The circumstance of my appointed field of labor being in a *slave-holding* State, may give importance to a few notes by the way. It would be in vain to essay to give a description of the deep emotions that thrill the soul when taking the parting hand of an affectionate father, a kind mother, dear brothers and sisters, and friends beloved; when bidding adieu to the hills, valleys, and streamlets, that were the associate of one's juvenile sports, and childish perambulations; the most vivid imagination and nervous language, are utterly inadequate to the task.— Such reflections as these are very natural. Am I looking upon these people the last time? — Shall I ever again meet a father's smile, or have the seal of maternal affection stamped on my cheek? May I ever again drink the sweet waters which flow in the channel of the society of those endeared by the tender ties of consanguinity? With these peculiar feelings and cogitations, on the morning of the 1st of October, I turned my face to go to the far South, to pronounce that Gospel which proclaims *liberty* to the captive, and the *opening* of the prisons to them that are bound.

I must needs go through Zanesville for my books and clothes, (it being my former field of labor.)

On Saturday evening I arrived at Zanesville, was kindly received by brother J. and family. On Sabbath evening spoke a short time from viiith chapter, 9th verse, second Corinthians. In improving the subject, I tried to show that Christ is our example — we must have His spirit if we would be His — it is a spirit to labor, suffer, for the good of man, — we must be willing to sacrifice property; He became poor. Reputation, He made Himself of *no reputation*; and person, He was wounded, bruised? chastised, and all for man, yea, for His enemies. He suffered patiently, suffered not unnecessarily, but in harmony with the will of His Father. Those who do not imitate Him are not Christians, whether individuals or organizations. Dear reader, how much are you willing to sacrifice? How much have you suffered in property, reputation or person, for the good of your race? Wherein have you denied yourself daily? — of what to-day?

I was detained till Thursday, waiting for a boat. As none came, I mounted the stage on Friday morning for M., a town at the juncture of the Muskingum and Ohio rivers, sixty miles below Zanesville. The day was wet, cold and gloomy, and the road rough. But as it followed the river, a person having large individuality, would delight himself in observing the flowing river; its little islands, adorned with the waving willow; the fading foliage bedecking its bank; together with the craggy hills, the rolling forest, the rich fields and green meadows, which variegate every succeeding prospect, Who can witness such a scenery and not mark the footsteps of the power, wisdom and goodness, of Him who bridles the waters, plows their channels, and determines their courses?

I arrived at M. about 9 o'clock, P. M., and not wishing to travel on Sabbath morning, I sought out the residence of Brother P., where I was made very welcome, and was able to feel at home, Brother P. is an efficient agent in the underground railroad. M. is the oldest town in Ohio; it is beautifully situated, built (in some respects) after the eastern style. There are a great many antislavery Methodists in this place, but they do not seem to see the incongruity of coming out of a pro-slavery political party, and remaining in fellowship with a proslavery Church. The Methodist Episcopal friends had their Quarterly Meeting on Saturday morning at 10 o'clock, M. T. Young, Presiding Elder, preached from Matthew xiv: 23. Subject, Private Prayer. In descanting on what we should pray for, he named the prosperity of the Church. On this point he manifested great earnestness, referred them to the past prosperous condition of the M. E. Church, compared it to the stone of prophesy cut out of the mountain, it had rolled on gloriously. That evening I had the happiness to see Ephraim Cutler, the only man living who helped to frame the Constitution of Ohio. He claims the honor of making it a free State; he sat up a whole night to frame arguments to accomplish that object. Honor to his life! When dead, peace to his ashes!

Sabbath, 11 o'clock, A. M., preached in town hall of Harmer, (H. is on the other side of the Muskingum from M.,) from Matthew vi: 9. After meeting, a Mr. S., Presbyterian, accosting me, said I must have the Methodist house that evening. It was obtained for 4 P. M. I spoke from Matthew vi:10. Here I tried to make it appear that the means ordained by Heaven for the establishment of Christ's kingdom were, the preaching of the Gospel, the whole Gospel, the practice of every duty, the right and faithful exercise of discipline, by which every sinner, of whatever kind, would be kept out of the pale of the Church; and those organizations which do not use those means cannot effect the object for which they organize. This was my last Sabbath in Ohio. I then waited (though very impatiently) for a boat, which did not come until Tuesday morning, 11 o'clock. In a very few minutes I was sailing down the beautiful Ohio. The day was wet and cold, a great many passengers, and an amount of vanity displayed, though I was pleased by the order observed.

On Tuesday night we were landed on the Virginia shores, at the mouth of the Great Kanahwa; here again we were detained until Thursday morning for a boat to go to C, sixty miles up this rapid river.

Thursday night got to C. in time to give ourselves to the faithful keeping of Morpheus, at about 1 o'clock, A. M.

Friday took stage for Lewisburgh, one hundred miles from C. After riding about thirty miles over a good road we found ourselves at the base of the Green Briar Mountain. The prospect now becomes indescribably romantic. The traveler seems to be environed at every point of the compass, by great piles of earth, covered with pines, which lift their hundred arms on high, as though they would grasp the clouds, or sweep the sky. The complete symmetry with which these piles are formed, coming to a peak with the order of a pyramid, will strike the admiration of every beholder. I would advise every one who travels this road to visit the Hawk's Nest, a precipice of rock piled on rock, to the height of nine hundred feet. Here you will fancy yourself at the jumping off place. To look down you seem to be lifted far above the earth, the head reels. The country is under very poor cultivation, and the minds of the inhabitants are no better. An old revolutionary soldier, bending beneath the weight of time, and trembling with age, got in to ride a few miles; he stated that they are beginning to raise wheat. (They formerly lived on bear's meat, and pone.) I remarked to the old gentleman, it was a long road from C. to L., one hundred miles, without any towns or villages; he replied, there was no place to put them. We lodged a few hours fifty miles from C, and by 1 o'clock, A. M., was in the stage again.

To-day, Saturday, feelings of deep sorrow, mingled with emotions of profound indignation, swell my bosom, while surveying the fallen and corrupt state of the Churches of our land, while I see them chattelizing humanity, and driving the iron chariot of oppression over her breast, while its massive wheels squeeze hissing streams of blood from the tender cords of her great heart.

Saturday evening arrived at L., where we spent the Sabbath. In the morning I attended meeting at the Methodist Episcopal Church; listened to a sermon from John 1st chapter, 38th verse.— The body of the discourse was very well proportioned, but if I am a judge, the body was all there was of it; I do not think it had any soul.

Monday morning, 1 o'clock, took stage for Fincastle. Our road was over the Allegheny ridge of mountains. The scenery was magnificently sublime. The air is highly salubrious, and the mountaineers are the Goliah's of the land. We had a few hours rest, about 12 o'clock mounted the stage for Lynchburgh. We crossed the range called the Blue Ridge, before day; here the sun rose on us in Old Virginia. The peaks of Otter on the Blue Ridge, are the highest of the Allegheny; being four thousand, two hundred and sixty feet high. A circumstance transpired here worthy of note. A colored woman was put in the stage at F., who said she was on her way to L., a town about thirty miles from F. On being interrogated, she informed us that she had been sold to a negro trader in L., her former master lived in F. She was leaving a husband, a mother, brothers and sisters, and the *grave* of a child. Are not such acts of cruelty enough to make us "sick of humanity, and blush to know ourselves men." She was a member of the Methodist Episcopal Church, and *he*, the man who sold her, of the Episcopalian Christians (by profession) selling God's own image, the purchase of the Savior's death, and the temple of the Holy Ghost, as beasts in market. Oh Shame, where is thy blush! I asked her if she did not mourn the loss of her babe! and the emphasis with which she responded No! made my blood run cold. She continued, I am *glad* it is gone, for it is a stranger to my sorrows.

What a horrible comment, this, upon the cruelties of slavery. The slave-mother's joy begins not like that of other mothers; "when a man is born into the world;" but when her infant is hurried out of existence, and its first faint cry is hushed in the silence of death! Why this perversion of nature? Ah! that mother knows the agonies, the torments, the wasting woes of a life of slavery, and by the bowels of a mother's love, and the yearnings of a mother's pity; she rejoices to know her babe shall never experience the same.

But will God be avenged on such a nation as this? The withering displeasure of heaven can be seen standing out in bold relief upon the whole face of the country. Their soil is rendered sterile by the burning foot of slavery. — Their fields are converted into forests; their *fences*, their *houses* and their *barns*, are dilapidated, and the very air poisoned with the effluvia from the mangled body of humanity which lies bleeding on every plantation. In a word, slavery, like the mighty *incubus*, standing with one foot on the neck of the master, and the other on that of the slave, crushes them physically, intellectually and morally into the very earth, and leaves them — *leaves* them, did I say? No! keeps them there struggling for life.

The evening of October 23d, I found myself at Indiana, having terminated a fatiguing journey of six hundred and fifty miles. I rested till Sabbath; in the evening, preached in the Methodist Episcopal house; I tried to enforce the doctrine of universal love and the duty of doing unto others as we would have them do to us, without reference to class, color or condition, etc. Some of them said "That was just what they always believed." There is much more anti-slavery sentiment in this part of North Carolina than I had supposed. This is owing, in a great measure, to the influence of the society of Friends. It is said the treatment of the slaves is much modified by their presence;and as they are numerous in this community, slavery is seen in its mildest form. It is somewhat amusing too, that I am taken for a Quaker, go wherever I will. I attended their meeting Sabbath morning, after my arrival, and even the Friends themselves, thought I was one. After hearing me preach in the Methodist Episcopal house, some of them asked if I was not a Friend. I went to Toledo last week, lectured on temperance, and there, *again*, I was thought to be a Quaker. This, I suppose, is owing some to the doctrine I inculcate, and partly to my plain coat. Upon the whole, the prospect is pretty encouraging; the hearts of many are open to receive the truth, and by the help of God's grace, I mean to sow the seed of the word, praying that the great head of the Church may give a *large* increase. And now, at the commencement of my labors, let me call upon the whole Church, and every lover of God, and friend of man, to send up their *earnest, faithful, importunate* and prevailing prayers, that Heaven would smile propitiously upon the cause in North Carolina; the good of our common Christianity and common country; the sacred demands of the trembling, weeping, bleeding, perishing slave, and the high and holy claims of the Holy One require it; yea, and future posterity will say, Amen.

It is not a little interesting, and amusing, to trace the rise and progress of the Church, in our state. Dr. Stanton, a Quaker, brought into this country some pamphlets, containing the address delivered by brother E. Smith, in the Sixth Presbyterian Church, in Cincinnati, March 19, 1843. from Rom. xiii, 10, — two thousand of which, were printed at the expense of the Society of Friends. The printer neglecting to state the *office* in which it was printed, Mr. C, the Methodist Episcopal preacher then traveling the Guilford Circuit, (who was silenced by a Conference, held at G. a few weeks ago,) faithfully charged his hearers not to read them, or even suffer them to come into their houses. He stated they contained no truth — were a mass of pernicious errors — were anonymous, and that it was not known where they were printed, etc. But alas! for him that he was not a *Pope*, for then would his *Bull*, have been *Law*. Nor would he have resuscitated these pernicious errors, and buried himself in the tomb he intended for them. What he said served to excite the curiosity of his hearers, which led many of them to procure the interdicted pamphlet, before they went home. They were read with avidity, and circulated with industry. The result was, they aroused the public mind with all the potency of truth, and many who had defended Slavery from the Bible, changed their language, and said, "No Slaveholder can be a Christian!" Brother Smith said, at Conference, he wished himself young, that he might go to N. C, but he was here several years before me, through the agency of his address.

The next circumstance leading the way to secession here, was the division of the Methodist Episcopal Church. The delegate from N. C, to the Southern Convention, was instructed to oppose a split, but he was influenced by the members of said Convention, to vote with the South, — so that the N. C. Conference was voted into the southern division, contrary to her wish, and instructions. I have been told the feelings of this Conference were so exasperated, that it refused to submit, and could not hold its succeeding session. Be that as it may, one thing is certain, it tamely consented for Bishop Andrew to preside at its last session. But when the division took place, the cherished - hopes of many, that the Methodist Episcopal Church would eventually free herself of the sin of making merchandise "of slaves, and souls of men" were completely blasted. Their first expedient was, to join the Northern Division, but soon found it impracticable. They then *Resolved,* (some of those many,) to form a third Church, which they did, and called it the Free Methodist Church.

"Up to this time, they had no knowledge of the existence of the Wesleyan Methodist Connection. By some unknown agency, (perhaps an angel of mercy,) they became apprised of it, — sent for our Discipline, — met in Convention, — read, approved, and adopted it, and at their request, came under the supervision of the Allegheny Conference. Since then, they, like an ocean rock, have stood unmoved, while the mighty waves of opposition have spent their furious power, in vainly essaying to overwhelm them; and blessed be God, they still stand, or rather move forward, despite of all that would oppose. On my arrival, the cry of 'amalgamation, nigger-thief, abolition,' which are synonymous terms here, went careering in frantic alarm through the entire community; but that has measurably subsided. On the whole I cannot complain, other churches have been pretty courteous, in opening their pulpits, especially the Protestant Methodist. Calls for me to preach are numerous — Congregations generally large. I seldom preach without denouncing the peculiar institution; mostly I have slave-holders to hear. We held our first quarterly meeting on the third Saturday and Sabbath in December; congregations full, and very attentive. Sabbath morning at 11 o'clock we had a meeting, weeping and rejoicing time. It was the first communion held by the Wesleyans in North Carolina. The Lord strengthened and comforted our hearts.

"Last Sabbath I read our general rules, to a large and deeply attentive concourse; indeed it was affecting to witness the profound interest with which young and old stood and listened for near two hours; I say stood, for there was room for only about half of the congregation in the house; so that I was under the necessity of standing in the door to be heard by those out as well as inside the house. When I read our rules on slavery, I pledged to prove before I took my seat that the Wesleyans occupy the platform erected by primitive Methodists, on the subject of slavery, viz.: that they made slaveholding a test of membership. To prove which I read from Robert Emeroy's History of Discipline, stating the authority I gave was written by a Methodist Episcopal hand, printed on a Methodist Episcopal press, published under Methodist Episcopal authority, and issued from a Methodist Episcopal Book-room. After having shown from that, the action of the Church, *before, at,* and *after,* its origination, I claimed to have redeemed my pledge, with the clearness of demonstration, and if the countenance is to be taken as an index to the mind, I think the congregation was ready to give a verdict in our favor. We have subscriptions for the erection of three houses of worship; the parcels of ground on which they are to stand, are donated, and I think the prospects for success encouraging. It is the opinion of some of the most intelligent men of North Carolina that she will be a free State before many years; and that in the event of a dissolution of the Union, North Carolina will go with the North. The great spirit of Liberty is beginning to breathe upon the people. If her hosts but rally under her standard, inspired by a generous patriotism and noble philanthropy, resolved with the Spartan soldier, to return '*with* our shields, or *upon* them,' the day is not far distant, when, under the smiles of the *God of Liberty*, her fair tree will shoot its top to the sun, and cast its cooling shades over the oppressed of every land. We believe the death warrant of American slavery is sealed in heaven, and the angel of mercy commissioned to execute it speedily.

"I think I never enjoyed more deep and constant communion with my Savior than since I came to North Carolina. 'Jesus all the day long is my joy and my song.' My daily prayer is,—'O, Lord, revive thy work.' I long to see the pillar of divine glory rise, and the ark, and people of the covenant move forward. May the Lord speed the day.

Dedication of The First Wesleyan Methodist Church In North Carolina.

"With grateful emotions, I take my pen to give the readers of your excellent sheet, a statement of the dedication of the first Wesleyan Methodist Church in North Carolina, with a brief history of our success. Our Second

Quarterly Meeting, which commenced the third Saturday in March, was held in a new house erected for the worship of Almighty God, through whose sovereign clemency, and the liberality of the friends of God and Man, in the community, it was completed. The dedicatory discourse was pronounced from 1st Tim. iii: 15. The use made of the text was, to show *The office of the Church,* — viz. first, to support as a pillar, — secondly, to elevate, — and thirdly, in times of trial, to stay, the truth. This is to be done, first, by not shunning to declare the *whole* counsel of God, — secondly, by the practice of all Christian duty, — thirdly, by the *faithful execution* of Discipline,— and lastly, if need be, meekly and patiently suffering, for so doing.

"The position was taken, that an ecclesiastical organization, not maintaining the *whole* truth, must support some error, there being no neutral ground on any moral question. 'He that is not *for*, is against me. He that gathereth not with me, scattereth abroad,' said Jesus. From all this, the following conclusion is unavoidable: *That it is the imperative duty of Christians, to disconnect themselves from corrupt Churches!* To be in connection with such a Church, is to support it,— to support it is to support error; for it *is the pillar and stay of error*: — hence, the solemn command from Heaven contained in Rev. xviii: 4.

"The Quarterly Conference gave me leave to visit Virginia, some time this Summer, as I received a call from the mother of Presidents to that effect. Sabbath, I spoke to a large, attentive, and deeply affected concourse, from Isaiah xxv, 1: — I am told it had the happy effect of killing much prejudice. We were favored with the acceptable labors of our worthy brother, D. Wilson. He is one of the Spartan-like band, who dared to brave the popular current, and boldly fling the Wesleyan flag to the breeze, and manfully maintain its claims. Brother W. preached on Sabbath night, when the Lord graciously poured out His Spirit and dedicated the house, by filling it with His glory, and one professed to find peace. The meeting was protracted ten days. I have no recollection of having witnessed such displays of the virtue of love divine? to subdue the carnal mind. An incident occurred on Wednesday, worthy of note. A woman, who had belonged to the Methodist Episcopal Church, a number of years, became so deeply convicted at home, she had to quit work — sent for her neighbors to pray for her — said she had been trying, for a long time, to get to Heaven in her own way? but saw she could not succeed. She came to meeting that night, and as I arose to preach, her feelings so completely overcame her, that without regard to the order of the meeting, she arose and made her way to the altar. I invited the mourners forward, stating the Lord would not let me preach that night. The house and surrounding country was soon rendered vocal with the cries of seekers, and the shouts of saints. During the meeting, *twelve* touched by faith, the sceptre of mercy and were at peace. The same number joined. — nine from the world, two from the Primitive Methodists; and one from the Episcopal Methodists. All glory to Him whose wing of love overshadowed us.

"On last Sabbath I formed a class of twelve members in R. county, which promises an abundant increase. Father Briles, who has been a standard-bearer in the Methodist Episcopal Church for about forty years, said, 'we must build a *large* church, — oh! I feel such an interest I could almost build it myself.' An old gentleman, who had seen me but once, rode ten miles to hear me preach, gave us his name. I asked him if he enjoyed the comforts of religion, — he answered satisfactorily. Are you coming from another church? — I inquired. 'No,' said he, 'I never could join in consequence of war and slavery!' There has been *thirty-two* accessions this year. We have raised the walls of a second church. It is not yet covered. Blessed be Israel's Keeper, while watering others, I have felt the refreshing showers of grace in my own soul. I want to be more and more given up to God, — more and more conformed to his likeness every day. The opposition is great, but He that is for us, is greater than all that can be against us. He that binds the mighty deep with sand, saying thus far shalt thou come, and here shall thy proud waves be stayed, has decreed that the wrath of man shall praise him, and the remainder of that wrath he will restrain. I would earnestly call on the readers of this, to join with me in praying for our enemies, and. blessing those who curse us, — remembering the prayer that went up from the cross, Father forgive, they know not what they do. I subscribe myself, the servant of God, and friend of Man.

Opposition.

"I need not say that the opposition to my course is great. My image was tarred and feathered in this town. [Jamestown.] I saw it the next day as I rode by the place. It was leaning up against the fence. Some of my friends are beginning to tremble for my personal safety; but my trust is in the Friend of the poor, the Deliverer of the oppressed.

"The law is very strict with regard to the circulation of papers, etc. Efforts have been made to put those laws into execution on me, but failed. Meeting-houses are generally closed against me? unless it is the Friend's, I have received upwards of fifty members. We now number between ninety and one hundred. I expect to visit Grayson county, Va., in a few weeks.

"I will tell you a little about the pious slaveholders. One man, a member of the Presbyterian Church, said he would shoot his slaves before they should be free. (See how these Christians (?) — love Slavery.) A Methodist preacher tied up his slave, whipped him a while, and then prayed for him; then whipped and prayed for him, whipping and praying alternately. (His name is Lumsden.) Another by the name of St. Clair took his wife and child with him around his circuit, and his slave girl must frequently run through the mud and cold barefoot, in the Winter. Another instance of cruelty: A slave-trader was passing through this county last Winter with a drove of negroes. One of them, (a man,) got an axe and cut his hand; several licks drove the axe through it, thus rendering it useless, doubtless, for ever. For this he was beaten and kicked without mercy. These things transpire where slavery exists in its mildest form, and if this is its little finger, what are its untold horrors? It seems to me I hate slavery more every day.

"Let the note of '*The Clarion*' wax louder and louder; and as the walls of Jericho fell by the sounding of rams' horns, so by the proclamation of the truth lay the walls of slavery to their foundations.

"As I write on business, I would say for the satisfaction of our Zion, and in Reform generally, that the state of our work, in these parts, is encouraging. Our Third Quarterly Meeting was held last Saturday and Sabbath. We had a 'feast of fat things.' Two joined. One was Wm. Anderson, a licensed preacher from the Primitive Methodists, the other from the Methodist Episcopal Church. The meeting was held at Flint Hill School-house, where a Church of twenty-three members has been recently formed, and trustees elected prospectively, I think the circuit is in the most prosperous condition it has experienced since its formation. We number about one hundred members, fifty-eight of whom have united this year. The harvest is great, but the laborers are few. My exertions have been more than my physical abilities justify, and yet calls for service are multiplying. Some think there is a field for *two* or *three* active men.

"I propose visiting Virginia next week, and may, perhaps, stay a month. If I succeed in forming a circuit, or mission, in that part, (Grayson county,) of the *Old Dominion*, it will greatly advance the cause here, by having two fields sufficiently adjacent, to enable the preachers to visit and assist each other in holding meetings, &c.

Visit to Virginia

On the morning of the 17th of June, I set out to plant the standard of *reform*, on the tops of the mountains of Grayson County, Virginia. It is one hundred miles from this. The journey was somewhat lonely, having no company, but it is good at times to be alone. I passed at the base of Mount Ararat, or the pilot mountain. This is North Carolina's greatest natural curiosity. It is not attached to any chain of mountains— is near a mile in height, and on its brow, is a stupendous rock, rising nearly perpendicular to the height of three hundred feet. It is a matter of surprise to look to the tops of the loftiest peaks which seem to touch the sky; and find them under cultivation. The daring mountaineer builds his house where the thunder's fiery bolt leaps in sportive vengeance from brow to brow. The evening of the next day found me comfortably seated in the very hospitable residence of Isaac Moore. I need scarcely say the sparkling eye, beaming countenance, and warm embrace of the old veteran for truth, almost made me forget the fatigue of my journey. I here obtained the following information, viz: When the question of the division of the Methodist Episcopal Church was pending, the preacher in charge of Grayson Circuit gave the members liberty to vote to which party North or South, they wished to belong. The Presiding Elder on hearing this, and that many were opposed to the separation, issued his '*bull*' interdicting such procedure, thereby disfranchising those who had not voted. I am not sure that such a course is in strict accordance with 'Neither be ye lords over God's heritage.' It produced a shock from which many never recovered.

"A goodly number believing that *slavery* was the great wedge that split the Church, resolved to be disconnected from all Church organization until they found one free from the wedge of gold and Babylonish garment. The majority of the Hopewell Church took this stand. Here I organized a Wesleyan Church, first numbering eight members. During the next week, there were six accessions; so that when I left it numbered fourteen members, one of whom, (Isaac Moore) is an Elder. During my stay which was sixteen days, the spirit of the Lord was poured upon us, the Church was revived, and six professed to have found peace in believing. To God be all the praise.

"I am much pleased with this people. Their hearts, houses, and purses are open. Indeed, their kindness borders on enthusiasm. But the best of all is, they are full of faith and the Holy Ghost. A preacher is asked for the coming year. This will be a pleasant field in which to operate. My faith is strong that a glorious harvest may be reaped from these mountains.

"We held our fourth Quarterly Meeting, commencing on the fourth Saturday of July. I was under the necessity of leaving on the Tuesday morning following. At that time five were hopefully converted, and twenty-one had joined: ten from the world, and eleven from other Churches. Bless God, the bright rainbow of promise still spans our horizon. At the commencement of the year, there were four Churches, and forty members in North Carolina.

At present there are eight Churches; and including Virginia, one hundred and forty members. We have an increase of one hundred. I calculated when I came, if we held our own the first year, we would do well; but instead of the waves of opposition beating us back, the Lord has more than trebled our number. May we not join with the Psalmist?— and say, 'By this I know that thou favorest us, because our enemies do not triumph over us.'"

"As you are reappointed to the editorship of our' Church organ, and I to my previous field in Carolina, I am happy in the anticipation of extending my acquaintance with *you* as an editor; and while I return you my hearty thanks, for former indulgence extended to a young correspondent, I would beg the continuance in future of the same *indulgence* promising to aim at improvement,

"Brother Bacon and myself left our friends on the morning of the 2nd of October, to go to our respective fields; *his* in Grayson County, Virginia, *mine* in Guilford, North Carolina. We came by private conveyance, and found it much more pleasant and less expensive than by public; although not so expeditious. After having contended against hills, mountains and distances for fifteen days, on the evening of the 17th of the above written month, we had the gratification of being seated around the familiar hearth of the hospitable residence of my good friend Richard Mendenhall, in Jamestown. The same evening we visited our worthy brother John Sherwood, (also of Jamestown,) and found him over his *press, laudably employed* in printing *Free-soil Tickets.* The following Saturday, we commenced our first Quarterly Meeting (in the first Wesleyan Methodist church built in the State,) and protracted it six days. The congregations were large and deeply attentive. Brother Bacon preached with great power and acceptability. While breaking the bread of life to others, his own soul feasted on the rich blessings of the Gospel. During the progress of the meeting, the spirit of the Lord was graciously poured upon the people; ten professed to obtain peace in believing, and seven joined. On the next Saturday, we proceeded to Sandy Ridge, Here we held a few days' meeting, at which we were favored with the presence and labors of our good brother Amos Moore, from Virginia. The meeting resulted in the hopeful conversion of five, and addition of seven to the Church. To God be all the glory. In a sermon preached on Monday from John xv: 5, — "For without me ye can do nothing," Brother Bacon, in a very lucid *light*, showed up the grand *inconsistency* in which those involve themselves who say of a practice it is sinful, and yet claim that it is proper to acknowledge the Christian character of persons living in the habitual indulgence of that sinful practice. It was a most happy effort; which with his other labors of love here, will not be soon forgotten by us. While he was here, which was thirteen days, he delivered fourteen sermons which were crowned with fifteen *conversions* and fourteen *accessions.* I think the prospects for our future success good; and that we may bless God and take courage."

The Camp-Meeting.

"**With** grateful emotions, I lift my pen to inform the friends of Zion of what great things the Lord has done for us, that we may be thankfully glad. In harmony with the expressed wishes of our third Quarterly Conference, we appointed a Camp-meeting to be held at Union Meeting House, Guilford County, in conjunction with our fourth Quarterly Meeting.

"In a little time there appeared many prophets in the land, who were Wroth, and mocked the Wesleyans, saying, 'What do these feeble Wesleyans? Will they fortify themselves? Will they sacrifice? Will they make an end in a day? Even that which they build if a fox go up, he shall even break down their stone wall.'

"But we prayed to our God, (for we were despised) and built our tents, and all the tents were formed together unto the half thereof, for the people had a mind to work. Our meeting was to commence on Friday evening, 10th of August, at candle-lighting. By sundown, Brothers J. C. Bacon, Amos Moore, from Virginia, and myself arrived at the place of our feast of Tabernacles; found a goodly number assembled for Divine worship. Brother Bacon preached to an attentive and deeply affected congregation. Saturday 11, A. M., I tried to preach oil the subject of prayer. At the conclusion, the congregation, by rising to their feet, pledged to pray for a glorious revival during the meeting.

"Five, P. M., the rules for the government of the Meeting were read, and the entire congregation, and all succeeding ones, appointed a committee to see that they were strictly observed; (and I must give honor to whom honor is due.) So faithful were they in the discharge of their official duties that I had no cause to reprove an individual during the whole meeting. This was most agreeable. At candlelight, Brother Bacon delivered a solemn discourse from 2nd Peter, iii and 9, 'The Lord is not slack,' &c., to a serious congregation, after which the good work begun. A number came for. ward for prayers, and some professed to obtain mercy in believing. The meeting increased in interest as it progressed. More or less present for prayers every opportunity. The Angel of Conviction and voice of pardon went from the stand to the tents, from the tents to the houses, and from the houses to the fields and gold mines. What was it but heaven in miniature? — for the voices of old and young, male and female, fathers and mothers, husbands and wives, parents and children, neighbors and friends, to go up in bursts of hallelujah to God and the Lamb, Sweet was our camp-meeting, which lasted from the evening of the 10th till the morning of the 20th inst, during which about one hundred and fifty professed to be converted and seventy-six joined.

This was the best meeting I have ever attended, It was characterized throughout by large and attentive congregations, by far the best order I have ever seen at camp-meetings, deep and general convictions and clear and numerous conversions.— The conclusion was awfully impressive. A people about to part who will not all meet again in time! — The congregation assembled at the stand. Brother Bacon delivered a benedictary from Thessalonians. Brother Moore followed in some feeling appeals. The congregation in tears. The writer occupied a few minutes in returning his compliments to the audience for their good conduct through the meeting, to brothers Bacon and Moore for their attendance and labors at the meeting, and thanks to God for the out-pouring of his Spirit on the meeting, made allusion to Brother Bacon's trial which was to come in a few days, requested the audience to acknowledge their obligations to the brethren from Virginia, by promising to pray for them, which they almost unanimously did, with great feeling; then forming a procession, the preachers in advance, marched around in front of the tents, singing an appropriate hymn. The preachers halted at a specified spot, and received the hand of, and pronounced their blessing on all and parted, to meet not again, till we pass the portals of death, when we hope to strike glad hands and tune our harps to immortal songs, in the sweet grove of heaven, no more to sigh nor shed a tear, no more to suffer pain or fear, but sing anthems of praise, and doxologies, glory to God and the Lamb. Amen. It is reserved for the light of eternity and disclosures of judgment alone, to reveal the good done at the first Wesleyan Methodist Campmeeting, held in

North Carolina, but I think we may safely conclude that the gospel has been preached, sinners have been convicted, mourners have been comforted, believers strengthened, the cause of reform advanced prejudice crucified, (died a most ignominious death,) Christ to some extent has seen of the travail of his soul and is satisfied, pious intelligence gratified, and God's name glorified. The cause has been prosperous from its commencement. The increase of its membership the first year from forty to one hundred and forty, including fourteen who joined in Virginia last Fall, when brother Bacon took charge of Grayson Circuit. It reduced the Guilford Charge fourteen, leaving one hundred and twenty-six. There has been an increase this year of one hundred and forty-nine; so that, at this time, there are two hundred and seventy-five members on Guilford Circuit. Brother Bacon's Charge, last Fall numbered eighteen. It has increased to one hundred and eleven; so that the Wesleyans in the South, two years ago, counted forty, all told, enjoying the labors of one man the first, and but two the second year, now number three hundred and eighty-six, giving an increase of three hundred and forty-six. What now becomes of the objection that we can do no good in the South? Echo answers, what! And this is our infancy, while the Herods of the South have been trying to murder us» Blessed be the Most High, the Wesleyan Ship still bears up against wind and tide.

"I know I do not write with the feelings of a proud boaster, or unkindness for such as oppose our progress, but with sentiments of the greatest respect for all men, and of the most profound gratitude to God, the God in whom David trusted? when he encountered Goliath of Gath. And I write for the purpose of convincing our foes, that they have judged us wrongly, and treated us accordingly; and of inspiring in our friends a confidence, which the correctness of our principles, the rectitude of our procedure, the holiness of our cause, and the certainty of its triumph, through the omnipotence of truth, would warrant, and courage in proportion to that confidence; that they may lift their standard anew, unfurl its bright banner along the sky, with this glorious motto written in blazing characters of Love, glowing on its ample folds, ' Glory to God in the highest, on earth peace, and good will to man.' That, under Jesus, the Captain of our Salvation, we may travel to certain victory, with the panoply of heaven to cover, and glory imperishable to crown us."

Trouble

"It is among the probabilities that the readers of your luminous periodical begin to inquire, 'What has become of our missionary at the South? Is he dead? Has he left his post? Why does he not write?' &c. He is yet at his post. His reasons for not writing sooner are part for want of matter, and part, perhaps, from neglect. I will take liberty to say something of Guilford Circuit, under the zealous and very efficient labors of brother Mc Bride. It is, and has been, in a very prosperous state. During this Conference year, quite a number have professed to obtain peace in believing, and seventy-four have joined the Church. The prospects for a rich harvest this year are flattering. The heart and hands of its pastor are full of hope and of work.

"A few words relative to the mission, and only a few. As I accompanied brother McBride in his first visit round the Circuit, I did not strike out till the first of January. I have not as yet organized any Churches but expect to soon. There are six appointments which we will call regular, and several incidental. The extremes are about eighty miles apart.

"I am extending my operations Southward. Numerous are the misrepresentations; the opposition is violent, and some threats are being made. I will give you an instance: — On the evening of the 11th instant I preached in Montgomery county. After the benediction, a couple of notes were given me. One signed by B. W. Simmons, stated that the writer had just returned from the courts of Montgomery and Stanly counties, and was requested to say to Die by many citizens of those counties that should I attempt to preach at or near Lane's Chapel, in Montgomery county, my person would be in danger, as it was understood in those counties that I am an Abolitionist and Free-soiler. The other, written by the same hand and signed "Many Citizens of the counties of Montgomery and Stanly," reads as follows:

Rev. Mr. Crooks: Sir —

"I have heard that you are out preaching the True Wesleyan doctrines. I doubt it not, though am fully unformed that you are acting behind the curtain — a "wolf in sheep's clothing" — that you are preying upon the minds of the weak and innocent, and inducing them to believe that slaveholding is not only an oppression to the slaves, but to all those who do not hold slaves. The slaves hereabout are in much better condition than their masters or other citizens! Your doctrine, if carried out, would bring down vengeance upon the heads of your followers by amalgamation and otherwise.

"Our different denominations here are at peace with and among themselves. We do not believe you to be sound , but conscientiously believe you to be worse than a traitor. We are in hopes you will return from whence you came, or you will be dealt with according to the dictates of our consciences.'"

"The above needs no comment. Suffice it to say that by it we are reminded of the charge preferred against our Savior, of casting out devils by Beelzebub. In harmony with the wishes of many in that community, I left another appointment. The language of my heart is, 'The Lord is my light and my salvation; who shall I fear?' 'The Lord God is a sun and shield.'" Truth is mighty and must prevail, though its enemies may triumph for a little season.

"My earnest prayer is that the Great Head of the Church may guide us unto truth. Brother McBride and myself start for Virginia next Monday, to brother Bacon's trial, which comes on the first of April, and his third Quarterly meeting, which commences the first Saturday of April. Your readers will be advised of the result of the trial as soon as practicable.

In Bonds

"A few days since brother McBride advised your readers of his arrest and my indictment. Another step has been taken.

"As the writer left the pulpit, the second Sabbath of this month, he was introduced to two men, one of whom informed him that he must consider himself his prisoner, until he gave security in one thousand dollars for his appearance at the Superior Court of Forsyth county, on the second Monday after the fourth Monday of September next. Though in a community where my acquaintance is limited, the Lord raised up friends who gave bonds for my forthcoming at the above written time and place.

"The charge is **Misdemeanor**. I do not know what is the specification — I presume it is for being in company when brother McBride gave the '*Ten Commandments*' to the little girl. What the sequel of these things will be, is for time, the great advocate and publisher of truth to tell. It will do to say, I have labored to live in all good conscience before God until this day. This being the case, I am ' careful for nothing, but in all things make my request unto God.' Thanks to his name, my mind has been kept in perfect peace. We may be condemned by wicked men, our backs given to the scourge, our joints to the pillory, and our persons to a gloomy cell, and it matters but little, it matters nothing — prisons would palaces prove, for Jesus would dwell with us there. Let our destiny be what it may, the bonds of our habitations be where they may, the cause of God will be advanced. The wrath of man shall praise Him. Let the potsherds of the earth strive with the potsherds of the earth; but let not man contend with his Maker. The Psalmists prays, 'let not man prevail.' But shall man prevail? What says reason? Reason answers. Not until he clothe himself in thunder, and make the lightning his girdle; till he wear the sun for a crown, the moon for a breastplate; the stars costly jewels encircling his brow, and the rainbow as his phylactery; not until his ipsedixit cause the immoveable pillars and imperishable foundations of the throne of the universe to crumble, and his breath extinguish the fires of immortality which glow in the bosom of Diety.

"You have been advised of our arrest under charge of Misdemeanor, for giving the '**Ten Commandments**' to a little girl in Liberty, a village on the suburbs of Salem, the capital of Forsyth county.

"To answer the above charge, accompanied by Bro. Bacon, Bro. McBride and the writer made our way to Salem Forsyth county, on the 7th inst. This is a Moravian town of a population of perhaps fifteen hundred — rather a beautiful place for this country. The inhabitants are generally of Dutch descent. Though the Moravians, and even this Church in Salem, were once opposed to the peculiar institution of the South, many members of Salem Church are slave-holders. We had been in the place but a short time ere the news took the wings of electricity, and flew through the entire town, 'The preachers have come I! The abolitionists are here!!!' Great was the excitement among the people. Some said, 'They ought to be lynched!' others, 'They ought to be hung!' and other some, 'No attorney ought to appear for them,' &c, &c.

"Perhaps it would be interesting to the reader to have an introduction to his Honor, the judge who presided, and the lawyers who plead at the trial.

"The judge (Manly) is of medium size, elegant form, slightly round-shouldered, perhaps about forty-five years of age, bright keen eyes, large intellectual faculties, has great self-possession, and presides with dignity. From his decisions and charges to the jury, &c, the reader is left to infer his sense of justice.

"Messrs. Gilmer and Waddell were employed on the part of the State; the prosecuting attorney, Mr. Pondeqter, did nothing but assist in managing.

"The defendants employed two attorneys — Messrs Morehead and Mendenhall — the largest slave-holders in Guilford county. Mr. Morehead is brother to Ex-Governor Morehead, of N. C, is rising six feet in height, a very giant-like man; a full brain, gigantic mind, great courage, and is said to be the best judge of law in the State.

"Mr. Mendenhall is a little over six feet, well proportioned, very straight, has a round, high head, light auburn hair, mechanical and intellectual powers large; is a good reasoner, and quite gentle manly in his manners.

The Indictment

"Contains two specifications. The first charges 'Jesse McBride and Adam Crooks' of, with force and arms, knowingly, wickedly and unlawfully, with intention to excite insurrection, conspiracy, and resistance in the slaves or free negroes and persons of color within the State, bringing into the State with intent to circulate, a printed pamphlet named and styled the 'Ten Commandments,' the evident tendency of which pamphlet would be and is to excite insurrection, conspiracy and resistance in the slaves or free negroes and persons of color within the State, containing, with others, the following incendiary clauses: (Here are inserted some extracts from the pamphlet) Contrary to Act of Assembly, &c....and against the peace and dignity of the State.

"The second specification charges the said 'Jesse McBride and Adam Crooks' of, with force and arm; wickedly, seditiously, knowingly and intentionally circulating said pamphlet within the State, with an intent to incite insurrection, conspiracy and resistance in the slaves or free negroes and persons of color within the State; which pamphlet, with other seditious teachings and doctrines, contains the following: (Then follow various extracts from the pamphlet) which taken separately, or with the balance and other parts, have an evident tendency to excite, &c.....against the Act of Assembly, &c., and against the peace and dignity of the State.

Witnesses

"On the part of the State (the defendants had no witnesses) sworn and testify the following:

Washington Kenedy. That defendants stayed overnight at my house in Liberty. I left early in the morning; returned in the evening and found the pamphlet at my house. They behaved like ministers.

Lora Kenedy. — McBride gave me the pamphlet in the absence of Crooks. He said nothing to me when he gave it. I think this is the one he gave me; I put no mark on it by which to distinguish it from any other pamphlet of the same name. I go to Sabbath School; there, are no colored persons at school or at home.

Just here, by permission from the Judge, Waddell read the pamphlet in open court. This was done to identify it.

"Mr. Shore. — 'I saw this book at my house. I do not know who brought it. I did not read it or mark it. James Kenedy came to my house one morning and got it. I think this is the same.

"James W. Kenedy. — I saw McBride give a little book to my sister Lora. I was in the yard. Crooks was not in the house. My father sent me to Mr. Shore's after it. I brought it to Belo's store.

"Edward Belo. — I got this book of James W. Kenedy. It is the same; I put my name on it.

"Henry Marshall.— I heard McBride preach at ——. He said he was not in favor of amalgamation or insurrection; was opposed to war of all kinds; would not have the slaves take swords and guns and murder their masters; he was the friend both of the slave and his master. And he invited us to come to his trial at Salem; he was indicted for giving a little white girl the 'Ten Commandments.'

"David Idle. — Never had got a book, pamphlet, or tract from either McBride or Crooks.

"Smith's testimony about the same as Marshall's.

"George Fulk knew nothing definite.

"Newel Sapp.— Heard McBride say he would preach the truth independently, and Crooks that he would suffer his right arm to be cut off rather than with-hold the truth.

"Witnesses through; go to dinner; return; now pleading commences.

Mr. Morehead

"In behalf of the defendants, commenced his luminous plea by raising the following point of law. Though the indictment charges us with Misdemeanor, the statute makes it a Felony. Now in misdemeanors all are principals; but this is one of those felonies which admits of accessories. On this ground I demand an acquittal of Crooks. In order to convict him as an accessory, you must not only prove that he was in company at the time the pamphlet was given, but also that he was employed in advising or assisting to give it; but the very contrary is proven. This is necessary to make him an accessory, but he is charged of being a principal. But, gentlemen of the jury, the State has made a complete failure in point of sufficient evidence to convict McBride. It has not been proven that the pamphlet was brought into the State by McBride, so that it is impossible to convict him on the first charge.

"I now institute a question. It is this: — What constitutes a violation of the Act? I maintain the pamphlet must have been given with a wicked *intent.* If this is not so, then the lawyers, etc., who have been handing this pamphlet to and fro to each other are every one subject to indictment. The jury cannot convict McBride, unless it is in testimony that he gave it with an *intent* to bring about the evils which the law is intended to prevent. To prove this I refer you to the very familiar case of the law in England as to blood-letting. The law required that every man who let blood in the streets of London, should be hung. Now. though the design of the law is plain, that it was to prevent murder which so much prevailed in that populous city, yet there were actually three physicians hung for letting blood in the streets in order to save the lives of persons who were thrown from their carriages. This led to a change of the law, so that it required a compound offence, or the overt act with a criminal intent, to violate that law. I hold that this case is precisely parallel. Now, what is the evidence that McBride gave the pamphlet with a wicked intent? It was not given to a child whose parents held slaves, or where there were slaves. Lora Kenedy did not go to school where there were slaves; no slaves or colored persons about. McBride did not advise Lora to make an improper use of it.

"But again: if the pamphlet is an exposition of the 'Ten Commandments' then, sirs, the defendants are innocent. All Churches have an absolute right to publish their sentiments to the world. The pamphlet is not addressed to slaves, but their masters and freemen. (Here the speaker's manner grew quite animated.) The Constitution of the United States, and of this State, secures to every man the right to worship Almighty God according to the dictates of his own conscience. All the Churches but one of which I have any knowledge are, or profess to be opposed to slave-dealing — some more, some less, between the two extremes. Why tolerate all others and proscribe this? He showed, in a strong and happy light peculiar to himself, the glorious advantages of free discussion; said it had saved our necks from the galling yoke of the Church of Rome. Without free discussion we have no *Protestant Church*; we have no *America.*

"The 'Ten Commandments' is innocent in a political point of view. The liberty of speech and of the press are and ought to be tolerated. Upon this proposition the speaker mesmerized the tremendous concourse who were listening with mouth and ears. (Brother McBride at my side, whispered, 'What a pity he is not a preacher.')

"Mr. M. said witnesses were brought as a kind of key to show the intent of the circulation of the pamphlet, and they all show Mr. McBride to be an innocent and prudent man. Every man is an abolitionist who dare say one word about slavery. I have been called an abolitionist because I dared present a Quaker petition to the Legislature of this State, though every man is sworn to present every petition sent him. Slavery is a question we have a perfect right to discuss. Strange, indeed, if we dare not speak our sentiments. Not one of these men had at any time conversed with slaves in a low, sneaking way. Mr. M.'s speech occupied about an hour.

Mr. Gilmer

"Said he did not arise out of antipathy to the defendants, but from a sense of duty, &c. Said we had a right to speak of slavery privately, but never in the presence of slaves; that "knowingly" made the design of the law obvious; that Post Masters might hand out an anti-slavery document ignorantly, but the design of the law is to prohibit any and all circulation of anti-slavery publications, either among white or colored persons; that the law was established just after the Southampton insurrection, and was made with great care and caution; that these men certainly brought the 'Ten Commandments' into the State. McBride was recently from the State of Ohio, and the fact that he had it in his possession was legal evidence that he brought it into the State. A man found in possession of stolen goods was in law considered the thief, until he showed how he came by them. So, unless they show how they got this book, they must be considered the guilty persons.

"But it has been argued that the pamphlet was not given with an evil *intent.* The law supposes a man to intend all that may legitimately flow from his conduct. Look at the manner in which the pamphlet was given the child. That he did not say *one word* to her shows clearly his intentions in giving her the book. He did not ask her to read it when he gave it to her, nor did he on his return, at the time of giving the pamphlet to the other children, say, "Lora, have you read your little book? — how do you like it?" or anything of the kind. No! — but in a sneaking and sly way, when all were out but the little girl, slips to his trunk, and hands her this little book. Crooks, in order that he might appear innocent, stepped out of the house. No doubt but he was knowing and consentive to It all, and hence accessory. The fact of their having two buggies and separate trunks does not clear him. They travel together; what one does the other agrees to. (With great emphasis.) McBride says he will go ahead independently, law or no law. Crooks says he will suffer his right arm to be cut off before he will give up circulating such pamphlets,

"The speaker, rising in feeling, spoke of the dreadful consequences of circulating such incendiary publications; of McBride's preaching, said it would bring on insurrection. Knives, guns, swords, burning houses, cruelties and barbarities, were largely and fearfully described. Spoke about forty-five minutes.

Mr. H. Waddell

"Said — I have often stood in defence of criminals, but never felt so awfully as I do at this time. I am not defending one life, but thousands of lives. I am pleading for my country, for the security and safety of our wives and children The northern people are the last men to teach us morals on the slavery question, since many of them have got rick by selling their slaves. The abolition of slavery has been put off by Northern fanatics. I have heard a Rev. Mr. McDonnell give a full description of the Southampton insurrection a day or two since. He witnessed this horrible scene; at least he saw mothers and innocent babes lying in their blood, exposed to the flies, too numerous to bury. I think, said Mr. W., Nat Turner must have been a Wesleyan, and felt he was commissioned from on High to deliver his brethren. Read from Webster's Dictionary the definitions of the terms *insurrection; conspiracy,* and *resistance*; commented largely. Said though slaves were not in the pamphlet, advised to resist, yet, to let a slave know that he had no right to have his sweat and blood extracted, was calculated to make him resist.

"Why do we want men from Ohio to come and teach us morals? We have preachers enough of our own. Ohio is nearly or quite as bad a place on account of abolition as New England. Paul sent Onesimus home, but McBride would not, McBride called people cowards. What language for a preacher!! He (McBride) is a bold man.

"Here some pretty strong epithets were used, E. G. In speaking of anti-slavery doctrines, the speaker called them hellish principles, &c. The sympathies and fears of the jurors were loudly appealed to. Mr. W. said — if these men may go unpunished then have no law against the midnight assassin. The speaker called attention to, as supremely exceptionable, the words of Rev. John Wesley, in the pamphlet where he speaks as follows: 'Whatever it costs put a stop to its cry before it be too late — instantly.' The word *instantly*, Mr. W. thought was very significant. It seemed to be the Speaker's misfortune, during his entire speech of about an hour, to be so much excited as not to be able to master his feelings, arid of course neither the jury, the audience, nor his subject.

G. C. Mendenhall

"Arose with a countenance bespeaking mingled feelings of a profound sense of responsibility, and a deep determination to discharge his duty with firmness and integrity. Spoke of the great excitement and even prejudice against the defendants — even counsel is denounced within this bar, for appearing for them. Said Mr. M., with thrilling emphasis— God forbid that the time should ever come that a man, an *American,* arraigned before a court in North Carolina, shall appear without counsel because no man at the bar will open, his mouth for him. The man who has license in his pocket, or at home, and when called upon refuses to step forward in behalf of a criminal, and demand the court to show cause why he should be convicted, ought to be denounced everywhere, and scouted from the North Carolina bar.

"In the discharge of my duty as an Attorney, I appear to see that these men have a full, fair trial. Nor do I arise to try and please those around me, or to make half a plea. Said Mr. M. — Even this jury has been threatened, provided they did not convict these men. Mr. Waddell informed you that 'if you clear them, you may see the day you will bitterly regret it.' It has been charged upon them that they have come into our midst unasked for. Why, does not that gentleman know they are here as regular ministers of the Gospel; that they were sent for by your own citizens; that one has been here three years, and the other not quite so long? They preach against intemperance, and the Moravians ought not to oppose them on this ground; and against war, just as the Moravians once did. The Quakers, from which I sprung protest, and have for a hundred years, against *slavery.*

"For doing nothing more, these men must be dragged up before this court as felons, and compared with Nat Turner. I am sorry that a man (alluding to Waddell) who ventured to bring so large a book as Webster's Dictionary before this court, to teach us the meaning of words— and we acknowledge ourselves duly informed — knows no more about modern history than not to know the defendants are ministers of the Church organized in 1843. Here was given a short history of the Wesleyan Church.

"Is it in testimony that these men have at any time interfered with slaves? Where is the man who gave such evidence? Let us look at the intention of giving the pamphlet. By raking and scraping their Camp-meetings, and McBride's meeting at Bethlehem, not one word has been brought to show that they have any sympathy with insurrection, but right to the contrary. Is it in testimony that the pamphlet was circulated with an intent to have it get among, or into the hands of negroes? No such advice was given the little girl, who was herself a white girl; her father held no slaves and there were none about the house. These men have a right to use means to gain proselytes; and believing, as they do, that slavery is sinful, they have a right to convince masters and freemen that it is wrong. Mr. Waddell says, 'such a hellish firebrand as the 'Ten Commandments' was never circulated in this country.' I'll show him that other ministers have brought and circulated things as bad as this little pamphlet, and that every intelligent Methodist minister keeps and circulates books equally as strong against slavery. Presbyterians and Quakers do the same. And I'll show, too, that none of them are incendiary.

"Here, by permission of the court, Mr, M. read and commented on extracts from the writings and sayings of the following distinguished statesmen and divines, viz., Patrick Henry and Thomas Jefferson, 'the brightest stars which

Virginia has produced: The narrative of the doings of the North Carolina Yearly Meeting of Friends on the subject of Slavery within its limits; Husbands separated from their wives, parents from their children —printed in Greensboro' in 1848: Wm. Pinkney; Clarke's Commentary on 1st Cor., vii:23; — Petition of the Presbyterians to their General Assembly — printed in Washington and circulated everywhere, and equally as strong as the 'Ten Commandments;' John Randolph; Wm. West; Dr. Paley; Dr. Burgess; Bishop Horseley; John Jay; Broadnax, of Virginia; Clark's Theology; Governor Swain, of North Carolina, scorching; Digest of the Presbyterian General Assembly, as strong as the English language can make it; Address of Hon, Wm. Gaston, before the students at Chapel Hill, N. C. — clear, masterly, and pithy — circulated everywhere, admired by everybody. Fourth edition, printed at Raleigh, capital of North Carolina.

'Now, gentlemen of the jury, I have not read these things to convince you that slavery is wrong, but to show you that if the 'Ten Commandments' is incendiary, then these are equally so, and to show you that the defendants have done nothing more than other ministers do.

'But it cannot be that these men design to raise an insurrection; for they are here to suffer with us? and for what have they come?'— to set the slaves at butchering their masters? No! But having brought all their earthly crowns and laid them at their Master's feet, have come here as humble ministers of the Gospel of the meek Redeemer. Why, it is plain this pamphlet was not intended to go among slaves; for it is not addressed to them, but their masters. Again, the slaves cannot read, and there is no evidence that McBride advised the little girl to read it to them, but directly the contrary. I venture the assertion, that if this pamphlet had been given out by a Methodist Episcopal preacher, there would not have been one word said about it. And why is it, gentlemen of the jury, they have indicted Crooks? There is not one particle of evidence against him. Not any, I fear the object was to influence the jury to compromise, acquit one and convict the other. I have seen too many such compromises. Where is the witness to testify that either of these men brought the pamphlet into North Carolina? The State would have you believe that we must prove ourselves innocent; that the fact of possession is evidence. Have they nothing?— did they never have anything but what they brought into the State? There is something remarkable about the prosecution; — here are three of the wealthiest men in Salem, prosecutors. Was not one enough? But that would not give sufficient character to all this excitement. I fear, and I awfully fear, there is too much ground of fear, that there is a design in all this, to force a conviction on these men. Mr. Waddell, with the appearance of sincerity, told you not to suffer yourselves to be influenced by any appeals which had been made or which may be made on either side. No, no; that gentleman would not have you become excited. I bring up burning houses, streaming blood and dying men, women and children, but don't suffer yourselves to be excited.'"

"Mr. M. after reading from his notes fifteen reasons why the defendants should be acquitted, about 8 o'clock at night concluded his last manly defence of three hours and a half, which was delivered in a clear, dignified, and masterly manner: and, notwithstanding its length, was heard by all with the most profound interest and breathless attention. The pleading closed; the Judge delivered his **CHARGE TO THE JURY** which was as follows:— after reading the law, the Judge observed, — The indictment contains two charges. The first, of bringing into the State, with intent to circulate, a printed pamphlet, the evident tendency of which, would be to excite insurrection, conspiracy, and resistance in the slaves. The second charge is, of circulating said pamphlet within the State, and so on. We will reverse the thing, and take the latter charge first. You will first consider the contents of the pamphlet. Has it an evident tendency to excite insurrection, or is it an argument couched in respectful language as to the morality of slavery, or of the best method of doing it away.

'You will then consider the evidence in regard, to circulating the pamphlet. Did he give (lifting the 'Ten Commandments') this pamphlet to the little girl? Next, is this the same pamphlet? As to the contents of this book, after the most serious and critical examination, I give it as my judgment, that it does have an evident tendency to excite insurrection. As to the question of his giving the pamphlet to the girl there can be no doubt. It is not my opinion that to violate the law, is necessary to circulate incendiary publications among the blacks. The design of the Legislature, no doubt, was to prevent the circulation of such things among the white, as well as the black portion of the community. Such productions tend to excite the master to treat his slave in such a manner as to create dissatisfaction in the slave with the treatment of his master. That this is the same pamphlet which McBride gave the girl, seems to be clearly proven by all the witnesses, who testified to that point.

'If Mr. Crooks was present and advising, or aiding Mr. McBride to give out the pamphlet at the time it was given, ho is equally guilty, but I believe the testimony is, he was not present. If from the evidence you think the defendants brought the pamphlet into the State, say so, and if not, say so. Giving the jury the papers he ordered them to be conducted to their room.'"

"The court arose, to sit next forenoon at 10 o'clock. Bro's Bacon, McBride and the writer retired to our lodgings; committed ourselves to God; slept securely till morning; at ten o'clock returned to Court: the Judge in the chair; the Jury report they are agreed upon a

Verdict

That 'Crooks is not guilty. McBride not guilty of the first, but guilty of the second charge, and ask for him the mercy of the Court.' The sentence was not immediately pronounced. About eleven o'clock Bro. McBride's counsel, Mr. Morehead moved for a new hearing, and required the State to show cause why it should not be granted. A new hearing being refused, the Judge passed

SENTENCE

That Brother McBride shall stand at the pillory one hour, receive twenty stripes, and be imprisoned in the county jail one year, and that the Sheriff proceed to inflict the penalty immediately. Whereupon an

Appeal

was taken to the Supreme Court of the ' State, which holds its session at Raleigh, on the 30th of December next.

GROUNDS OF THE APPEAL

"We think the court erred in the following:—

1st. The court permitted the whole of the pamphlet to be read in evidence, when only a part of it was set forth in the indictment.

2d. That giving the little book to a child was not putting the same into circulation under the act of Assembly.

3d. As a matter of law, the evident tendency of the book was not to excite to insurrection, conspiracy, and resistance.

4th. That the penalty of the Act was incurred by circulating the book among white persons, without reference to an intention that it should be circulated among persons of color. The appeal being entered,

A MOTION TO FORBID PREACHING AND CIRCULATING BOOKS.

"By Mr. Waddell it was moved that the court for bid Mr. McBride to preach or circulate books till the next session of the court 3 or for six months, on which he made a fiery appeal to the passions of the court, and *ad captandum vulgus.*

"Followed by Morehead in a thrilling address, in which he commenced by saying, 'Surely we have got into strange cities,' spoke in a pathetic manner of McBride's innocence, of his great loss and sore affliction in the death of his companion; of his separation from a lovely daughter; called upon them to point to an immoral act of his life, or an improper word from his lips.

"Mr. Waddell was very reluctant to protract this unhappy discussion, but he had been called upon to 'point out an immoral act.' The speaker referred to the meeting in Jamestown, published by Montgomery. McBride might be honest— he was sure he was misguided. 'I,' said W. 'revere the holy religion of the Bible as much as any man ...I know no master but the law, and that we make ourselves,' &c, to the end. The court decided it was not proper to forbid McBride from preaching as he had not been tried for that; but he should consider himself $1000 in debt to the State of North Carolina, if he did not appear at this court at its next session, or did circulate the Ten Commandments or anything similar, between this and then. Securities given. We went out from Salem, praying God's blessing upon His enemies and ours, and if not rejoicing that we were counted worthy to suffer for his 'name's sake,' at least. 'Submissive, I trust to the will Divine.'

"The moral elements are in commotion, but God rules the storm, bless His name! He has thus far said to our hearts 'fear not.' Let all who truly fear God and love man, join us in praying and laboring, and if need be, suffering, to bring on that happy day, when every system which arrays one portion of the human family against the other shall be extinct, and love's golden chain bind all in its sacred inclosure.

Other Persecutions

"Ecclesiastical history not {infrequently furnishes matter alike interesting to the Christian and lovers of the novel. The following may to some extent be of this character.

"Meetings are held in this State under the innocent name of Fairs, at which pilgrims from various parts of North and South Carolina assemble; some for the laudable purpose of selling various articles of food, and other some for the less praiseworthy motive of gambling, horse swapping, trafficing and drinking intoxicating liquors. At these almost every thing is *fair*.

"On one of these noted occasions, in Montgomery Co., a council was held to fix upon some plan to stay the progress of Wesley an ism in these parts? which resulted in the appointment of a Committee to wait on the writer, and request him to absent himself from the State of North Carolina by the 1st of February next. Accordingly, on the 27th of December, eight souls, the number saved in the ark sought, but found not the object of pursuit, he not being at his usual boarding-house; so they left a letter, stating if they did not get an answer they would meet me at one of my appointments. The following is a copy of their letter, including orthography and prosody.

'"North Carolina, Montgomery Co.
'We the undersigned Committee having been appointed, by a large meeting of the citizens of Montgomery, and the adjoining Counties, to wait on Adam Crooks, abolitionist? and request him peaceably to leave the State of North Carolina, by the 1st of February next, and we demand positive answer from the said Crooks whether or not he intends to comply with the requirements of these few lines, this 27th of December, 1850.'   [Signed by eleven names.]

"An answer was prepared, but not being sent, on Sabbath, the 12th inst., six men came to the meeting-house just as services commenced, but did not come into the house. Meeting being concluded, Mr. B. desired Mr. Byrns to introduce him to the preacher.

'I'll do no such thing; why did you not come into the house like a man?'
'Is your name Crooks?'
'That is my name.'
'My name is Bright. I wish to have a word with you. We are appointed by a meeting of Montgomery county, to request you to leave the State of North

Carolina. We think you are doing no good, and for the sake of the peace and harmony of the community, we desire you to leave.'

'I received a letter to that purport a few days since.'

'Yes, but we got no answer.'

'I prepared an answer, but had no opportunity of sending it. I am of the same mind as when I wrote it; and in it I decline complying.'

'Then you do not ask any set time, only till you see cause to leave?'

'All I ask is the rights of any other preacher of the Gospel. All we ask is the rights of the State. I have not, nor do I have any disposition to violate these rights. Good day, gentlemen.'

"All left, but Mr. O., the writer of the above note.

'Mr. O., I believe you are the writer of the letter received.'

'Yes, sir.'

'I have written an answer, and as I hold your letter, you can have the answer, if you desire it.'

'I should like to have it.'"

"Whereupon the following was given.

Valentine Moore's, Mont. Co., Jan. 6th, 1851.

"To the Committee appointed by a large meeting of the citizens of Montgomery and adjoining counties, to wait on Adam Crooks, abolitionist, and request him peaceably to leave the State of North Carolina, by the 1st of February next.

"Sirs: — Your by no means polite note, bearing date of December 27th, is before me, which I will endeavor to answer, in the meekness of humility, and kindness of charity, as well as in the frankness of honesty and plainness of sincerity.

"And 1st: — As to the language of your letter, it is well calculated to extort the exclamation, *Mirabile dictu!* You begin with a request, and conclude with an absolute demand, which your own good sense must teach you had not the least shadow of a right to make.

"2d: — To the implied charge of abolitionism, I am free to acknowledge, I believe with Benjamin Franklin, George Washington, Thomas Jefferson, Patrick Henry, William Pinkney, John Wesley, Richard Watson, Adam Clarke, and others, philosophers, statesmen and divines, to whom the world owes a large debt of gratitude, and to whose names posterity will gladly pay its *devoir,* of a place on the fairest page of fame, on the subject of American slavery. In the fullest sense, I subscribe to that ever memorable instrument, the Declaration of Independence; written, using the language of figure, with the point of the sword in the blood of the heroes of seventy-six, who appealing to the Searcher of hearts to witness the rectitude of their intentions, with the American flag majestically floating in heaven's free air over their heads, and the watchword liberty, blazing in capitals from its ample folds, nobly wrote: 'We hold these truths to be self-evident, that all men are created equal, and endowed by their Creator with inalienable right to life, liberty, and the pursuit of happiness; that to maintain these rights, governments are instituted among men, deriving their just powers from the will of the governed.'

"And is this, in the estimation of their sons, an offense, a crime meriting exilement? If so, as Croesus cried out, 'O Solon! Solon! Solon!' may not we with equal propriety, though opposite emotions, exclaim 'O Fathers of the revolution! Fathers of the revolution! Fathers of the revolution!'

"3rd. With regard to your request, for three rea,, sons I can not comply.

"First. There is no insignificant number of as loyal citizens, and some as orderly Christians as crown this or any other State, desire my ministerial services; and because I can not be false to these, false to myself, false to my office, to the Church, and above all, false to God, I can not comply.

"Second. As an American citizen, pursuing a laudable, not to say charitable occupation, to a self-constituted tribunal, recognized by no law-governing civilized nations, I can not yield the right to try without notice, convict without a hearing, and banish without crime. To do so would be to offer a base indignity to our nature as men, and character as Americans.

"In the third place, I can not comply with so unreasonable a request, because as a Christian and Christian minister I will not surrender to any earthly power, and more especially to illegally assumed authority, the right given by our Almighty Creator, and secured by the government under which it is our privilege to live, to worship Almighty God according to the dictates of conscience.

"I am bold to declare that no true American or genuine Christian, will either make or submit to such demands. The pen which recorded the sur. render, would be quite as dark as the page which chronicled the requirement. What would such procedure be, but a re-establishment of Inquisitorial Councils? — the re-kindling the consuming fires of religious intolerance? — the annihilation of the Protestant reformation and all its glorious blessings, and the resurrection of all the bloody cruelties of the Papal persecution? Would you have the ignominious tragedy of the reign of Henry VIII, Queen Mary, and James II — the reign of terror — re-acted on American soil? If so, who will tell the mournful catastrophe? Who will give assurance that your children's children will not drink the fatal dregs of the poisonous cup first presented by their erring fathers? If there are such things as weeping in heaven, and sorrow in the tomb, might not sainted spirits find occasion here to drop a tear over the grave of slaughtered freedom, and the bosoms of illustrious dead to heave a sigh for departed glory?

"Than that such should be the case — that the clarion of freedom should cease to whisper in our breezes, and murmur along our stream s, the free born conscience enslaved; liberty's self murdered in the house of her friends, and by hands which should cherish her; her garments stained, and home drenched with the blood of the martyrs of Jesus; the name of our loved, our idolized America, should be written on the page of infamy, and be a hissing and by -word among kings, princes, and autocrats; every man's hand of the

American people be turned against his fellow, and they fall victims to the evils of intestine broils, and the ravages of international wars; — I say, before these things come upon us, let the sun refuse to look upon us; the stars represented on our country's flag, withdraw from the firmament; let the American name be blotted from the archives of nations; the American people fall beneath the devouring pestilence from God; our fair cities, flourishing towns, and peaceful hamlets become one unbroken desolation; and fruitful fields, green meadows, and majestic forests, a theater of the sports of wild beasts, and return to the uninterrupted dominion of the untutored savage.

"Permit me to ask, in all kindness and candor, may not your procedure, if prosecuted, prove to be the precursor and even the prelude, to all these dreadful calamities?

"That the above indifferently described evils be averted, and their opposite blessings secured, may the American people, ever proverbially sensitive to the least seeming encroachment on their individual or national rights, insure their enjoyment to themselves and posterity by uniformly respecting, as no less sacred, the rights of each other; worshiping as seemeth good unto them, and allowing their neighbors the peaceable enjoyment of that exalted privilege. And if at any time they differ in opinion, as in our imperfect state we will be certain to do, let us pray for and reason one with another; thus at once obeying the heavenly command, and imitating the glorious example of Him who causes His sun to shine on the evil and the good, and rain to bless the just and unjust, and died for us when we were enemies, remembering that if any man have not His spirit he is none of His.

"I will conclude this scroll, the length of which please excuse, by referring you to the wise advice of Gamaliel, Acts v: 33-39; the woe pronounced against the offender, Matthew xviii:1-7; please ponder well Matthew xxv:31— 46.

"We have erected two meeting-houses this Winter, one in Montgomery and the other in Randolph Co. We anticipate a visit from our deeply injured? hut highly esteemed Brother McBride on the first and second Sabbath of the next inst., at which time we purpose holding protracted meetings. May the Lord greatly revive his work, Amen."

It was during this visit of Brother McBride's, in February, 1851, that, as they were going from one appointed place of meeting to another, each in his own carriage, as they came to the top of a high hill, they saw in the valley below, three men, armed with guns, standing across the road. Evidently they were waiting for them. Brother McBride said,

"Crooks, do you see those men?"

Mr. Crooks answered, "Yes."

That was all that passed between them, but their hearts were lifted in silent prayer to One who is ever ready to help his children in time of danger. When they came to the place where the men stood, two passed to one side of the road, and one to the other.

Mr. Crooks said, "Good morning, gentlemen."

The men answered, "Good morning."

As they ascended the opposite hill, before they passed out of sight, they glanced back, and saw two other armed men coming. They heard afterwards that five men had pledged themselves to meet there, and waylay and kill Mr. Crooks, as he regularly passed that way to attend his appointments. Two of their number were tardy. McBride was a stranger. The three probably feared to act alone and through Providence their plans were brought to nought.

Religious Intolerance In North Carolina

"Nothing in all the book of common sayings is more true than that 'Coming events often cast their shadows before them.'" In nature the morning star proclaims the approach of the superior splendor of the solar orb. The semi-decomposition of his rays forming divergent milk-colored lines in the vapory air, precedes the darkening heavens, the red lightning, roaring thunder, dashing rain, and the sweeping tornado. The rumbling of the volcano is precursory to the vomitings of the clouds of smoke and ashes, showers of burning stones and rivers of fiery lava.

"In the progress of human affairs, circumstances intrinsically of little or no importance, in their relations to mighty movements, are fraught with interests boundless in extent and endless in duration.

"The fact that pieces of carved wood, a canoe and two human bodies differing in complexion from Europeans, had been driven by westerly winds upon the shores of islands contiguous to Europe, was important only as to its influence upon the observing mind of Columbus, in leading to the discovery of an unknown hemisphere,

"The falling of an apple is a simple and common occurrence, yet it taught Newton, priest of nature, the great law of attraction by which the mighty God governs the grand machinery of the heavens.

"The burning of Andrew Oliver in effigy, in Boston, on the 14th of August, 1765, and the breaking open of three hundred and forty-two chests of tea, and emptying their contents into the ocean the 18th of December, 1773, trifling as they are, serve as a thermometer to indicate feelings which throbbed through the veins and arteries, and nerved the arm of the United Colonies — feelings which brightened till they produced throes which shook the foundations of the mightiest throne on earth, and gave birth to a nation no less powerful.

"And the formation of the Jacobin club in France in 1790, in itself appeared unimportant, yet it was the shadow of coming events which convulsed the world. Considered as the unobserving eye of the multitude beholds human transactions — separate and disconnected, uninfluenced and uninfluencing, the subject of this communication is comparatively local and unimportant. But viewed as the true philosopher, wise statesman, and enlightened Christian are wont to look upon passing incidents connected, linked, bound to, influenced by, and influencing all the movements of men; and as a milestone marking the progress of civilization, and enlightened liberal and Christian principles, or of political and religious degeneracy, it is infinitely otherwise.

"It is the seizure and forcible commitment to prison, in Montgomery Co., North Carolina, on the Sabbath, by professors of Christianity and officers of the law, without the forms of law; refusing bail of a free born American and Minister of the Gospel uncondemn ed, which it is the painful task of my pen to record.

"The morning of Sabbath, the 15th of June, as if unwilling to be a spectator of the transactions of the day, the sun arose behind a cloud. The air was cool, as if chilled by the inhospitality of the hearts of the oppressors.

"The rumor that a mob was to be at the Lovejoy Chapel, to transport him beyond the limits of the county, induced him to leave his horse at Brother V. Moore's about a mile from the Chapel, and go to meeting early before the mob could arrive. By ten o'clock quite a number of the loyal band landed, and fifteen minutes to eleven, the balance, numbering in all according to their supposition one hundred and seventy-five; ten of whom were magistrates. The preacher was sitting in the pulpit, when the mob, headed by S. Christian, a "Justice of the Peace" and a negro-trader as their orator approached and accosted him with: —

"Is your name Crooks?"

"That is my name."

"My name is Christian. The Methodist Episcopal Church North and South are divided. They have agreed on a line, and this very subject of slavery has divided them. The North would not have a slave-holding bishop. Andrew, being a slaveholder, was deprived of his office, and on this account the Church split. The slavery question is agitating this whole nation."

"Yes," said Crooks, "it is convulsing it from center to circumference."

"And you have come amongst us preaching against slavery — violating our laws — breeding disturbance. I have no doubt you preach the Gospel, but we are not heathens, we are a Christianized people. You are making interruptions in families, in neighborhoods, and Churches, (wonder if he is not a regular descendant of some chivalric knight,) and causing us to abuse our servants; for they have got to know you are preaching that they ought to be free, and it makes them unruly; so that they have to be abused. And now, what we want of you is a solemn promise that you will leave the county forthwith, and never preach in it again."

"You, Mr. Christian, are mistaken as to Bishop Andrew being deposed. He was a bishop at the rise of the General Conference of 1844. In answer to three questions it was ordered that his name should remain with the other bishops — he should receive a bishop's pay; the work he did to be subject to his discretion in view of the action of that Conference. But that matters not, it being merely a fact of ecclesiastical history. As to my having violated your laws, your conduct to-day vindicates me from that charge."

"I think not."

"Evidently," continued Crooks, "for had I broken your laws, you would not have been under the necessity of violating them and adopting the sublime *modus operandi* of Mob Law to punish me."

"Some of the company. — 'We did not come here to have a debate.'"

"Certain charges have been preferred, and it is the undisputed right of every man to be heard before being judged; and I am going to be heard. As to breaking the peace; you have acknowledged I preached the gospel. As to your not being heathens but a Christianized people, your conduct in trying to drive out of the county a man for preaching the gospel, is more like that of heathens than of Christians. Not a drop of blood warms my heart, or courses my veins in favor of insurrection. Were you to take my advice there would be no danger of such an event,"

"What would that be?"

"Do by your slaves as you would they should do to you,"

"Explain."

"It needs no explanation. It is so plain a wayfaring man though a fool shall not err therein."

"Now, see there!"

"With regard to leaving the county, etc., it is my right, in common with American citizens, to come and go at pleasure. The Constitution of the United States says, the citizens of each State shall have all the privileges and immunities of the citizens of die several states."

"Mr. Cogins, [a magistrate and slave-holder, was once class-leader in the M. E. Church, is not now a Church-member.] "Did you not agree to leave Guilford, and never return?"

"Mr. Cogins, I do not wish to be interrupted, tout I answer, I did not."

"I am informed you did."

"I know what I did, — and I know I did not. To give a promise never to preach in this county, is a demand you have no right to make, and one to which I as a Christian minister have no right to submit. I trust I shall ever be ready to go where God commands, and should I feel it my duty to preach in Montgomery County, by His grace assisting I shall try. The right to worship according to dictates of conscience, with other rights, was purchased at the expense of blood, lives and treasures, of our revolutionary fathers, and should not be surrendered but with life. The Constitution of North Carolina, which some of this company have taken a solemn oath to support, secures this right. Here a number of persons commenced asking questions at the same instant, having one employed in penning down the answers given."

T. Halton— "Brother Crooks—"

"O, don't call him brother."

"Yes, let us call him brother. Brother Crooks, did you not preach to servants not to obey their masters?"

"I did not."

"I did not hear you, but heard you did."

H. Hulen to Haltom — "Don't you interrupt the man,"

"Haltom, much excited, shook his fist, stamped his foot to the floor, and striking the book-board, declared he was at home on his own premises.

Crooks, — "O, men! — keep calm!"

O. Hulen. — "Men, are we in Court? If so let the judges call the court to order; and if we came to worship God, let us do it."

Mr. Bright. — "O, men, do your duty for which you come here."

Mr. Christian. — "Well, can you comply with our request? "

"I have answered that question."

"We have extended the olive branch of peace to you, and if you do not receive it, you must abide the consequences."

"Crooks now for the first time rises from his seat; — "I extend the olive to all men. I have lived in all good conscience to God and man since I came amongst you — feel resolved despite of all opposition, to do the will of God and make my home in the cloudless regions of undying delight."

Mr. Cogins — [in an excited tone.] "Who are you — what were you before you come here, — have you papers to show?"

"I have."

"By whom are they signed; — the Governor of the State?"

"By members and ministers of the Methodist Episcopal and Methodist Protestant Church, and the treasurer of the County Court. I have them in my pocket, if you wish you can see them."

"Who knows by whom they are signed."

"Mr. Christian: — Aaron Burr was once a good man and afterwards guilty of treason."

"Crooks: —Aaron Burr was once a good man and afterwards guilty of treason, therefore, O. Hulen is a bad man, Aaron Burr was once a good man and afterwards turned traitor, therefore S. Christian is a bad man. Is not that strange logic?"

"Mr. Bright:— men, perform the duty for which you came!"

"Mr. Cogins: — Were you sent for to come to this State?"

"I was."

"By whom?"

"Forty persons in Guilford."

"Name some of them."

"Well, Mr. John Sherwood of Jamestown, and Rev. D. Wilson of Guilford."

"Was Wilson a preacher in the Methodist Church."

"He was."

Mr. Bright:— "Did he not apply for license, and it being refused, get mad and leave the Church?"

"He was a preacher of the M. E. Church."

"I heard it otherwise."

Mr. Cogins: — "Did not the Annual Conference pass resolutions condemnatory of your course?"

"Yes sir.   The North Carolina Yearly Conference of the Methodist Protestant Church did pass sentence of condemnation upon us."

"No, but one of the Northern Conferences of the Wesleyan Methodist Church."

"No sir."

"The papers say they did."

"If they do, they say that which is untrue,"

"Did you not write to the editor of the Wesleyan, that O. Hulen told you of a man in this county tying up his slave, putting a log of wood between his feet and whipping him to death? "

"I wrote no such thing."

"No, not that he whipped him to death, but gave him five hundred lashes."

"If you, Mr. Cogins, have a paper having ^such an article, and my name attached to it, perhaps I wrote it."

"Now, just see there."

"One of the crowd; — "O. Hulen is here, he can speak for himself."

"O. Hulen, did you give Mr. Crooks such information?"

"Are we in court? — Who is the Judge?"

"One says, "Christian; — let him show his authority. Oh — we have nothing against Mr. Hulen."

"During a miscellaneous interchange between the contending parties. Mr. Crooks, resuming his seat, seemed to lift his heart in devout but silent prayer.

"As the preacher had but one answer to their demand, four men were ordered to take him from the stand. Orders were instantly obeyed.

"O. Hulen. — Men, take notice who takes hold of that man by violence."

"Crooks wished to get his hat and books.

"From the crowd. — 'Yes, let him get them.'"

"As they descended the pulpit, Win. Hurley wished to know what they were going to do.

"Oh, get out of our way!"

"But stop, you don't run over me. What are you going to do with the preacher? "

"Going to take him to Troy."

"Well, can't you take bail? "

"We want no bail."

"Crooks is led or rather dragged from the pulpit into the yard. All is confusion. Some are rushing for their horses, others are screaming, and still others prostrated, motionless and speechless.

"Where is Crooks' horse; where is his horse; where is your horse? "

"Where I left him, I expect."

"Where did you leave him?"

"Where he is welcome."

"Has any person a horse and buggy to take this man to Troy?"

"He is taken to Luther's vehicle. Luther is ss magistrate, a slave-holder and one of the brave four.

"Let us have help to put this man in the buggy."

"Oh, he will get in!— Get in!"

Crooks remaining motionless and silent.

"Let us have help to put this man in the buggy."

"Oh, he'll get in,— he'll get in!"

"Crooks remaining motionless and silent.

"Let us help to put this man in the buggy."

"Oh, he'll get in,— he'll get in!"

"With emphasis and anger — 'Get in, get in I Come here, some four or five men and help to put this man in the buggy!'"

"He is hoisted to a seat.

"O. Hulen. — 'Men, take notice who forces this man into that buggy.'

"Mr. Cogins, — 'I will help to put him in, now do your d—ndest.'"

"Said Crooks, — is there no means of conveyance for S. W. L., my friend from Randolph? None being obtained, in company with three brethren, L. walked to Troy, a distance of six miles. But one of Crooks' friends (O. Hulen,) in company from the Chapel to Troy, those on foot taking a shorter way.

["Conversation on the way.]

"Crooks. — There is a day approaching when there will be an account to meet for this day's work.

"Luther. — Yes, and you will have to answer for your conduct.

"C. I hope I shall be prepared to do so.

"L. Those who have taken you have done God a service.

"C. Our Saviour has told us the time would come when those who kill his followers, would think they did God service. But that question will be settled at the Judgment, and the Judge will consider treatment to his servants as done unto Him. Now if he were on earth again would you drive Him from the county?

"L. 'I don't know what we might do, if he were an abolitionist. We are going to have perilous times, and we are bound to keep them off as long as we can. You would bring them on before the time.'"

"C. 'That's what the devils said to Jesus — "Thou art come hither to torment us before the time."' But if you would take my counsel all clanger of perilous times would vanish. Your conduct to your slaves make them your enemies. Were you to treat them with justice and kindness they would become your friends. You remind me of the saying of a heathen philosopher. 'Whom the gods would destroy they first make mad.' To prevent an insurrection you banish a man for advising you to pursue the only course which can secure you against such a disaster.

"Nothing can be more certain than that slavery will prove fatal to the South if it is not peaceably abolished. The war between the antagonistic principles and interests of liberty and slavery, is bound to go on till one destroys the other. As well attempt to reconcile God and the devil, as to establish peace upon a permanent basis between liberty and slavery, and it is for every man to say which side he will take in the contest. Slavery will destroy the country if the country does not destroy slavery.

"*L.* I have some slaves, but I wish there was not one in the United States.'"

"*C.* And yet you will drive from the County a man for advising you what you wish was done. But I notice when a slave concludes to leave, you do all in your power to bring him back.

"*L.* The slaves of the South in general, are much better off than the free niggers of the North, and men of intelligence and candor from the North admit it.

"*C.* Perhaps these intelligent and candid gentlemen are not competent judges; — one thing is undeniable, and that is, there is not a single instance of a negro's fleeing from liberty to slavery, while there are numerous cases of an opposite character.

"*L.* I treat my slaves as well as I could wish them to treat me.

"*C.* Were you a slave, would you not wish to be free.

"*L.* Yes.

"*C,* Why, then, do you say you use them as you would be used, while you refuse them their freedom?

"*L.* O. If I were *black*, I don't think I would wish to be free. Your preaching makes the slaves dissatisfied, [They are wonderfully well satisfied] — we have the gospel preached by others.

"*C.* Well, it has been admitted that I preach the gospel. Why punish me for doing that for which you honor others?

"*L.* They preach the gospel of peace.

"*C.* If they do you have a poor way of obeying them.

"Christian, with an affected smile, I heard quite a good joke the other day about you and myself.

"Crooks, very seriously— 'Ah! what was that?'

Why, I heard that you are in my employ; preaching against slavery, that I may purchase below par; and then we divide profits.

"*C.* That is doubtless as true as many other things you have heard.

"Now, Mr. Crooks, you must know that your preaching is contrary to our laws, for they are in favor of, and you preach against slavery.

"Not any more contrary to law, Mr. Christian, than for temperance lecturers to proclaim against the license law, and for Whigs to denounce laws enacted by Democrats, or *vice versa* — -the law does not enjoin but permits slavery.

"But you violate the law by disturbing the peace of Churches.

"You, Mr. Christian, cannot be ignorant of the fact that the law establishes no form of Church government.

"*C.* Yes, it does.

"Show the chapter, section, and paragraph. Our laws allow all Churches the privilege of fixing their own terms of communion and membership., and every individual the right to worship according to the dictates of conscience. You say you believe slavery is right. I believe it is wrong. The law allows us an equal right to our faith.

"You know your course is contrary to law, for McBride was convicted of a violation of law.

"True it is, a jury of twelve men gave it as their opinion that McBride had broken the law, but an appeal being taken to the Supreme Court, his prosecutors unwilling to abide its decision, raised a mob and drove him from the State. They knew right well he was an innocent man: — the leaders of the mob acknowledged they believed him to be a gentleman and Christian; and one of them said, as soon as he saw the grounds of appeal, he knew they could not convict him by law. The means you adopt to support your cause is a virtual acknowledgement. You must not be offended, Mr. Christian, at me a prisoner, for talking so plainly to you, for really I feel I am conversing with an equal, and nothing more.

"*C.* No, not at all; I travel a great deal; I have been in almost all the States in the Union. Don't you believe George Washington is in Heaven?

"Well, what if I do?

"Why, he was a slave-holder. "George Washington willed his slaves their freedom.

"*C.* No, he did not.

"He most certainly did; I know whereof I affirm.

"Are you in favor of the Fugitive Slave Law?

"I am not. Now, you see that was passed by *Congress*, and it is the best thing that has ever been done; had not that law passed, the Union would have been dissolved, and if it is repealed it will be dissolved.

"That is a matter of opinion, and I very much differ with you. I have never been able to persuade myself, the South is so foolish as to dissolve the Union. I would be opposed to the Fugitive Bill, if for no other reason, because it does not respect the rights of conscience.

"Luther. — Mr. Christian, where will we stop? Mr. Crooks says he is hungry, and I want my dinner.

"Christian. — Well, he must have dinner, Where do you usually stop?"

"Where it happens."

"The prisoner was taken to Luther's, and after washing himself, was desired to read from two papers relating to the notorious abolitionists, McBride and himself, one of which articles was headed in large letters, "**Damn Crooks**," — which he did.

"*C.* I had noticed how that was headed; it must be by mistake.

"*Prisoner.* — I suppose it was intended for a burlesque, but it matters nothing.

"Seated at the table, Christian requests Crooks to ask a blessing, which he did.

"Dinner over, Mr. J., an official member in the Methodist Episcopal Church, and one of the mob, thought it a reasonable request which had been made; wished to know the meaning of abolition; was informed by the prisoner it was a derivation from abolish, which means to destroy, to do away, and is most commonly applied to slavery.

"Sheriff Sanders. — (also a member of the Methodist Episcopal Church, and one of the mob.) "Yes, that is its meaning."

"*C.* You, Mr. Crooks, must know that your Church is contrary to our laws, for they favor slavery, and your Church opposed it.

"*C.* As before stated, Churches are at liberty to make any terms of membership they see proper, and individuals to worship as they may deem is right. If you believe it right to hold slaves, there are Churches where you will be readily received. We believe we are equally entitled to a Church whose doctrine and discipline prohibit slave-holding — a Church according with our religious convictions.

"But if the Wesleyan organization is contrary to your laws, because it makes slave-holding a test of membership, what will you do with the Quakers' Church which does the same?

"*C.* Oh! — the Quakers hold slaves.

"Under what circumstances? Dying persons sometimes make them their agents in securing the freedom of their slaves; this, at times, proves the occasion of lawsuits; they hold them till the suit is decided, and if in favor of the slaves their liberty is given them.

"*C.* If it is right to hold them a little while, it is right to hold them always.

Sanders. — [spoke in the positive] "Almost all the Quakers hold slaves. They are in favor of slavery." [A strange declaration for a professed Christian to make.]

"*C.* I stayed overnight with Mr. H., a Quaker, and he said they were as much opposed to the Wesleyans as to any denomination; that he believed there are many slaveholders good Christians, and that he would advise everybody to keep the Wesleyan preachers out of their houses. [It is never necessary to make false statements to support a righteous cause.]

"*C.* Why do you not go to South Carolina.

"I have never been invited, nor have I felt it my duty to go.

"You talk about *duty.* What if you should feel it your duty to tell my slave to kill me.

"*C.* Should you find me about your stables stealing your horses, or about your kitchens, or any where else violating the law, I refuse not to suffer in a legal manner. You talk of violating your laws, and you have every one broken your own laws this very day, and you know it, and you know that I know it.

"Sheriff Sanders.— If we have we are willing to abide the consequences.

"Crooks,— So I say."

"To Wm. Hurley. — What is the reason you could not stay in the Church you first joined?

"Why, I have ever been opposed to this thing.

"What thing?

"Why, slavery; but I wished to belong to some Church, and as there was none in my reach that suited me better, I joined the Methodist Episcopal Church.

"Well, if you believe slavery to be wrong, you need not hold them, it does not hurt you.

"Well, but for me to support a thing I do not believe in would not be right. And you can have your privileges and let us have ours.

"Would you receive a slave-holder into your Church.

"No, that is not our way.

"Well, would you receive a slave?

"Yes, if we believed him to be a Christian.

"What! — receive a nigger and not a white man? That is a grand insult depriving us of our rights.

"Not at all. We do not say you shall not hold slaves; all we want is to keep clear of supporting it.

"Well, if that is your principle you ought to leave the State.

"I was born and raised here — pay for my privileges under the law, and it is a hard case if I am to be deprived of them.

"(To S. W. L.) — Well sir, where are you from.

"Randolph County.

"What business have you here?

"I thought I was a freeman.

"Sheriff. — Well, but you are here violating our laws.

"I am not convinced of having violated your laws.

"Bo you ever preach?

"No sir.

"Do you exhort?

"I never have.

"Do you ever hold meetings?

"No sir.

"Squire Harris. — Well, you pray for him sometimes when he asks you to, don't you?

"I have done the like. [What an incorrigible sinner.]

"A voice. — He came to see Crooks out; we will serve him the same as we do Crooks.

"During the foregoing there was much anger as well as insolence exhibited.

"Well, Mr. Crooks, will you give us a promise that you will leave the county and never preach in it again?

"That question has been answered. When you found me, you found me a free man; when you leave me, you will leave me either a tree or a dead one.

"Christian. — [to mob] Well, it will not do to commence a thing and not go through with it.

"After a few minutes consultation, four magistrates ordered the Sheriff to take the preacher to jail.

"The Sheriff. — I command all present to assist me.

"(To L.) Do you wish to go to jail?

"I believe not.

"Orders are immediately obeyed.

"The Sheriff. — We are not going to allow bail; this case is too bad for that."

"Well, Paul was imprisoned.

"Yes, but them times was different from these.

"And these times are no less different from those.

"After ascending a pair of stairs.

"Sheriff. — [to jailor.] Where shall I put him?

"Put him where you please, I will keep him where you put him. [Hesitating a few minutes whether to commit him to the dungeon or debtor's room.]

"Well we will put him in here, [the debtor's room.]

"Introduced to Mr. Gad, a young man awaiting his trial for assault and battery. How do you do, Mr. Gad? A hissing sneer, such as devils use when they receive to their dark abode a lost spirit, was indulged in by the rabble.

"The doors are locked, Crooks is confined in a gloomy prison.

"Now we have got him and we are going to keep him, and North Carolina, not Montgomery County, will have to pay the expenses.

"L. is left to choose between leaving the place in fifteen minutes and going to jail. As he had nothing to detain him he chose to leave.

"The room in which the preacher was confined, is about 9x13 and 7 feet to the ceiling above. His fare, or more properly his *foul*, was, for bedding, some blankets directly from the dungeon, which were ponderous with dust, and so offensive as to be sickening; these spread upon the floor. His portion was two meals per day; breakfast and dinner. The food was passable, the floor was his table, his finger served instead of a fork, and pocketknife for a table-knife; a plate and bowl his dishes. His friends might furnish him with superior if they saw proper, which they were going to do,

"A committee was appointed to read any and all writings which passed between him and his friends, who were not permitted to visit him.

"None but his enemies could enter that *sanctum sanctorum*. The committee was further instructed not to release their prisoner till he signed a bond like McBride's.

"Monday, A. M., the jailor, or rather his deputy, who was one of the mob, and addicted to habits of inebriation, entered the jail about 7 o'clock.

"Good morning, Mr. Crooks.

"Good morning, sir.

"How does your pulse beat by this time in regard to leaving?

"As it did on yesterday.

"You had better leave; they are determined you shall not preach any more in the county.

"Ah, indeed!

"Nine o'clock, some seven or eight persons among whom were Mr. L., a merchant in the place, and Mr. H., a Baptist, both slave-holders, and principal men in the mob, visited Mr. Crooks; were very sorry to see him in that unhappy situation; had no doubt that every man of honorable feelings and honest heart was sorry.

"Mr. C. No doubt of it at all.

"You are being imposed upon by your professed friends; you are a stranger and they pretend they will do a great many things; but they are not to be depended on; they are the very dregs of the county. You cannot get them to be any thing that is good; those who are against you are the best men of the county. They are determined you shall preach no more in the county. There is no more possibility of success; you can't get justice, and you had as well attempt to set this jail on fire with cold water as to accomplish any good.

"You say I cannot get justice; I will be convicted whether there is anything proven or not; will not men respect their oaths? If my friends are as ignorant and wicked as you say, they are the very people who need preaching. What I wish to know is, what is my duty; at present I do not think I can ever say, I will never preach in Montgomery County, or any where else.

"You will have to come to that at last. Well, good morning,

"Good morning.

"After remaining from Sabbath till Tuesday P. M,, consulting his friends, who advised him to do all his conscience would permit to get his liberty, and being fully convinced that his rights would be protected neither in the court, or out of it, he desired an interview with the committee appointed by the mob, which was readily granted.

"Dr. C. — I am very sorry, Mr. Crooks, to see a man of your profession and qualifications for usefulness in your situation.

"To be taken from my work, my friends; my liberties taken from me, and I confined in this gloomy cage, is sir, by no means congenial to my feelings. But here I have been put, and here it appears I must stay.

"Dr. C. — Oh, we would be happy to release you; it can be a pleasure to no one to see you here.

"Nor can it be a pleasure for me to remain; nor would I do so, were I permitted to leave upon conditions not involving a surrender of my liberties as a man but more especially as a Christian minister.

"Of course we will require nothing unreasonable.

"It has been done.

"Well, we will ask nothing that we Carolinians consider unreasonable.

"I have been trying to look at things as they are, and to invoke the Divine guidance, and have come to the conclusion that I can be more extensively useful elsewhere than in this county, and hence to leave, intending not to preach in this county again.

"We were instructed to require a bond.

"I do not believe the bond, if given, would be worth a fig. Nor should I consider any instrument of writing more binding than my word.

"We believe you will do anything you promise, but we must go according to orders.

"I should like to assist in wording the bond.

"We will write the bond and then you can see if you can sign it.

"Very well.

Whereupon the following was drawn:

"Now the condition of the above bond is such:— That, whereas the above bounden Adam Crooks has been advocating and preaching abolition doctrine contrary to our laws and institutions, and this having been made known to him and strictly enforced on him to desist and leave this county and never again to preach in said county, and he having agreed to do so * * * to be done in ten days.

"After the reading of which, Crooks stated that two things must be changed before he could sign the bond.

"First: You say, I have advocated and preached abolition doctrine contrary to our laws and institutions; laws must be struck out. I do not believe I have violated your laws, and a man is judged innocent till proven guilty.

"Dr. C. — I suppose he does not like to leave the county under the stigma of having broken the law.

"That is not the point with me, doctor. It is a matter of veracity. Not believing I have violated, I cannot say I have.

"William McKay — the [jailor, and he who drew the bond.] We think you have.

"I do not ask you to say I have not, but to relieve me from saying I have.

"Being put to vote, all but one voted not to have it erased.

"Well, said one, we can discuss the question.

"Crooks.— The question being decided, is no longer open for discussion; to bring it before you for that purpose a motion to reconsider must be made by one who voted with the majority.

"The matter dropped here, and 'laws' struck out.

"The second change which must be made before I can sign this bond is, the conjunction "and" must be erased, and the participle "intending" inserted, so as to read k 'and leave this county intending never to preach in said county again,' instead of " leaving this county and never," &c.

"My reason for asking this is, because, as a minister called of God to preach his gospel, I have no right to, nor can I say I never will preach any where.

"Believing I can be more useful elsewhere than in this county, it is my present intention to leave intending not to preach in it again; this I can *say*, or have it written down. Duty may require, and things may so change as for it to be desirable that I should preach in the county.

"This change also being made, the bond was signed, and Crooks permitted to go forth again to mingle in the mighty conflict which now convulses the moral world. His heart was deeply pained to leave the Church in Montgomery; nor would he have done so, only from a clear persuasion that he would not have been permitted to be useful to it.

"I was released from confinement in the Montgomery jail, on the evening of the 17th of June. While visiting and bidding adieu to the much-injured friends in that county, there was an instance of moral heroism which it affords pleasure to record. After taking my leave of Brother V. Moore's family, I was called back to write in the class-book, the name of his daughter C, who belonged to the Methodist Episcopal Church, but would continue such connection no longer — joined the Wesleyans, though deprived of the privilege of preaching, and threatened to be of holding prayer and class meetings.

"On the ensuing Saturday and Sabbath, I had meeting at Bethel, in Randolph Co., a mile or two from the Montgomery line. The congregations were large, and appeared to be deeply afflicted; one brother joined the Church.

"A portion of the Montgomery mob, met some distance from the meeting, but concluding they were too few, disbanded. Being invited, I agreed to attend a funeral in Davidson, to be preached the following Sabbath, by B. L. and A. K., Baptist ministers, I too preached after them, and before the congregation dispersed. This meeting was to be held in a neighborhood where I had never been. Threats were made if Crooks came he should be tarred and feathered inside and out, and such like.

"The hour for meeting arrived, and with it an overwhelming congregation; two officers were on the ground to see that the laws were respected, and the rights of the writer protected. The mob did not appear. While speaking from 2d Cor. 4th and 5th, a glorious unction rested on the audience.

"By this time, a feeling of deep indignation and strong opposition towards the conduct of the mobs began to develop itself; indeed, ere I came out of prison, without my agency, or even knowledge, a company was being raised to get me out peaceably if they could, forcibly if they must. Forcible resistance or violence I felt it my duty to discourage.

"Tuesday, had a meeting in Davidson, but about a half mile from the Montgomery line. Violent threats were made on both sides. One party swore if Crooks attempted to preach so near to Montgomery, he should be taken back to Troy. Another, if they come for that purpose they should have hot shot. This meeting also passed 'without interruption.

"Next day, meeting at Union, in Randolph County. There Z. N. made an effort to get up a riot, but failed. Thank God, his royal presence was signally displayed.

"The following Saturday and Sabbath, meeting at Franklinsville. Saturday a Doctor from Chatham came to town for the purpose of raising a mob; but not succeeding, he came to meeting and appeared during the sermon, to be much agitated with mental agony.

"From the 17th of June to this, the 6th of July, I traveled alone. Brother William Yestal now, became my traveling companion.

"Tuesday, we had a precious time at Freedom Hill, in Chatham County. Two joined the Church, whom may God bless. The house at this place was threatened, but I guess it stands yet.

"Wednesday, I had the pleasure of meeting Brother Wilson, who is employed on Guilford circuit, with whom, we went to 'Cool Spring,' in Randolph County, preached a funeral sermon to a large and deeply attentive auditory. The funeral was of a child, a namesake.

"Thursday, Brother W. preached (I was sick and unable to preach) at Craven's School-house, where some months since my buggy was much abused. A good sermon and a good meeting.

"Sabbath, meeting at Caraway. Text, "Finally, brethren, farewell." A large and tender congregation.

"Report said, the Guilford mob was going to be there, and join a wing from Randolph, but to the credit of Randolph, I will say it was not disgraced by a mob, nor did, it to any considerable extent, sympathize with mobocracy. No interruption, except some conversation during worship outside of the house.

"Wednesday evening, we went to Abel Guardener's in Guilford.

"Thursday, went to Jamestown. News is immediately conveyed to Greensboro, that A. Crooks is at Jamestown. Here I saw and conversed for a few minutes with G. C. Mendenhall, our counsel, who informed me he could not get McBride's case before the Supreme Court. One man gave me quite a philippic, on learning that I was a preacher, and taking it for granted that I was a pro-slavery one, but on learning who I was, offered his services to head a company of armed men, and protect my person wherever I might wish to go. This, of course, I did not wish to encourage.

"We, Vestal and myself, left town, the sun about fifty minutes above the horizon; thought of lodging with Mr. B., about a mile from town, but concluded my property, if not my person, would be in danger that distance from town; went three miles to Brother P's., did not yet feel satisfied, and travelled eight miles to Brother W.'s. and in Randolph staid till next evening, when we went to Wm. L.'s.

"Saturday morning, went eleven miles to T. P.'s, in the neighborhood of whom, on the Sabbath, I organized a Church of ten members.

"Monday, I went to the S. W. part of Randolph County, to my post-office, and got a letter from Brother Bacon, stating that all things were peaceable on his charge, and that he expected to remain another year, etc.

"Tuesday morning, early, received by private conveyance a letter from G. C. Mendenhall, Esq., urging me for my own sake, for the sake of my friends, the public peace and of religion, to desist attending a Quarterly-meeting which was to be held at Union, Guilford County, the following' Saturday and Sabbath; a meeting which that gentleman knew I designed attending; and if I entertained any doubts as to my duty, to come and see him forthwith. If I desired he would come out of Guilford, the county in which he lives, into Randolph to see me, etc. I started immediately to see M. u Mr. Mendenhall assured me that such was the excitement in the public mind, that my presence in Union, on Saturday or the Sabbath would be the occasion of bloodshed, that there were two parties equally determined, one that I should be arrested, and the other that I should not. That no pains had been spared in making preparations for my arrest, that the probability was, there would be thousands from Alamance, Chatham, Randolph, Davidson, Forsyth, Rockingham and Guilford counties for that purpose, that not a few looked upon the conduct of the mob as contrary to law, in violation of the Constitution and their rights as citizens, which the Constitution and those laws were designed to protect, and who were determined to die in their defense; that these were not Wesleyans^ and iii order to prevent the most sanguinary scene that has ever transpired in the county, it was the wish and request of my friends for me not to come to the meeting.

"I suggested that perhaps the Constitutionalists might be dissuaded from their purpose to resist.

"All present agreeing with Mendenhall that if I were at Union no earthly power could prevent the effusion of blood, and that I ought not to go. I gave Mr. Mendenhall leave to make it known that I would not be at the meeting, and of my purpose to start for Conference shortly.

"On receipt of this information, Mr. Gilmer declared I should not be interrupted according to law or otherwise till the 10th of August, and that he would make every possible effort to prevent the meetings from being interrupted. In view of every circumstance, I thought it would not be amiss to let my whereabouts remain a secret, which I did. I was confirmed in this belief by information from a friend on Friday, that the day before; some men came to Mr. L.'s, inquired for Crooks, said they had a warrant, and it was their business and duty to arrest him, made search, and left "without aid or comfort."

"Saturday morning, ten o'olock, a company numbering about three hundred, came from different counties armed with clubs, pistols, dirks, etc., not expecting, as they said, to find Crooks, but they heard that Bacon would be there, and were resolved that no Northern Abolitionist should preach in the Country.

"A company was also there armed with guns, etc. determined that Bacon, nor any orderly man, should be abused if they could prevent it. Besides these there was a large congregation who had come with other intentions from different parts of the circuit.

"Before separating, the mob arranged to have a circular printed and scattered broadcast, in which they entered into a resolution to give their continued and united efforts to expel Adam Crooks and J. C. Bacon from our State— *peaceably*, if we can, and *forcibly, if we must.* — And to affix a reward of two hundred dollars ($200.) for their apprehension, or one hundred ($100.) for either of them, if taken anywhere in the State, after the 5th of August.

"On Monday morning I commenced getting ready to depart for Conference; took my buggy to R.'s, about five miles from Greensboro, to get it repaired; staid at R.'s till Tuesday, a.m.; then started for my trunk in the southwest of Randolph. On my return, when passing a house, I spied Mr. Stead, making towards his barn, which is about eighty yards from the road, as I came opposite which, from behind a stack issued stones which fell around but did not hit me. These were hard arguments, but are never needed in defense of a good cause.

"When I landed in Guilford, I was informed that, notwithstanding the mob had entered into resolution to give me to the 5th of August to make my arrangements to leave, and that I should not be interrupted according to law or otherwise, till after the 5th, an effort was made to raise a company in Greensboro, on Monday night, to take me at R.'s, and that on Tuesday morning a slave came to R.'s shop, inquired if he had a large two-horse carriage for sale, a thing never made in that country unless ordered. Seeing me, the boy asked if that was Crooks; was answered in the affirmative. About an hour after, the officer in company with the slave, his master, and others, rode up to R.'s, inquired if Crooks was there. William R.'s son answered, "He is not." This seemed to cause great surprise; and the officer manifesting a disposition to search the house, was told if he attempted it without a search-warrant he must kill or be killed. He did not insist. William told the truth; I was not there, being on my way after my trunk; a happy escape from officers of injustice, while disappointment was the reward of their faithfulness to their own resolution.

"The object in getting out the warrant was not to give me the benefit of a trial according to law, but as a pretext why I should be taken without resistance, and when they once had me in their power, they could do as they pleased with me. Some threatened to hang, and others to tie a rope around my neck, fasten me to a buggy, and take me where I could be transported to an uninhabited island, from whence I would never return to North Carolina, No doubt they intended not to let me leave without at least entering into bonds not to return. But they did not get me, and may I not say with the Psalmist, 'By this I know thou favorest me, because mine enemies do not triumph over me.'

"Saturday evening the second of August, left B's., a distance of about nine miles, for my buggy; got to R's. by twelve at night, and deeming it unsafe to remain, accompanied by my friends, I started for J. Stanley's, a distance of thirteen miles, where we landed all in safety at break of day, and from which on the morning of 4th., of this instant, I started for this place, where I landed after a lonely journey of five hundred miles, performed in eleven and a half days — and was cheered by the smiles of my relatives and friends, among whom, besides my parents, and brothers and sisters, I will name Rev. J. Phillips, Rev. J. McBride, and Rev. A. R. Dempster.

"As this letter is already too lengthy, I forbear indulging remarks as to the happy effects the conduct of the mobs has had in directing the public eye to the enormities of a system which has long warred against the throne of God, and rights of man. They intended to prevent investigation, but God, who causes the wrath of man to praise him, and taketh the wise in their own craftiness, has caused it to have the very opposite effect. Never did the Carolinians think as much on that subject as they now do. Never did they hate Slavery as they do now.

"I entertain the confident hope, that ere long American Slavery will expire amid a nation's joy."

Observations

Mr. Crooks finished his Conference year fully. During all his difficulties, he never neglected one of his own appointments. Those meetings he was persuaded not to attend, were upon brother McBride's work. He had numerous calls, which he did not and could not obey. During those four years of arduous labor and almost constant danger, his mother fasted twice a week and prayed for the advancement of the cause, and the preservation of her son. He left North Carolina with sorrow and sadness, feeling that the friends of Jesus and suffering humanity were left as sheep without a shepherd, and among wolves. He left many warm personal friends. Among them he counted one of the lawyers employed in his trial, George Mendenhall, Esq., and his estimable wife. They were extensive slave-holders. Their slaves came into the family by a former wife. The present Mrs. Mendenhall, was a Friend, and opposed to chattalizing human beings. As soon as they could do so they set their slaves all free. Their riches consisted in slaves and land. The earnings of the slaves were carefully saved, and as soon as enough money was accumulated, a company was started for Ohio and Indiana. Thus they liberated nearly eighty thousand dollars' worth. They were years in doing the work, and it was not all accomplished when the South seceded at the commencement of our last war. The last load was ready and started, hoping to be allowed to cross the lines, but they were sent back. They were in the care of Mrs. Mendenhall. We received a visit from Mr. and Mrs. Mendenhall, when we were living on Delaware Circuit, The journey from the South was made in carriages and covered wagons. When at our house they had about twenty slaves, old and young, with them. Several years before the work was all accomplished, Mr. Mendenhall was drowned while attempting to ford a swollen stream. When found his arms were thrown upon the bank, and in his hands he held his satchel containing manumission papers for all his slaves, who were still in the South. The family were very great sufferers during the war. When Mr. Crooks bade them farewell, to come North, Mrs. Mendenhall placed in his hands a paper, containing the following poem, beautifully engrossed.

> May He whose care
> Surrounds the little sparrow when it falls —
> Who hears the nestling raven when it calls,
>   Still prompt thy prayer!
>
> For He will own
> All that His holy Spirit inly breathes —
> That through the windings of the heart enwreathes
>   A sigh — a groan.
>
> Look round and see
> The passive dew-drop on the lily rest;
> The active lightning flash from east to west;
>   So may'st thou be.
>
> So be thou taught —
> "Instant in season, out of season" too,
> Vocal like thunder, silent like the dew
>   With blessing fraught.
>
> O! let thy will,
> Thy *all* of self upon the cross be slain,
> That *all* of death may die,— that Christ may reign,
>   And man 'be still!'
>
> Words may not tell —
> Not e'en the unseen, silent, parting tear,
> How earnestly we bless thee — brother, dear!
>   Farewell! Farewell!

D. E. M.

Guilford, N. C, 7th mo., 1851.

Further Activities

The first year after his return, he was appointed to Zanesville Charge. As the membership was small, they were not able to support even a "single man." He told them if they would board him, he would teach school, in order to earn enough to defray his other expenses. He commenced a private school. Very soon he gained such a reputation for managing bad boys, that his school was largely composed of boys who had been expelled from the public schools of the city. He was very much interested in the teacher's work.

In August, 1852, he was appointed preacher in charge of Medina, or what was called the Granger and Huntington Circuits. Rev. George W. Bainum was his assistant. He was also elected one of the delegates to the General Conference, which held its session in Syracuse, within a few weeks. The appointments on his charge were many miles apart, making long, hard rides. His home was at River Styx, Medina County, in the family of brother Turner. He could be there but little, as the work on the different parts of the field required his presence. During the Winter, they held several protracted meetings, with good success. At Lodi there were numerous accessions, and in the Spring following, a new edifice was built.

His Marriage

The third of May, 1853, he was married to Elizabeth Willits, student and teacher of Leoni Institute. In a book presented to his bride, these lines are written: —

A HUSBAND'S GIFT TO MRS. E. W. CROOKS,

Presented on our wedding-day,
   Which as you see,
Is the third of May,
   Eighteen fifty-three.

And as my parents say
The same is my birthday,
   In eighteen twenty-four.
   Which makes me one score,
   Plus nine, and no more.

As the gentle shower
   Descending from above,
Cheers the bright May-flowers;
   So shall I, my dear,
   Seek thy heart to cheer
   By kindnesses of love.

For eight years he had been a traveling minister without home or home-comforts, literally fulfilling the injunctions — "Take neither purse nor scrip, for your journey." "Eating what is set before you asking no questions." Sometimes faring sumptuously, and sometimes otherwise; meanwhile laboring hard in the vineyard, and resting wherever night, overtook him.

In speaking of this experience he said, "He learned to call each 'sweet spot' a home, and every man a brother." He always said he never felt like complaining, for he fared better than his Master, who had not where to lay his head. He always found a friendly roof to shelter him. Though at times very poor in this world's goods, yet the kind Father always provided for his necessities.

At the Conference held August, 1853, he was appointed to Huntington Circuit alone. Here, the last of September, his own humble home was first established. Here his own family altar was first erected, upon which ever since, continually have been offered sacrifices to the Most High — the fire upon that altar never grew dim. — The house-keeping was commenced, as a light purse would dictate — very plainly. It was a settled principle, "There shall be no debts." If there was not ready money to get all we wanted, we denied ourselves, or waited until means were given. He remained on this circuit two years. Quite a number were added unto the Lord, and a new church-edifice was built at Huntington. We found many devoted friends; among them were Timothy Burr and wife, of precious memory. It was hard to leave them; but as there was some difficulty in supplying the work of the Conference, and this Charge could be supplied by those who lived near, and did not wish to move, we were appointed to Delaware Circuit. Here three years were spent pleasantly, and with profit. Several new appointments added to the field, and some of the old ones were greatly enlarged.

Trials and Triumphs

At Bennington, the house of brother Marcus Philips was used for service. The congregation was small, but they had precious meetings. Not far away, at the corners, stood an old, dilapidated Methodist Episcopal meeting-house. There had been some difficulty. The ministers had left, taking the church records — even the class-book. For eighteen months the house had been opened only for funeral services. Some of the Christians in the neighborhood sent an invitation to Mr. Crooks to come and preach to them. A protracted meeting was held, souls were saved, Christians were encouraged. By request, the appointment at brother Philip's was changed to the church. The membership greatly increased. By this time, the Methodist Episcopal brethren thought the people ought to be looked after. They sent a preacher once in two weeks, and where there was no service at all, now the pulpit was supplied every Sabbath. They reorganized their class, and some thought should close their doors upon us; but we had sympathy of the community, and they waited until they thought it would be safe. When there was a change in the pastor, they shut their house against us. The result was, we were able to build a beautiful new church.

A meeting of great interest was held in a new place, (Fairview,) lasting seven weeks. There was a Presbyterian church in the village, and not far away a Baptist, but no Methodist. There had been no revival there for many years. Eighty professed to find the Savior. There was scarcely a family in the whole neighborhood, but were subjects of the Spirit's influence. There were many heads of families. Many homes were changed. The world had held sway, but now God was worshiped. Fourteen were sprinkled, and seventeen immersed in one day. A class was organized, and a church built. Some of those brought to Jesus then, are now singing his praise around "The great white throne on high."

The woodland home of the Rev. Edward Smith was near Bloomfield, where his remains are now interred. We visited him several times. During his last sickness, we spent three days with him. He sent word to the brethren, that "If I die of this attack, all is well." He died July 6th, 1856. Mr. Crooks preached his funeral discourse from

2 Timothy iv: 6, 7. 8. The sermon was repeated by request during Conference, at the memorial service. In his death, the cause of reform lost one of its most fearless advocates, and the Church of God one of its strongest pillars. Mr. Crooks was one of the delegates to the General Conference held in Cleveland, in the Fall of 1856.

At the Conference of 1857, Mr. Crooks was Chairman of Committee on Reforms. This is what he wrote then, eighteen years ago.

On Slavery

"*Resolved,* — That all our former declarations of hatred and opposition to the system of American Slavery, are by us most emphatically re-affirmed. We still believe slavery to be evil, and only evil, opposed to the well-being of the enslaver, as well as the enslaved; opposed to the prosperity of the nation, to the spread of the Christian religion, and to the salvation of men.

Resolved, — That there is a oneness of sentiment, on the subject of slavery, among the Wesleyan Methodist Churches; that we have peace in all our borders, while other denominations are convulsed throughout, in consequence of this accursed system having a place within their pales.

Resolved, — That we deeply sympathize with our much beloved brother, John G-. Fee, of Kentucky, in the recent outrages that have been committed upon his person; and shall most earnestly pray the God of Daniel to keep him from the power of the enemies of truth and righteousness, while thus pursuing his labors of love, in planting the standard of the Redeemer in that land of bondage.

Resolved, — That the recent decision of the Supreme Court of the United States, in the Dred Scott Case, in which it is declared that ' the Negro has no rights that the white man is bound to respect,' is a disgrace and a burning shame to the nation, at war with the Christian religion, and strikes a blow at the rights of man, and should therefore be disregarded and scouted by every lover of the Bible.

On Secret Societies

Resolved, — That we will firmly maintain our disciplinary rule against the admission or retention in our Churches of persons holding connection with secret oath-bound societies.

Resolved, — That we believe the principle of secrecy, a3 developed in the various secret organizations of the day, to be fraught with evil, dangerous to political purity, to national virtue, to the rights of man, inimical to the cause of liberty to the oppressed millions of our land, and above all, opposed to the spread of that light which is the life of men.

On Temperance

Resolved, — That we are as much as ever convinced of the great evil of the sale and use of ardent spirits as a beverage — And

That we will oppose it in every reasonable, and lawful way. We will lecture, preach, pray, and vote against it, and recommend to all those over whom we may be able to exert an influence, to forsake, and oppose these evils."

About this time be furnished a number of articles for the Wesleyan, on "True Politics;" also, took some part in a discussion upon the question, — "Is the Twenty-first Section of Discipline, on Secret Societies, law?" He was present at the General Conference when this subject was discussed, passed, and by a majority declared to be law. He took the position in his argument, that if *it was not law*, we should spend our time and talents in *making it such*, not in attempting to prove it a nullity.

The next Conference year was spent on Licking Circuit. The friends were very pleasant, but during the Winter, the Small Pox raged in the village where we resided. Great fright. prevailed, and there would have been great suffering, only that Mr. Crooks, (who had this disease while in Allegheny City) spent a part of each day visiting the sick, burying the dead, and encouraging the living. A number said they believed they should have died of fright, if it had not been for his words of comfort and hope. As a matter of course he could not attend his appointments, for the inhabitants of the country and towns adjacent, would not attend Church, Thus the year passed without any marked revival, yet the children of God seemed to gain strength and grace. During this year, Mr. Crooks spent all his leisure time in reviewing President Finney's *Systematic Theology.* Afterwards, parts of this review were given in the Wesleyan. He has since said that "this close consecutive thought was a school to fit him for his work years after."

Labors at Cleveland, Ohio.

In the fall of 1859, he left Licking Circuit to become pastor of the Church in Cleveland, Ohio; five years were spent with this good people; true hearts were found — noble men and women; those who for the right and truth were willing to be "little and unknown," if the cause of God and humanity could only be advanced. For years, this Church had stood a moral "beacon light" to all other Churches in the city. Here the first church edifice was built by the "people called Wesleyans." When it required moral stamina to bear the name Abolitionist, here was a band of braves, who boldly flung to the breeze the banner of liberty to all alike.

Soon after we arrived in Cleveland, John Brown made his raid into Virginia, was taken prisoner, and the 2d day of December, 1859, witnessed the death of this earnest friend of enslaved humanity. We assisted in the preparations for appropriate memorial services. The following is an extract from a daily paper of the times: —

"IN MEMORIAM.
EXERCISES COMMEMORATIVE OF THE SACRIFICE OF JOHN BROWN."

"Across Superior Street, from the Bennet House to the Rouse's Block, was stretch a banner deeply bordered with black, with the words of Brown, 'I do not think I can better honor the cause I love than to die for it.'

"Several places of business in the city were closed during the day.

"Melodeon Hall was draped in mourning for the meeting held there in the evening. The stage was hung with heavy folds of crape caught up with white rosettes. Around the gallery were folds and festoons of crape with white rosettes. Festoons of crape hung from the walls, the girders and the chandeliers, while the pillars were wound with the insignia of mourning.

"Over the center of the stage hung a large and fine photograph, of the Hero of Harper's Ferry, encircled with a wreath. Above this was the motto: —

"'Amaricus humanis generis.'

"On the left of the picture was — 'John Brown, the Hero of 1859,' and on the right — 'He being dead, yet speaketh.' Still further to the right were the following — 'The end crowns the work.' 'If I had interfered in behalf of the great, the wealthy and the wise, no one would have blamed me.' — John Brown to the Court of Virginia; and on the left the following — 'Remember them that are in bonds as bound with them.' 'His noble spirit makes despots quail, and freedom triumph.'

"The whole was arranged with fine effect, and showed that the ladies had been in no wise inattentive.

"The Meeting. — The number of persons present, and the character of the meeting is stated as follows by the Cleveland *Morning Leader*: —

"'As early as half-past six o'clock the dense throng crowding into the "Melodeon" testified the universal interest felt in the nature and objects of the meeting, and at seven o'clock there was not a vacant seat in the Hall, and the standing places were all occupied. There were not less than 1400 persons in the Hall, about one-third of whom were ladies. The strictest attention was given to the exercises throughout — deep, earnest attention.

"' J. H. W. Toohey called the meeting to order, and introduced tie Rev. Mr. Brewster, of the Wesleyan Church, who read the following passages of Scripture — "Epistle of James, v: 1 to 18; First Timothy, iv: 10 to 18; First Corinthians, xv: 19 to 34."

"The Throne of Grace was then addressed by Rev. Mr. Crooks, in an eloquent prayer, acknowledging the hand of God in all the events of life, and his dealings with the children of men. We, as a nation, the ministers, the Churches and people, are guilty of the crime that has this day been done, in the execution of him who, responding to his promptings of conscience, endeavored to set the bondmen free. He closed with the prayer that all present might so live that they might die in the hope of the Gospel."

Mr. Crooks was one of the speakers of the evening. He also prepared a sermon to be delivered to his own people the next Sabbath evening, but was invited to use the hall, which he did. There was a full house, and close attention. His text was — "He that departeth from evil maketh himself a prey" — Isaiah lix: 15. From this sermon, the following are a few extracts:

"Again, how are we to honor Lafayette, who, from pure and unselfish devotion to the holy cause of human freedom, left the security and quietude of a princely home, came to a land not his own, and threw himself into all the dangers and hardships of tent and field, that he might bestow upon an oppressed people, the priceless boon of freedom; and then brand with "traitor" an American citizen for a devotion no less pure, and a bravery and a magnanimity equally exalted? Why cry a *crown* for one, and a *halter* for the other? Or, how are we to transmit to posterity, as worthy of imperishable glory, the names of Eaton and Decatur, who displayed such distinguished bravery for the rescue of enslaved American citizens, from Tripolitan masters; and then, upon the same page, seek to couple the name of Brown with lasting infamy and substantial disgrace? Or, how lavish our sympathies upon Poland, Hungary, or any of the European nations struggling for freedom, and then unsparingly censure Brown for his *more practical* sympathy for the oppressed millions of our land?"

"He had seen that the purpose of the party dominant in the nation is to, as tar as possible, enlarge the area of slavery, legislate directly for its protection in the Territories, and to re-open the piratical foreign traffic in human "beings. He had seen the ermine of the Supreme Federal Judges stained by a decision which would have shocked the moral sensibility of even the Jefferies — making the administration of justice depend upon complexion! He had seen that slavery is an element of discord and strife in the bosom of this Nation, and the mortal foe to the prosperity and even the perpetuity of this Confederacy. He had seen that there is no political party, of any considerable numerical strength f which even professes to seek the overthrow of this monster iniquity. And last, but not least, he saw that the vile man -thief enjoys unobstructed access, to even the "high places" of our popular Zion, and that the oil of our incense is largely mixed with the sweat, blood and tears of the poor oppressed. Knowing and seeing all this — as a last forlorn hope, he and his less than Spartan band, made deadly assault upon the myriad robbers of their brothers' right. And, like Leonidas, he fell a sacrifice to his native bravery and noble love of liberty; and like him, he fell to be loved and honored. Henceforth let Harper's Ferry be styled the Thermopylae, and John Brown the Leonidas of this nation.

"But the truth, alike shameful and apparent, is undeniable; that it is owing to the pro-slavery character and action of this Government, together with the faithlessness of the popular Churches, that John Brown, and his unfortunate coadjutors died upon a Virginia scaffold.

But American Slavery cannot be eternal. God's justice will not sleep forever; aid God is against slavery. His word is against it; His government, both moral and providential, is against it; the prayers of his people are against it; the common, unperverted conscience of mankind is against it; and the cry of the poor op-pressed is going up continually against it. It is doomed to a speedy, and, possibly, violent dissolution.

"The iron chariot of oppression is not always to roll its ponderous cylinders over the prostrate but sacred form of humanity, squeezing hissing streams of blood from the life-cavities of her great heart. God is already shaking the nation, and the pro-slavery Churches, from center to circumference. Speaking from his throne, ere long, he will say, as anciently: 'I have seen; I have seen the afflictions of my people, and am come down to deliver them.'

"And when that time comes, as come it must, the names of Pierce, Douglass, Buchanan, and H. A. Wise, together with all those of the servile tools of the Slave-power, will be but synonymous with 'cruelty,' 'infamy,' and "misanthropy," and suggestive of whatsoever is odious; while that of John Brown, associated with the names of those who have been distinguished for fidelity alike to God and humanity, will be resplendent with the imperishable honors of Corinthian Lau-rel."

At no time during his labors in Cleveland was there a great revival; yet there was a steady growth, both in spirit and in numbers. Souls were con-verted, and there were quite a number of accessions to the Church. The church-edifice was removed, repaired and refurnished. The congregation was much increased. All seemed to have renewed zeal to labor for God. A prayer and class meeting was established in the suburbs where a number were converted, An appointment, five or six miles in the country, for preach-ing Sabbath afternoons, was added to the work.

Several of the early supporters of this Church have received their "sum-mons to the mansions above." They have laid aside the weapons of warfare, and have gone to that home where the "wicked cease from troubling, and the weary are at rest." Their record is on high. In that great day of final account, Jesus shall say to them: "Well done. Enter thou into the joy of thy Lord."

During our residence here, our Nation became involved in our last "terri-ble war." All loyal hearts were burdened for the salvation of our Country. Our sympathies were greatly enlisted for our "brave boys in blue," and for their dear ones at home. A number of those dear to us were called to sacrifice their loved ones for their Country's good. With aching hearts and tearful eyes we carried them to their last resting place.

Many tokens of kindness and sympathy were received from the friends here, and it was with sorrowful hearts we left them, knowing little of the tri-als, burdens, and conflicts before us; but the path of duty seemed to lead us away.

In July, 1863, Mr. Crooks received the following letter from Adrian College:

Adrian, Mich., July 3, 1863.

Rev. A. Crooks, Cleveland, Ohio: —

Dear Brother: — At the late Annual Meeting of the Trustees of Adrian College, you were regularly elected to the honorary degree of " Master of Arts," together with Rev. L. C. Matlack, W. W. Lyle, and Jas. J. White, of Cincinnati, Ohio, which was duly announced by the President at our recent Commencement.

The Board is pleased to tender this expression of esteem for yourself personally, and to convey to the public this assurance of confidence in your literary and moral standing in society.

Respectfully and Truly Yours,
John McEldowney, Sec'y.

Election to The Editorship

The General Conference, held at Adrian, Michigan, June, 1864, elected Mr. Crooks Editor of the *American Wesleyan.* Had he felt free to follow his own preferences, he would have still remained a pastor. His heart was in that work. He had been told that in all probability he would be one of the candidates for the office of Editor. He did not believe it would result in his election. Among his last words, as he left for the Conference, were these:— "Do not feel troubled about this matter, for I am confident that there are those who will stand before me in the minds of our people. There is no danger of my being called upon to occupy that position." He stated to the Conference his preference to remain in the pastoral work. But the Conference decided to elect him Editor. He always made it a principle to follow the leadings of Providence — to walk in the path opened before him. He accepted the position, returned to Cleveland, and commenced arranging his affairs, preparatory to leaving, as he was needed at the office immediately. His Church and congregation were wholly unprepared for this change. Some of them felt that it ought not so to be; and to human eyes it seemed to require great self-sacrifice. The Church was in a prosperous condition, spiritually and temporally. The house of worship had been put in good repair. All was pleasant between pastor and people. "Peace was in all her borders, and prosperity within her walls." But God, who sees the end from the beginning, and judges righteously, knows what is best for his children, and where he can use them for his own glory, and the upbuilding of his cause and kingdom on the earth. It is his prerogative to guide, and ours to follow.

June 23d, he left Cleveland to commence his duties in the office of the *American Wesleyan*, in Syracuse, N. Y., and on the 28th of June appeared the following: —

"SALUTATORY."

"In entering upon the untried duties of his office, the ' new Editor' will be expected to state, at least in general outline, his views of the objects to be secured, and of the principles and policy which should govern, in the performance of those duties. As this expectation is most reasonable, it shall be met at once. Then,

"1. Being the organ of a Connection of Christian Churches, the *primal* objects of the *American Wesleyan* should be the success of Christian enterprise — 'the spread of scriptural holiness, over these lands'— consisting in *piety* and *purity*, correct faith, genuine experience, and corresponding practice. ' Holiness unto the Lord' should radiate from ever issue.

"2. As the organ of the Wesleyan Methodist Connection of America, the paper should more immediately serve the interests of this particular Christian denomination, promoting its peace, purity, unity and prosperity, advocating its doctrines, propagating its principles, and chronicling its triumph. Yet at the same time, as a public religious journal, it will take pleasure in recording the achievements, moral and spiritual, of sister denominations. It should be a medium for the diffusion of general Christian intelligence.

"3. The organ of a denomination eminently reformatory, as heretofore, so in time to come, the *American Wesleyan* should speak no ambiguous language respecting the great reforms of the day. As our Connectional banner — battle-torn though it be — it must continue to float from the foremost and highest battlements of Zion, defiant of all sin, as when first given to the breeze. These are not the times in which to haul down our flag, use Quaker ordnance, fire-blank cartridges or offer truce or amnesty to rebels in arms against any claim of God or interest of humanity. Slavery must not be allowed to revivify. Its utter extinction must be rendered certain. Unrelenting warfare must be waged against the monster iniquity — Intemperance. The spirit of violence must be rebuked and checked — the arbitrament of the sword, treated as a calamity finding its dreadful necessity only in sin, and to be remedied by the Gospel; and all 'unfruitful works of darkness' must be 'reproved.' All this means work and conflict. The apostolic order, 'First *pure, then* peaceable,' is not to be esteemed either obsolete or inappropriate.

"Most obviously, dissensions and needless divisions among Christians are to be deplored as depleting, uneconomical and schismatic. From the first, our existence as a distinct organization was felt to be a painful necessity. Union, both in fact and form, among the disciples of 'one Lord,' is to be encouraged and promoted. Yet it should not be forgotten that true Christian unity— 'the unity of the spirit' — is accordant with, and tolerant of variety, and hence, in some sense, of dissimilarity. At the same time it should be remembered, that any real union between moral opposites is not possible; and if even possible, yet not desirable. Our motto shall be, — *Union at the expense of right, never; hut for the sake of right, always and everywhere.*

"The *loyalty* of the *American Wesleyan* shall be unconditional. Committed to the support of no political party, merely as such, it shall yet not be indifferent to 'that part of ethics which consists in the regulation and government of a nation or state for the promotion of its safety, peace and prosperity; comprehending the defense of its existence and rights against foreign control and conquest, the augmentation of its strength and resources, and the protection of citizens in their rights, with the preservation and improvement of their morals.' (See *Webster's Definition of Politics.*) It shall oppose as destructive of the interests of the Nation, all corruption, whether of private morals or in public life; and inculcate, as a Christian duty, the exercise of the elective franchise for the elevation to positions of honor and trust 'men who fear God and hate covetousness.' It shall seek to fan the fires of intelligent patriotism

— strengthen the hands of the Government in its efforts to suppress rebellion; and especially a rebellion having for its object the establishment of a government, the chief corner stone of which, is the iniquitous system of human chattelization. It shall denounce, as traitors to God and enemies of mankind, all, of every latitude, who either openly or covertly sympathize with the present rebellion. And it shall seek to nerve the heart and arm of the living, and speak words of comfort to the dying patriot soldier; and bestow upon his friends at home, its warmest and most Christian sympathies. Most happily, in all these respects, the Wesleyan Methodist Connection of America, is a unit. Thank God, there is not a traitor in the entire body.

"The *principles* governing in the composition of the *American Wesleyan*, shall be such as most fully accord with the foregoing objects.

"Its *spirit* and *policy* shall be liberal. Both sides of all questions proper to be considered shall be heard at reasonable length. This being the case, the Editor is not to be held responsible for any sentiment which he does not *personally endorse*. Christian courtesy must characterize style and matter. Investigation, rather than disputation, shall be encouraged. General interests, and not individual wishes, are to be consulted in determining what shall be admitted and what excluded. The rule shall be to disallow the discussion of all merely local and personal differences. The door may not readily open for the admission of careless writers. Records of grace victorious, whether as seen in marked conversions, beautiful lives, or triumphant deaths, are insured a hearty welcome.

"It is with great diffidence and self-distrust that the new Editor assumes the duties and responsibilities to which he has been called, and especially so, in view of the corps of able editors preceding; Scott, Lee, Matlack, and Prindle. But when he remembers that the inexperience in the chair is fully atoned by the large experience of our excellent Agent, Bro. Prindle; that, adopting military phraseology, he is to be supported by such staff officers as Dr. Lee, W. W. Crane, W.H. Brewster, L. C. Matlack, W. W. Lyle, and H. B. Knight, as Corresponding Editors, together with many competent field officers in the form of contributors; and that his readers are too intelligent and liberal minded to either require or expect *perfection* in any human production, his heart is more than doubly assured. For mere frigid critics, he has neither fear nor fellowship, but only indifference. He can promise only to *do his best* to send to its readers the *American Wesleyan* laden with 'food convenient' to make them intelligent, hopeful, happy, zealous, efficient, and mature Christians. Then, trusting not to his own, but to Divine wisdom, and asking and expecting the sympathies, counsels, and above all, *prayers* of his readers, the new Editor assumes the duties and responsibilities of his office."

The work was new, and his duties arduous from the first; for in connection with his editorial work, he had all the proofs of the two papers to read and correct. Very soon calls to attend Quarterly Meetings were received, to which he responded. He and Dr. Prindle together supplied the pulpit at Seneca Falls, for a number of months.

His heart was alive to the condition of our Nation, For years, dangers had threatened on every hand; traitors were at home and abroad. Only confidence in the wisdom and power of that God who *never* fails, kept up his courage. From an editorial, published July 20, 1864, we give a few leading heads:—

"The demand of the times."

"1. A primary demand of the times is, that the masses be made to comprehend the events transpiring, 'to know in this our day, the things which make for our peace.' In times of such weighty significance, this is often important even in a Monarchical Government; in a Republic, it is absolutely indispensable. Ours is a government of the people, and the hands of the people must be made skilful to guide the Ship of State amid rocks? and darkness and tempest. They should be made intelligent not only in history, and the philosophy of history, but in the rich and deep philosophy of the eventful present. They should be made intelligent as to the wicked moral forces which have caused this rebellion, the hellish purposes of its guilty leaders; and its inevitable results if successful, upon their position, pecuniary and social, and even liberties for generations to come. And that the people may be thus instructed, the very air should be rendered vocal with truth uttered from street, and cottage, and counter, and platform, and pulpit, and press. This is no time for either indifference, silence, or inaction.

"2. The popular conscience needs to be enlightened. The nation needs to be taught the inviolability of the Divine law — that 'though hand joined with hand, the wicked shall not go unpunished;' and that no nation can long survive persistent departure from the eternal principles of rectitude. Upon this subject we must have 'precept upon precept, precept upon precept; line upon line, line upon line," until this truth permeates the national heart, and becomes a sovereign sentiment.

"3. The times imperatively demand that positions of public trust be filled with men of incorruptible patriotism, broad, enlightened and statesmanlike views, and of inflexible integrity; while all unprincipled demagogues and political gamblers, of whom it may well be said, as of Leo X., that they 'get into office like a fox, rule like a lion, and die like a dog,' should have their part in the place kept for the burial of strangers. They should be esteemed the Nation's worst enemies, and treated accordingly.

"4. An all-ruling and undying patriotism, a patriotism which *'endureth all things,'* is another requisite of the times. The rebellion with which the Nation is grappling in life struggles is of unprecedented proportions. Hundreds of thousands of lives; husbands, fathers, sons, brothers — and hundreds of millions in money have already been given, and the end is not yet. Hundreds of thousands more of husbands, fathers, sons, and brothers, and hundreds of millions more of money may yet be required before we realize the right solution of 'the grave problem — If the Nation is to live; if Freedom is to die! Heaven grant that our integrity to the interests involved may abide the seven-fold heated furnace.

"5. The times demand a *United North.* "Divide, and conquer' was the motto which shaped the policy of ancient Rome. United, Carthage and Syracuse would have been invincible against Rome, but enemies, and divided, they fell victims to their common foe. For the last fifty years, the South has practiced this policy against the North, and in the interests of slavery. The political parties have unwittingly been our Carthage and Syracuse.

"There are those in our midst, whose names need not be written, but who share the protection of our laws, enjoy the immunities and benefits of our liberal institutions, and subsist upon the bounties of our plentiful Country, who nevertheless, like ingrates, prove themselves enemies in this, the hour of our Country's peril. To us, these are far from being an element of strength, but like others, they can expect to stand only upon their good behavior. For the Nation's sake, for the sake of the blood and treasure already expended; for the sake of coming generations, and for the sake of the dearest interests of humanity, *'as far as lieth in us,'* let there be a *United North*. Let not the prophetic words of our Washington be unheeded, that 'United, *we stand*, divided, *we fall.'*

"6. Another demand of the times is *continued liberality*. We say *continued* — for in the past, in the form of the Sanitary and Christian Commissions, and the numerous other concerted and individual schemes for the protection and comfort of our brave soldiers, say nothing of what has been done for their families at home, there has been a munificence of liberality displayed, for which the history of the world has no parallel. This should not be allowed to suffer any abatement.

"7. The times demand an unfaltering faith in God, and in the final triumph of the right. 'This is the victory that overcometh, even your faith,' In the absence of faith there can be neither courage, nor purpose, nor endurance nor efficiency. The times require that in all these respects we 'show ourselves men.'

"8. Our manifold sins of profanity, pride, self-adulation, worldliness and oppression, together with the fearful retributions of Heaven, call loudly for deep humiliation and true penitence, including a purpose and determination to 'break every yoke and let the oppressed go free.'

"9. Last, but not least, the demands of the times must fail of being met, without a stronger faith, more fervent piety, more all-consuming zeal, and a deeper baptism of the Holy Spirit."

In an editorial, written after our national skies were brightening} giving our position as a nation a few years before, and our then present prospects, he says:

"MORAL PROGRESS OF THE NATION."

"Through our highest courts we had declared that a 'man of color has no right which a white man is bound to respect;' and in violation of plighted faith, we had opened the virgin soil of Kansas to the ingress of slavery, and persistently employed the powers of the Government for the infliction of slavery with all its untold horrors upon an unwilling people. And with but few noble exceptions, the religious bodies of the land were acquiescent. Thus both Church and State were criminally in the interests of slavery. Here is where we were when the present war commenced. But we thank God, a brighter record awaits us.

"Maryland has enrolled herself among the Free States; Missouri, Arkansas, Louisiana and Alabama are moving in the same direction. The Methodist E. Church has closed its communion against all slave-holders; other Churches are uttering words of denunciation against the system, merited and distinct; and as a crowning act, by a large majority of both Houses of Congress, the infamous Fugitive Bills of 1793 and 1850 are wiped from the statute books of the Nation, and the repealing act approved and signed by the President. Three years ago, in the eyes of the Nation, slavery was legitimate, petted and defended; now it is well-nigh esteemed an outlaw and rebel against God; the Nation, and the interests of humanity.

"More than twenty years ago, Orange Scott? and other true prophets of the Lord, clearly saw and foretold, that 'the days of American Slavery, were numbered; that its death-warrant was sealed in Heaven.' We had hoped, however, to bring about the work of repentance to the extent that its *execution* would not subject the *Nation* to punishment, nor -peril its existence. But in this respect our hopes were not to be realized. We were doomed to disappointment, sad and grievous. God be praised that we are learning obedience by the things we suffer. Fruitless regrets aside, God does not needlessly afflict the children of men 'True and righteous are his judgments.' May we, as a nation, speedily show mercy to all the afflicted, that mercy may be shown us. Amen!"

Later he said: —

"The dark clouds are fast lifting from our Country's horizon. Victory seems to crowd upon the heels of victory. Let grateful thanksgiving continuously go up to God for benefits bestowed, together with fervent prayers for the speedy bestowal of a righteous and perpetual peace."

Still later he wrote, as follows: —

"HOPE FOR THE NATION."

"Watchman, what of the night? Is there hope for the Nation? After all that has been expended in blood and treasure must we still perish? We have survived the conflict of arms; shall we be adequate to the perils of peace? These are questions of appalling significance. Our enemies in Europe answer, No! Is the wish parent to the prediction? We believe that the lap of the future is freighted with good for our Country. Reasons: —

"1. The Nation is forever redeemed from the curse of slavery. The war, the Proclamation, and the Constitutional Amendment settle that question beyond all peradventure. Liberty is now and ever shall be in the ascendant.

Thank God, in this Country she has secured a continental home. We shall never have another rebellion in the interest of slavery. The body politic is forever relieved of this great element of unrest.

"2. The Nation is likewise purged of the essentially disintegrating element of the doctrine of State Sovereignty, in its perverted application.

"3. The aristocrats, anti-republicans and factionists of the South, who have ruled the Country for the last half century, are forever dethroned.

"4. In this Country patriotism is no longer to be an empty name; but is to be a living sentiment forever entempled in the Nation's heart.

"5. In our own eyes, in the eyes of the world, and in *reality*, we are stronger to-day than ever before. Stronger, because relieved of those internal elements of revolt, slavery, perverted state sovereignty, and their fruits and necessary adjuncts; pride, contempt for honest toil, impatience of restraint and the spirit of domination.

"6. It is to be hoped that politicians have learned a lesson of prudence and caution. Hereafter, let political leaders adhere to the truth, address reason, and not appeal to blind passion.

"7. Not only has the Nation been purged, politicians taught wisdom, but we rejoice to believe that our *religion* and our *Churches* have been improved. Thank God, that at last the distinct utterances of the Pulpit, the religious Press, Doctors of Divinity, and ecclesiastical assemblies, are no longer in the interest of the wealthy and proud oppressor, but unqualifiedly in favor of the poor and oppressed. This single truth lights the whole national heavens with a glow of promised good! Let heaven and earth rejoice at once over a disenthralled Nation and Church.

"Finally, There is hope for our Country, because, as our national currency attests, 'In God we trust.' He has not put us in the furnace for *destruction,* but for *purification.* A brighter era is just before us! This glorious truth murmurs in every brook and streamlet, whispers in every breeze, and makes glad music in the interior of every soul. God has great thoughts and purposes of good for this Nation. There is hope for our Country, for our children in coming generations, and for liberty in all lands!

Denominational Union Movement

Mr. Crooks had not been in the chair editorial many months, before the subject of our union with some other denomination began again to be agitated and as the prospect of our Nation's final release from the "sum of all villainies" became more and more apparent, the matter was urged more and more earnestly. When freedom to the millions of slaves was proclaimed, the friends of the "union movement" said: "Slavery, the primal cause of our organization as a body of Churches, is dead, and there is nothing to be gained by our continued existence. We can now disband consistently." They forgot that in destroying our little Zion, they were destroying the religious home of our people, the most of whom had never known any other. For this cause they had fought "many a battle sore," had "many atrial," "made many a sacrifice," and the little home, though humble, was very dear to their hearts. Many could not, in conscience, go to any other, and would be left homeless and uncared for during their journey to the better land.

It was asserted, time and again, by those who ought to have known the truth, that "Our people, as a mass, are ready for the change." Under these circumstances, Mr. Crooks could do nothing but "let the people *speak* for themselves, and decide for themselves."

The battle raged long and fiercely. Many seemed to forget that Jesus taught: "And unto him that smiteth thee on the one cheek, offer also the other." Some of us then learned the lesson — If we hope to be forgiven we must forgive.

He stood between the two fires, and tried, with constant, unceasing prayer to God for help, to hold the balances. If ever man sought to deal justly in this matter, he did. God alone knows the trials of those days and months; God alone knows the heavy blows which fell upon his devoted head, and burdened heart. When I remember those days of conflict, I am filled with wonder; how could he have borne all be did? He could not, only God was with him.

In looking over files of letters, I find copies of some of his replies to those who wrote him on the subject of the "Union." I give a few extracts to show his spirit:

June 8, 1869.

"Wholly aside from any conviction of right and wrong in the case, I cannot but regard it [the 'Union Movement'] as unfortunate at this time. Reasons: —

"1. It is not spontaneous with our people. It originates with the few; hence, the many are not ready for it.

"2. It involves a question which has heretofore distracted us, and concerning which many of our people are strongly bound in conscience.

"3. This being true, it puts the unity of our own people in imminent peril. Unless the greatest prudence is exercised, we are to be exploded, and with all the prudence possible, we are to be distracted and alienated. This at a time when we should be joyful over past achievements, and active in doing the work of the hour for the freedmen.

"4. It puts Adrian College, now in its infancy, in jeopardy, when it needs all the help of all the people. When our attention should be eminently fixed upon it, we are occupied with this 'Union' matter. Thus our people are distracted, and in suspense, and indeed, being alienated, when they should be a unit, both in heart and effort. The Convention (Cleveland) *must not ignore* the voice of the people, and Adrian College must act so as not to lose the confidence of our people.

"5. Five years ago, when every prominent man among us favored the 'Union,' it could not be effected. These facts have their significance, and on these accounts I tremble for results. *God help us* all to *act wisely*."

"I shall be as prudent as possible, but violate my conscience, or be dishonest *I will not.* The Lord helping me."

"God is witness, I have tried to be impartial. If I am supposed to be opposed to the publication of anything on either side calculated to throw light on the subject of duty as to this matter, I am the worst misunderstood man in the Connection. I have been pained tenfold more because of the profound silence of the authors of the 'Union Movement,' on the subject in its moral aspect, than by all other considerations combined. No, I shall most gladly welcome truth from either side. My heart has "been as a furnace, because of the aforesaid silence. I wish you would immediately send a statement of facts as to what was done respecting Adrian College. If anything decisive has been done, it looks badly. 1st, — Because of profound silence. — 2d, — It looks like an attempt to *almost force* 'Union' matters, and 3d, — To make the College practically sure to those who go into the 'Union,' and as a denominational enterprise *lost* to those who do not go in. It has a terrible bad countenance. If a full statement of the facts will satisfy our people, you do *yourselves* and *them* great wrong in withholding it. If it will not, then God help us.

"Another point: — Our people are far from being ready for concerted action. Not a few are opposed to the 'Union' entirely; others favor a union of all Methodists, and others of only non -Episcopal bodies. In a very few years lay delegation will be incorporated into the Methodist Episcopal Church. This will make the existence of the new body either sickly or temporary.

"In view of all these facts, is it wise to press the 'Union Movement' to a speedy consummation? I cannot so regard it. Rocky roads require slow and careful driving; rapid driving will be damaging, may be fatal to the vehicle. There are times when it is the dictate' of the highest wisdom to 'make haste slowly.' Delay may secure concert; haste will surely be fatal."

"You know my heart in relation to this great question how I desire that God should guide you and me and all of us in the right way. . . As to our 'fate being sealed' — that 'we cannot live' — I do not believe a word of it. If we but do the work of a Church of Jesus Christ, we will be subject to the law of increase."

"By some I may be judged as self-seeking. God forbid! I do not seek ease, nor shun toil. Following the pillar of God's providence, I went and remained in North Carolina at the peril of my life, and now I am where God and the brethren have put me. I never sought position, and I shall antagonize nothing nor any one, hut as duty may seem to impel.

"I would not let myself think otherwise of thee, my brother. His will as known, to be our law, may He keep us ever in this spirit. -With you, I do not know what I shall do, *only* that I shall seek to please God."

Also, in another of the same date, but to another person, he says: —

"In an emergency it is no time to seek new friends, but to depend upon old ones, true and tried. When those who have been sapping the foundation of confidence in our perpetuity, get through with that kind of work, if they ever do, then we may hope to succeed in enlarging our list. You say you 'want the Wesleyan to live.' Those with whom you are in correspondence, boast that 'the *Way of Holiness* has gone down, and the Wesleyan soon will.' If I wanted a house to stand, be assured, I would not keep incessantly digging away its foundation.

"Reverse our position and relations, and let me pursue the course you *have* and *are* pursuing, and as a man of sense, I ask you what you would think of me? [Would you still think me acting the part of a brother?] I allude both to your conversation and correspondence."

In October, 1866, Dr. Prindle resigned his position as Agent, at the meeting of the Book Committee. At the same meeting, Mr. Crooks was appointed Agent. His first editorial after his agency commenced, was

"EARNEST WORDS TO WESLEYANS."

"Beloved Brethren and Sisters: — Just at this point in our history there are evils to. which we are greatly exposed and against which we should be strongly fortified. We will name some of them.

"With us as a denomination, the last twenty months have been months of earnest, and in some instances, we are sorry to say, caustic controversy. As in the case of Paul and Barnabas, the contention became 'sharp.' There is danger of protracting these contentions to our own injury, as also of fostering feelings not compatible with Christian charity and fraternity. Having been thoroughly canvassed, may not these questions of controversy be profitably dismissed, at least from the field of disputation? We are confident that this is intensely desired by a large majority of our people. And awarding integrity of motive to all, shall we not rise to an altitude of Christian charity and magnanimity which will keep our hearts united in unabated Christian fellowship and esteem? We are brethren. Wesleyans must not fall out by the way. In matters of such vast moment, blind passion may not innocently be consulted. Let us earnestly covet and devoutly pray for the 'best gift' — that without which by the verdict of inspiration, we are nothing.

"We should give no place to needless discouragements. We cannot free ourselves from the conviction that undue emphasis has already been given to discouragement. We have even heard it more than whispered, that our continued existence as a separate organization is not possible. Duly sensible as we believe we are to all that tends to discourage, our faith in the possibility of a continued useful existence has never for one moment faltered. Viewed and judged from a merely human stand-point, our prospects are vastly better than were those of Israel at the Red Sea, or the disciples after the Crucifixion, or of Luther at Worms, or yet of the Wesleys when they first entered upon their career of grand spiritual achievement and triumph. What, if for some years past we have been under the law of diminution: the same is true of larger, sister denominations. These have been years of special trial to all Churches. Moreover, there is a diminution which contributes to strength and perpetuity. All new bodies are less or more the victims of a kind of floating capital, to be relieved of which is a real deliverance. Of this class of character, Wesley and have had their full share. *If we will but faithfully do the work of a Christian Church, multiply converts and build up believers in all the Christian graces, we will quickly pass from under the law of diminution and come under that of increase.* Our continuance and growth under God, therefore, is with ourselves. If we deserve an existence our extinction is not possible.

"As in former times, God has made us his vanguard in his great battle for the temporal deliverance of his oppressed poor, may he not have in reserve for us a future of a still higher and more glorious significance; the calling of his people to a larger spiritual liberty? For years there has been imbedded in the Christian consciousness the conviction that the Churches are signally failing to fulfill the great mission of evangelizing the world. We have churches and pulpits, and preachers, and learning and talents and sermons enough, but conversions are few, and in too many instances only partial. A higher and better state of things must be inaugurated, or otherwise the conversion of the world is not even the subject of reasonable hope. What is the great defect? The ready answer comes, Want of the spirit of power on the part of God's minister's and people. Other reasons there are; but the great foundational and all comprehensive reason is found here. 'Not by might nor by power, but by my spirit, saith the Lord.' God will not share his glory with another. In the work of saving men too much must not be awarded to human, nor too little to Divine agency. Hence, in his great wisdom God chose the 'foolish things of this world to confound the wise; and God hath chosen the weak things of the world to confound the things which are mighty; and base things of the world, and things which are despised, hath God chosen, yea, and things which are not, to bring to naught things that are.' Hence, too, men of great power with God, are invariably men of much prayer. To us it was cause of exceeding joy as we visited the Conferences at their recent sessions, to find that many of our ministers are coming to the apprehension of this great and vital truth. It was in harmony with this apprehension, that having resolved to continue its present ecclesiastical relations, the Iowa Conference immediately adopted the following: 'Here and now, to the glory of God and for the salvation of souls, we consecrate ourselves renewedly to the work and service of Christ, trusting not in forms or usages, but in the Holy Ghost, for success.' Also many of the members of the Michigan Conference renewed their ordination vows; and the gracious influences of the Holy Spirit descended and rested richly upon them. Yet as it respects this subject, we only see men as trees walking. May the entire ministry renew their covenant vows; and may Heaven bestow upon us and upon all the Churches, abundantly, the baptism of zeal and of power! And let all the people say, Amen!"

Part of editorial, January, 1867.

"'UNION MOVEMENT' CALLED CONFERENCE.

"From the first we deprecated the 'Union Movement,' so called; fearing it could only work disaster. The sequel proves that these fears were well founded. But we supposed that in the absence of general harmony, the enterprise would be abandoned. In this we were sadly disappointed. Opposition soon began to develop. Both sides were allowed an impartial hearing. For many months the contest raged around our head, and we remained silent. It becoming apparent that opposition was formidable, Conference after Conference *Resolved,* 1st. Not to compromise any of our positions on moral questions; and, 2d. Not to destroy our own denominational unity. Hence, we were confident that the Cincinnati Convention would meet, consult, and pray over the general subject of Christian union, and part, leaving each denomination with integrity unimpaired; just as brother Matlack afterwards said he advised. But as is well known, this was not the policy adopted by the Convention. Soon it became apparent that in the Convention there was disagreement on moral, and even patriotic questions. We believe that no single paper introduced by a Wesleyan on either of these subjects, passed in the Convention without encountering opposition. As must have been the case, Conference succeeding Conference which had hitherto favored the movement, now withdrew that favor. Some individuals still felt themselves bound in honor and in conscience to press the measure to consummation. As a concerted movement it is now abandoned. This movement was for a union of all the non-Episcopal Methodist bodies in this Country.

In this issue of our paper will be found a Call for a Conference of all Wesleyans in favor of uniting with the Methodist Episcopal Church. We give the Call insertion, not because we can go into such Conference, but for the reason that we regard religious -denominations as voluntary associations, and for the further reasons, that however regretful we may be, yet we are willing that all those whose tastes or convictions of duty would lead to the Methodist Episcopal, or any other Church, should conform to those tastes or convictions.

"What we would desire, is that those who go out from us do it quietly and peaceably. There is no beauty in, nor just occasion for distracting or mutilating. The Methodist Episcopal Church needs neither our ministers nor members. And on the other hand, we would have no one, minister or member, leave the Connection as the mere result of panic. 'Stand still, and see the salvation of the Lord.' There is no necessity for haste. Do nothing now which may lay the foundation for future fruitless regrets. Let no Church, minister, or private member leave, merely because they hear that others in other localities, are going to do so. Such rumors may or may not be true. Let every one be fully persuaded in his own mind, and act out his highest convictions of right. And let no one fear to do right. A religious denomination fully devoted to the edification of its members in all the Christian graces, and in the salvation of sinners, may duplicate in three years. 'Trust in the Lord, do good, so shalt thou dwell in the land, and verily thou shalt be fed.' 'They that trust in the Lord shall be as Mount Zion, that cannot be moved.' The Lord give us the victory of Faith.

"In these days we are ever and anon reminded of the appalling report by the spies sent by Israel to spy out the land of Canaan. There were great, walled cities. There were giants in the land. They said 'we were in our own sight as grasshoppers, and so we were like grasshoppers in their sight; we had better return to Egypt.' Also are we reminded of the mockings of Sanballat and Tobiah — 'What do these feeble Jews? will they fortify themselves? will they sacrifice? will they make an end in a day? will they revive the stones out of the heaps of rubbish which are burned?' 'That which they build, if a fox go up, he shall even break down their stone wall.' The sequel of both of these cases is well known to the Biblical student. But we confess that we are growing weary of hearing our own funeral sermon repeated so often. The good folks will please desist, and neither administer upon our estate, nor any part of it; nor yet observe our funeral rites until our demise is officially announced.

"Men and women of God, the world is before us. Souls are perishing all around us. In many places Zion is a waste. Life is but brief. Time is swiftly passing. What we do to rescue the perishing, or edify the Church, which is the body of Christ, must be done quickly. Then 'rich in faith,' strong in purpose, and led by the great Captain of our Salvation,

> 'Indissolubly joined,
> To battle all proceed:
> But arm yourselves with all the mind
> That was in Christ, your Head.'"

"And if, in the providence of God, our forces are in the future to be united with other cohorts, we should hold ourselves in cheerful readiness for such event But Providence should never be anticipated; only patiently awaited."

THE RALLY AND RESTORATION OF CONFIDENCE.

The people rallied bravely. Expressions of confidence were given. Every man who remained seemed to feel he had something to do. His labors were very arduous, having all the editorial and publishing interests to care for, and at the same time, be prepared with weapons furnished by faithful brethren, and his own, to meet all the attacks made by those who had said we must disband; and of course we would have to do so, if they, by any possibility, could bring it to pass. In connection with all the rest of his labors, he served the Church in Syracuse as pastor, one year, and at the same time, attended regularly a temperance meeting, held on Sabbath afternoon, in one of the Halls of the city. This last organization being in its infancy, he was anxious that it should be a success. He often addressed it, and served it one term as President. He continued to meet with it until his frequent absences from the city made it impossible to do so longer.

He seldom rested one Sabbath, for his calls to the Churches became more numerous than he could respond to. Far and near he went to attend Quarterly -meetings, and encourage weak Churches to rally to the work. Of course, this I made extra work — requiring very much night, or early morning work. He would not write evenings, because so weary. After a few hours sleep, he would awake refreshed, and could accomplish much more in a short time. Many mornings he has arisen at one o'clock to write, or prepare "copy." Indeed, nearly all his editorials during these years of conflict, were written by lamp-light, in early morning. The matter for the paper must be furnished in time — the affairs of the Office must be attended to, supplies must be kept on hand. Thus the dollars must be made to go as far as possible. Retrenchments in every way must be made. All his energies, all his time and talents were given to the cause. He could talk of nothing, think of nothing beside, and the burden of his prayers was for direction and help in the work before him. Memory brings to mind seasons of earnest pleadings for wisdom, for a *constant* guidance, for he did not want to go forward except he heard the command "Go forward," from his leader, God.

During one of the sessions of the Allegheny Conference, the way seemed blocked. The powers of darkness for a time appeared to prevail. He felt that he could not go forward unless he had some token, that it was Lord's will. He spent the entire night in prayer. Alone, nearly all the time with God, like one of old, he felt he could not let him go except he bless. His prayer was, "Oh Lord *show me the path of duty. Give me the light to walk in.* If it is thy will that *we,* as a *denomination, should disband, make it plain to me; if not, open the way. I cannot give it up — I must know thy will. I cannot— I will not go forward unless thou dost direct the way.*" All night was spent on his knees pleading. Just as daylight appears to drive away nature's darkness, so the "light of God" shone around him, making duty plain. Almost an audible voice said "Go forward; I will never leave thee nor forsake thee." From that time, no matter what the opposition, or how great the obstacles, he felt the calm assurance that God was with us, and "who can be against us." He walked constantly in "that light," feeling that "one with God, is a majority." He would often hear of unkind letters having been written, unkind personal remarks having been made, but I never knew him to manifest a spirit of retaliation. He almost always used to say "I am so sorry for them, they are not happy, or they would not say such things." Many times he used this language in his prayers, "O Lord, bless our enemies, if we have any. Touch their hearts, change their language and save their souls."

One who left the Wesleyans during this movement, said to him, "Now, brother Crooks, you are ambitious, and you can take a high position in other Churches, and why do you remain with those who are left. They are poor, illiterate and humble, and you cannot expect eminence if you remain with them." His answer was, — "I am ambitious only to do God's will. I want to fill the place he has for me; to do the work he gives me to do. God will take care of me and my reputation."

When our people took courage, and began to build churches, he was sent

78

for, far and near to dedicate them. I think it was in the Winter of 1867, he went to Iowa. It was extremely cold. He had to work early and late, to be able to leave the Office. He was gone six days, of which he rode five days and nights. He took his luncheon along to save expenses, as they were not able to do more than barely defray his expenses. In 1873 he went to the same State, was gone seven days, and rode five days and nights. He never spared himself if he thought the cause of God needed his labors. If expostulated with, he would say, "It is labor here and rest hereafter." There was so much to be done — so much that would have to go undone, if he did not step forward and do it, that he could not rest. It is easy to stand and look on, and enjoin care of self, but it is hard for an earnest worker to see the cause of Christ suffer for the want of efficient laborers, or for the want of means to pay others for doing the work a Many, very many times he stepped forward to lift the burdens for others, when he ought to have been relieved. During his ten years and over, of hard labor at the Wesleyan Office, and his attention to the interests of the Connection, he never had one week's rest; not one week in which he could lay his cares aside and seek repose. When the pastors of the various Churches of this city would be taking their Summer vacations among green fields and pleasant surroundings, it was a heavy cross for me to see my precious one toiling on, regardless of heat or dust— weariness of body or mind— every day using *all* his strength. Sometimes it seemed to me that ail the change for him was added care, or a little more work.

At the General Conference held in Cleveland, Ohio, in the fall of 1867, he was re-appointed Editor and Agent. For more than five years he had the entire charge of the Connectional interests. He was editor of two papers; manager of finances, both of Publishing Association and Missionary Society. He also carried on an extensive correspondence with all parts of the work. He was ready to entertain all who came, and had a cheerful, hopeful word for every one. During these years he often had ague and fever; also, was subject to attacks of bilious colic, when, for a few hours, he was a terrible sufferer. He did not take much medicine; for rest of body and of mind was what he most needed. He could not believe that his constitution was being undermined; that the seeds of disease were being sown, which would destroy his strong, healthy body. His heart and hands were so full of "labors more abundant," that he did not take time to realize his danger. When sick, his greatest anxiety was to get well for fear the work would suffer.

In the spring of 1868 the first National Anti-Secret Convention met in Pittsburg, Pa. He was a delegate, and in 1869, a State Convention of the same kind was held in Syracuse, over which he presided. I give the resolutions passed by the State Convention held in Rochester a few days after his death; also a few of his reasons why Christians should oppose those societies.

PREAMBLE AND RESOLUTIONS

"Whereas: — In the midst of our rejoicings in prosperity, the pall of an inexpressible sadness has been recently spread over us, in the event of the death of

Kev, Adam Crooks, one of the most able and efficient members of our State Association, —And,

"**Whereas:** — In early life Brother Crooks identified himself with the cause of reform, and with heart, and pen, and voice, has ever stood in the forefront of every great moral conflict, battling for God and the right; and he attended the first National Convention Opposed to Secret Societies, held at Pittsburgh, Pa., and was elected one of the officers of the National Association then and there organized, — And,

"**Whereas:** — From his early association with this work of reform, and the great abilities and devout piety he brought to the work, we had learned to look to him as one of our most honored and trusted leaders, — And,

"**Whereas:** — A God of infinite wisdom and unbounded goodness has called our dear brother from the conflicts of earth to the rest of heaven, your Committee have appended the following resolutions — if it please the Convention for their adoption: —

"*Resolved*— 1. That in the death of Rev. Adam Crooks, from his great force of personal character, his superior abilities, the efficiency of his pen, we feel deeply, as a Convention, oar great loss.

"*Resolved* — 2. That inspired by the example of Brother Crooks, and others who have fallen at their posts, we will close ranks, lock shields, and press in the name of God to victory.

"*Resolved* — 3. That our warmest sympathies are tendered to the widow of Brother Crooks, and all afflicted in the death of members of this association during the year last past; and we do most earnestly pray that Divine grace may prove their sufficient support and consolation.

"All of which is most respectfully submitted.

N. Wardner, *Ch'n Com.*
D. Kirkpatrick, *Pres.*
Edwin Barnetson, *Sec'y.*"

Extract from Supplement to "An Inquiry into Freemasonry and Oddfellowship."

"The Wesleyan Methodist Connection of America does antagonize those fraternities. In all kindness, yet with much plainness, the following pages set forth some of the prominent reasons for such attitude. We write with the single object of serving the interests of Christ's kingdom. Read and ponder with the candor of Christian honesty.

"I. In its pretensions to great antiquity as also in the history of its degrees, Masonry evidences a criminal disregard for truth. Instance a few examples; and only a few. As every person intelligent upon the subject knows, Masonry professes to date back to the days of Adam and Enoch, and narrates how by the agency of the latter its 'precious jewels' were preserved through the flood.— That it has its A. L.— Year of Light, dating back 5874 years, — That it teaches that Solomon and cotemporaries, Hiram Abiff, the widow's son, and

Hiram, King of Tyre, were three Grand Master Masons, — That Hiram Abiff was cruelly murdered by three Fellow Crafts, *Jubela, Jubelo, Jubelum,* for firmly refusing to give them the Master's word, and for which they respectively suffered the dreadful penalties of the first three degrees of Masonry, — That anciently the Word of God was preserved from being lost through Masonry, — That the omission of the name of Jesus in the Blue Lodge prayers is owing to the fact that Masonry is more ancient than Christianity,— That the two Saints, John the Baptist and John the Evangelist were patrons of Masonry,-— and very much more of like character.

"Speaking in unvarnished terminology, the Editor of the *American Freemason*, a Monthly, published in the interest of the Fraternity, said of the story of the murder of Hiram Abiff, parroted as history in the lodges every week, that its ' every sentence is a lie.' And as every scholar knows, *Jubela, Jube. lo, Jubelum,* who according to Masonic lore murdered Hiram Abiff, are not Tyrean but Latin names, and that the Latin language did not have existence till some three hundred years after Solomon and the two Hirams; and that therefore the story is not only false, but ridiculous. But in the presence of such boastful pretensions to antiquity, what are we to think of the following confessions to the recent nativity of Masonry? Steinbrenner, an able Masonic historian, admits that Speculative Freemasonry dates no further back than 1717 — less than 160 years. Now what becomes of the stories about Enoch, and Solomon, and Hiram Abiff, and *Jubela, Jubelo, Jubelum,* and the preserving the Word of God from being lost, and of the omission of the name of Jesus because of the superior antiquity of Masonry, and of the two Saints John, and of its 'Year of Light?' But Dr, Dalco, compiler of the book of Constitutions for the State of South Carolina, meets these pretentious claims with a direct contradiction. He says, 'Neither Adam, nor Noah, nor Nimrod, nor Moses, nor Joshua, nor David, nor Solomon, nor Hiram, nor St. John the Baptist, nor St, John the Evangelist, were Freemasons. Hypothesis in history is absurd. There is no record, sacred or profane, to induce us to believe that those holy men were Freemasons; and our traditions do not go back to those days. *To assert that they were Freemasons may make the vulgar stare, but will rather excite the contempt than the admiration of the wise.'*

"II. Profanity is specifically forbidden in the Word of God. 'Thou shalt not take the name of the Lord thy God in vain; for the Lord will not hold him guiltless who taketh his name 'in vain.' Ex. xx: 7. Jesus is very specific and minute. 'But I say unto you, Swear not at all, neither by heaven, for it is God's throne; nor by the earth, for it is his footstool; neither by Jerusalem, for it is the city of the Great King; neither shalt thou swear by thy head; because thou canst not make one hair white or black. But let your communication be Yea, yea; Nay, nay; for whatsoever is more than these, cometh of evil.' Matt, v: 34, 35, 36. And St. James emphasizes this prohibition in the words following: 'But *above all things*, my brethren, swear not; neither by heaven; neither by the earth; *neither by any other oath.*" Jas. v: 12. The duty of the Church to prohibit profanity no person of common intelligence can doubt. But Freemasonry is built upon swearing. Every distinct obligation in every degree is taken by swearing. In the first seven degrees there are over half a hundred distinct oaths. And this terrible swearing is going on throughout the Country in all the Lodges, every week! Every person must know, upon a moment's reflection, what must be the influence of such familiar use of the name of Deity. With so much swearing in the Lodges, no marvel that the earth almost groans beneath abounding profanity. Hence, in-so-far as it is the duty of the Church to prohibit profanity, it is her duty to protest and oppose Freemasonry; seeing that every stone in this superstructure, from foundation to capstone, is laid in profanity — *swearing authorized, by no law, either human or divine.*

"III. The obligations of Freemasonry are taken in ignorance, and under circumstances which preclude the possibility of the due consideration of their character. Still further: The higher degrees rest upon and are supported by the lower; and the members of the lower degrees are assumed to be in utter ignorance of the obligations of the higher. Thus, by the very organic structure of the institution, the members of the lower degrees are supporting under oath and death-penalty, *they know not what.* That the Church cannot innocently tolerate such reckless disregard of the sacred obligations of morality and the valued interests of mankind, is self-manifest.

"IV. But not only are the obligations of Freemasonry assumed and supported in ignorance, but some of these obligations are essentially criminal. We instance the obligation to keep the secret of a brother Master Mason, communicated as such, as inviolable as in his own breast, murder and treason only excepted; and in the Royal Arch degree, ' murder and treason not excepted,' — that to flee to the relief of a brother Master Mason giving the sign of distress, at the risk of life; and this wholly irrespective of what may be the occasion of his distress — and. that to espouse the cause of a companion Royal Arch Mason engaged in any difficulty, so far as may be necessary to rescue him therefrom, *whether he be right or wrong.* [See Morgan's Expose of Freemasonry, pp. 74, 75; Light on Masonry, pp. 74, 75; Finney's Letters, pp. 90, 91. Also xiii Wendell, pp. 9 — 26.] Palpably, such obligations are alike incompatible with the duties of the citizen and the Christian, obstructive of the just administration of civil and ecclesiastical law; and therefore essentially subversive of both Church and State. Civil Government is as really ordained of God as is the marriage relation; and hence, it is as much the duty of the Church to maintain the former as the latter. Therefore, by all that binds the Church to maintain its own purity and life, as also the integrity of the State, it is bound to antagonize Freemasonry.

"V. Everywhere the Scriptures teach to hold in sacred regard, human life. But everywhere Masonry pawns the lives of its votaries. We enumerate some of its horrid penalties. — The throat cut across — the tongue torn out by the roots — the left breast torn open and the heart and vitals' taken thence —

the body severed in the midst and the bowels burned to ashes — tongue split from tip to root — the skull smote off, &c, &c. No reflecting mind can fail to see how essentially anti-Christian and barbarous are such penalties; nor yet how barbarizing the influence of making the mind familiar with such monstrous mutilations. What kind of imprecations are these for civilized men; saying nothing of Christians and Christian ministers? Thus while Christianity enjoins love, blessing, and forgiveness of enemies, Freemasonry binds to **vengeance** and **murder!**

"VI. But this thought gathers additional emphasis from the well-authenticated facts of history that Secret Societies have been the foster-nests of Jacobinism, Communism, Political Revolution and every form of Skepticism. Read Barruel's four volumes, and Robinson's Evidences of Conspiracy against both Civil Government and the Christian Religion. Hence, naturally enough, Voltaire, D'Alambert, Diderot, Condorcet, Robespierre and fellow conspirators, called into requisition secrecy, for the effectuation of their diabolical purposes. Even Communism is but Freemasonry gone to seed. For, from the Masonic position of a belief in *some* God, but *utter indifference as to which*, there is but a single step to the position of *no* God. Hence, to an extent which the masses but little suspect, Freemasonry and *free* thinking (Skepticism) are confederates. And this connection is both philosophic and historic. Hence, too, Communists are Atheists of the coarsest type. Only think! — in his great work on Modern Doubt and Christian Belief, page 30, Christlieb makes note of a Secret Society in a Prussian gymnasium, consisting of boys between thirteen and fifteen years of age, the very first paragraph of its rules commencing with — 'Any one believing in a God is thereby excluded from this society.' Thus, boys in their first teens are committed to the dogma, fatal as it is senseless, of 'no God!' But none can doubt that this society is modeled after one whose initiates are 'boys of larger growth.' Hence, as the divinely appointed conservator of all interests sacred to either God or humanity, it is the high duty of the Christian Church to antagonize such fraternities.

"VII. Again: As Secret Societies are organized favoritism, which ever and anon pushes justice from her throne; puts one up, and another down not because of personal merit, but the senseless figments of grips, signs and passwords thus unsettling the eternal sub-basis of the whole social fabric — community, Church and State; and, as the God-appointed work of the Church is to 'establish judgment in the earth,' in the very nature of the case, her divine mission cannot be accomplished without the overthrow of these societies. This single fact makes her duty plain.

"VIII. The Bible teaches everywhere the inseparableness of *purity* and *acceptable worship.* If we regard iniquity in our heart, the Lord will not hear us, 'Holiness becometh thine house, Lord, forever.' 'Worship the Lord in the beauty of holiness.' 'He that turneth away his ear from hearing the law, — even his prayer shall be abomination.' But aside from its caricature of the Bible narrative of Moses and the burning bush, where puny man is heard saying, 'I am that I am,' as in the Royal Arch degree; aside from their mixing repeated falsehood with the exclamation — 'Holiness unto the Lord!' as in the pretended finding of the Ark of the Lord containing the Law, the manna and the rod that budded; from the admixture of prayer and unmanly mummery; and aside from the mimic performances of the visions of the Revelator, as in Rev. v, vi, and vii: in which four old men with *inflated bladders*, represent the four angels of God, having in command the four winds of heaven, and worthy Masons in white robes, coming up to the throne, ' having washed their robes in their own blood!' — Aside from all these performances, revolting to every sentiment of reverence, these secret orders divorce, in the sanctuary of the soul, the divinely united ideas of purity and worship, by frequently appointing lips notoriously profane to parrot prayers into the ears of Jehovah; thus perverting the heart and mind in their deepest fountains — obliterating all just conceptions of acceptable worship. This single fact might well cause holy angels to weep, and sufficiently defines the duty of the Christian Church.

"IX. By all its multitudinous oaths, frightful death-penalties, and tormenting dread of the various vengeance of the Craft, Freemasonry seeks to bind the soul for life, in the holy sanctuary of its convictions of right. It may be filled and thrilled with horror in view of its obligations and associations, and yet find itself fastened to f this body of death' by cords of more than steel. This lamentable truth addresses itself not only to the conscience of every Christian, but also to the heart of every true American. The true Church everywhere cries out — l Loose the human conscience, and let it go free.'

"X. While seeming to reverence the Bible, as containing the revealed will of God, Freemasonry in reality degrades it to a level with the Veda, the Shaster, the Koran, the Zen Davesta, and the sacred books of all nations. In this regard, no distinction is made between the true and the false, the clean and the unclean. With this institution, all are of like authority; or rather *want* of authority, as having the Divine sanction. Proof: — *Chase's Digest of Masonic Law*, page 207: 'In fact, Blue Lodge Masonry has nothing whatever to do with the Bible.' Of course he means, as of divine authority. In *Masonic Jurisprudence*, Mackey lays it down as a fundamental Landmark in Masonry, that a 'Book of the Law' shall constitute an indispensable part of the furniture of every Lodge.' — That is, 'that volume which, by the religion of the country is believed to contain the revealed will of the Grand Architect of the universe.' — Pages 33, 34. Mark — believed 'by the religion of the country' — *not by the Masons.* To tamely acquiesce in this degradation of God's Holy Word to the level of the Hindoo Shaster, the Zen Davesta of the worshipers of fire, and the oracles of all the false religions would outrage even manly honor, to say nothing of Christian consistency.

"XI. The religion of Freemasonry is a rival to Christ's religion. That it intrudes upon the domain of Religion is manifest from its creed, altar, prayer, priesthood, &c. Chalmers I. Paton, an English Masonic writer says: 'It needs little proof to show that Freemasonry is essentially and thoroughly of a religious nature.' 'Religion is inwrought into the whole system of Masonic ceremonies.' Again: — 'It everywhere exhibits the same religious nature.' [See his work on its Symbolism, Religions Nature and Law of Perfection,' page 447, and first paragraph in Preface.] Rev. Geo. Oliver, Lieutenant Grand Commander of the Supreme Grand Council of the Thirty-third Degree for England and Wales, says — 'Freemasonry was revealed by God himself to the first man.' 'Masonry, in the first ages of the world, was therefore a pure religion.' 'The Order of the Royal Arch is founded exclusively on religion.' Star in the East, pages 2 and 8. Now, if a religion at all, it must be a rival religion — (1) By claiming time, attention, money, devotion. (2) By, in some sense, ministering to man's religious nature and thus tending to satisfy it. (3) By claiming to do for man all that Christ proposes — found a universal brotherhood — establish universal peace— regenerate — free from sin — insure a passport from the Lodge below to the Grand Lodge above. We have room for but a few quotations. Mackey in his *Lexicon of Freemasonry*, page 16, says thus: 'Acacian — A term derived from 'innocence,' signifies a Mason, who, by living in strict obedience to the obligations and precepts of the fraternity, is *free from sin*.' In a recent work by L. E. Reynolds, P. M., and P. H. P., and recommended by the *Masonic Trowel* of June 15, 1870, as 'void of ostentation, candid in statement, and worthy the study of every Mason who desires to take a comprehensive and philosophical view of great principles, and all students and reasoners will be delighted with its unfoldings and processes,' we find the following remarkable avowals: 'Masonry does not deal with the perversions of things, but is only illustrative of the regenerate man.' 'A Lodge in general signifies heaven, or the dwelling-place of the Lord, and includes all on earth who are being prepared for heaven.' 'Each man who is about to be regenerated, is led by his guardian angel to the door of the Lodge, of which it is said, 'Seek and ye shall find; knock and it shall be opened,' 'Regeneration or Masonry proceeds in progressive order or states' (degrees.) 'Man cannot work or correct the irregularities of life, until he is clothed with innocence or the badge of a Mason.' He then becomes a divine, spiritual man or Master Mason.' pp. 101, 237, 188, 219, 214, 131. Now, is not this very candid, and unostentatious, and philosophical? And in his 'System of Speculative Masonry,' page 79, Salem Town says: l Then (in die fourth degree) the Freemason is assured of his election and *final salvation*.' But (4) It claims superior merit. Steinbrenner, in *Origin of Masonry*, pages 13, 14, styles it 'that *higher* religion, which indeed embraces the *lower* religion of creeds and sects;' and in the category of sects, it places the Christian religion. And Rebold, in the *History of Freemasonry*, decries the Christian, Jewish, Mohammedan, and all other religions, and extols Masonry as destined to supplant them all, and become the 'Universal Religion.' And finally: As a matter of positive experience, in both Germany and France, the Lodge is largely supplanting the Churchy especially in the larger towns and cities. Thus; just as the Lodge goes *up* the Church goes *down*. And John D. Caldwell, 'Grand Secretary' of 'Select Masters' in Ohio, frankly avowed that in this Country also, Masonry is '**Disintegrating the Church**.' Shall the Church of Christ tolerate, caress, and warm into life this destructive rival? Shall its life-blood continue to be drained thus, as by a vampire? Shall it commit suicide by default, and basely and unresistingly deliver to its enemies 'the last hope of humanity?' May a merciful God avert such dire calamity! Surely all *true Christians* must say, *Amen*.

"XII. Being a *rival* to Christ's religion, it is a *false* religion, and lures to ruin.

"1. Its claims to establish a Universal Brotherhood are false. (1) In its very nature it is restricted to the few. Excluding all women and children, all cripples, and all the aged and indigent, it cannot be universal. (2) The basis is false — seeking to unite moral repellents — light and darkness, Christ and Belial. Where is the wisdom of attempting such impossibility? (3) The basis is *wrong*, if even possible. To treat the true and false, the good and the bad all alike is shockingly horrible; yet this is the Masonic mode of treating all religions.

"2. Its boastful claims of being cosmopolitan and of mutual toleration of all religions is also false. The Christian law requires prayer only in the name of Jesus.— 'No man cometh unto the Father but by me.' To such prayer in the Lodges the Jew, Infidel, Parsee, &c, object. Mutual concession would plainly say — 'Let the Christian pray in the name of Jesus, when he leads, and the Jew, &c, without it.'— A concession, by the way, Christians have no right to make. But does Masonry do this? By no means, The conscience of the Jew, Infidel, Parsee, &c, must be held sacred, but the law and conscience of the Christian must go into the dust, Thus does Masonry, down to the seventh degree, discriminate against our only Lord and Savior, and in favor of his enemies.

"3. *Its professions to save, are also false.* As seen above, it professes to 'free from sin,' regenerate, make a man divine, and insure *'final salvation.* But there is 'no other name under heaven given among men, whereby we must be saved' but that of Jesus. Acts, iv: 12. This name the religion of Masonry rejects.

"This conducts to the final proposition, viz: *Freemasonry is essentially anti-Christ.* Christianity proposes to bring man back to God *by Jesus Christ as the only way.* 'There is one God, and one Mediator between God and men, the man Christ Jesus.' 1 Tim. ii: 5. 'There is no other name under heaven given among men, whereby we must be saved.' Acts, iv: 12. 'No man cometh unto the Father but by me.' John, xiv: 7. 'Whatsoever ye do in word or deed, do all in the name of the Lord Jesus.' Col. iii: 17 'That at the name of Jesus every knee should bow, of things in heaven, and things in earth, and things under the earth; and that every tongue should confess that Jesus Christ is Lord, to the glory of God the Father.' Phil, ii: 10, 11. 'He is anti-Christ that denieth the Father and the Son. *Whosoever denieth the Son,* the same hath not the Father.' 1 John, ii: 22, 23. 'There shall be no false teachers among you, who privily ('stealthily and unobserved') shall bring in damnable heresies, even *denying the Lord that bought them,* and bring upon themselves swift destruction.' 2 Pet. ii: 1. 'But he that denieth me before men, shall be denied before the angels of God.' — Luke, xii: 9. In the face of all these passages of the Inspired Word, and others which might be quoted, Freemasonry sets up a religion professing to save men; but denies Jesus — disallowing the use of his name even in its approaches to God; and thus assails Christianity *in its divine Centre.* Indeed, in the seventh degree, it does not hesitate to cut his name from passages of his Holy Word which it professes to quote. [See Sickles' Freemasons' Monitor, pp. 50, 51.] True, prayer is sometimes offered in the Lodges in the name of Jesus, but only by sufferance, and in *violation* of the promise to 'cheerfully conform to all the ancient established usages and customs of the fraternity.' "Now, unless Christianity is a *farce* and a *cheat,* to ignore Jesus Christ in our approaches to God in prayer, is no less an abomination than are bold blasphemy and idolatry; and Freemasonry is defined and proven to be both 'a *deceiver* and *an anti-Christ.'* But in the degree of Knights Adepts of the Eagle or Sun,— The Key of Masonry— the fraternity speaks for itself. Hear its words. 'Behold, my dear brother, what you must *fight against and destroy,* before you can come to the knowledge of the *true good and sovereign happiness!"* Well, what is it? Harken! 'Behold this *monster,* which you must conquer— a *serpent* which *we detest as an idol that is adored by the idiot and vulgar under the name of* RELIGION!!!' (Revealed religion is meant.) 'Light on Masonry,' pp, 270, 271.

"There you have it in a nutshell, *in their own words!* Is it any marvel that the Lodge 'disintegrates the Church?' Is not this sufficiently *anti-Christ?*

"And it is but due to state that Odd Fellowship also excludes the name of Jesus from its authorized formulas of prayer. The same, we believe, is true of some of the Good Templar and Granger prayers. All these things being true, it follows with the force of irresistible sequence: —

"1. That whatever there may be in Freemasonry and kindred institutions that is commendable, *it cannot compensate for their demerits and essentially anti-Christian character,*

"2. That it is the sacred duty of all who are not entangled in the meshes of Masonry and kindred Christ-rejecting institutions to keep themselves forever free therefrom.

"3. That it is the sacred duty of all, especially of every patriot, Christian and Christian minister thus entangled, to *immediately* and *forever* terminate his connection therewith.

"That it is duty to repent of and not perform a wicked oath is palpable. Instance the oath of Herod to Herodias' dancing daughter, resulting in the cruel murder of John the Baptist, — that of the forty men to kill Paul; and that of David to slay Nabal, and all the strength of his house. 1 Sam. xxv: 22. — See also, Lev. v: 4, 5.

"4. That as Christianity is not only negative, but radically positive, it is the most sacred duty of every Christian, Christian minister and Church, to in every legitimate way, both by teaching and discipline, testify against and antagonize a religion which is at once without equity and without a Christ.

"5. That it is the plainly enjoined duty of every true Christian, whether minister or layman, to withdraw fellowship from all religious denominations which persistently refuse to thus testify against *monstrous sin.* — The Apostle, in a manner the most solemn, says: 'Now we command you, brethren, in the name of our Lord Jesus Christ, that ye withdraw yourselves from every brother that walketh disorderly.' 2 Thes. iii: 6. Again: 'And I heard a voice from heaven, saying, Come out of her, my people, that ye be not partakers of her sins, and that ye receive not her plagues.' Rev. xviii: 4. Thus it is clear that to remain in fellowship with religious bodies which tolerate great and crying sins, is to become partaker of such sins — is to virtually endorse them as not sins.

"The power we oppose is mighty. The princes and peoples of all provinces fall before it, as before the image of gold upon the plains of Dura. The populace have learned to list with silent awe and bated breath to its thundering laudations. It has superinduced its potent influence upon tongue, and type, and pulpit, and press, and platform, and colleges, and courts, and Congresses — every formative force in society — and thus well-nigh bound both Church and State as with fetters of iron. There is no moment to be lost in taking cowardly counsel of unmanly fears. If this foe is *mighty,* truth is *almighty.* Enough to know that our cause is just; and that immortal interests are involved, If we can innocently ignore Christ in prayer *once,* we can *always.* And there is no neutral ground. We must take sides. To surrender Christ, is *virtually to surrender Christianity.* In the name of all that is sacred in human destiny, these pages plead against a surrender so costly. With such a cause, shall we plead in vain? Ministers of the gospel, with the vows of God upon your souls, what do you say? Reader: the one question for you to settle is — **Will you at any cost be loyal to Jesus Christ?** He is appointed our final Judge. If we deny Him, He will deny us. The verdicts of Time are of little account. Be sure that your answer is such as the *decisions of Eternity* will approbate. Heaven, in mercy, impart the grace needed to fearlessly, and by all legitimate means, antagonize banded treason against the purity of the Church, integrity of the State, and the world's only Savior."

In June 1870, he wrote as follows: —

DUTY RESPECTING THE TEMPERANCE MOVEMENT.

"Now that the Heaven-insulting and Man-victimizing crime of chattel slavery has been abolished in this Country, the patriot, philanthropist and Christian can bestow more exclusive attention upon the soul-and-body-destroying evil of the rum-traffic. Human duty is one of the greatest thoughts that can occupy human attention. And duty respecting the temperance movement is well worthy the most candid and careful consideration.

"Begin with self. We need scarcely say that it is the individual duty to be consistently temperate. No man has a right to mar and scar the handy-workmanship of his Creator by self-inflictions in any form. Intemperance involves the highest possible inflictions upon the entire mam It is murder by protracted process, perpetrated upon his physical being, his social nature, his intellectual powers, and upon his deathless spirit. It is a matchless wrong inflicted upon self, which no man has, or can have, a right to perpetrate. Murder is the greatest wrong that can possibly be inflicted; and drunkenness is self-murder in the worst possible form.

"Next to personal, is parental duty. Those who are false to self, will not be true to family, or any other' interest. Heaven has committed to parents the fearful responsibility of training their children. Upon them devolved the un-speakably delicate duty of laying the foundation stones in the superstructure of their children's character, and thus to an extent in the presence of which an angel might well tremble, determine their children's' destiny, both for this and the future world. The fiery cup of death and damnation should be care-fully kept from their tender lips. Early in life, upon the father and mother's knee they should be made intelligent as to its dreadful effects, and taught to shun it as they would the bite of a serpent, or sting of an adder. All domestic wines or juices, having the least particle of alcohol should be excluded the domestic circle, as Satan and his legions were excluded from heaven. The principle of total abstinence from all that can intoxicate should be inwrought into the very web-work of their souls. What parent would not welcome the deadly knife of the assassin to the heart of his child, rather than the thrice deadly fang of this liquid serpent of perdition and the woeful fate of the drunkard? Then, by the love you bear for those precious, priceless jewels of immortal worth, see that no efforts are untried to fortify them against all possibility of a doom so dreadful. As Hamilcar pledged his son Hannibal, when but nine years old, to eternal hostility against Home, so in like manner, let all our children be pledged to ceaseless war upon this chief enemy of God and man. By every consideration sacred to a parent's heart, we solemnly ad-jure them all to the faithful performance of this duty.

"But the sphere of duty is not confined to self and the home-circle. There is the place to begin, but not to stop. We are interwoven with the warp and Woof of society. In spite of ourselves, our lives must, for weal or for woe, af-fect the fortunes of others. This fact constitutes the sub-basis of an enlarged area of obligation. (1.) We are to do others no harm. (2.) We are to do all pos-sible good, both to their souls and bodies; and (3.) We are to protect them against wrong at the hands of others. Not enough that we do our neighbor no harm. Not enough that we do him all the good we can personally. We may not innocently stand by and permit the infliction of injuries by others. These principles are fundamental to the social compact; and applied to the subject of Temperance, they (1.) Forbid all agency, direct or indirect, in the manufac-ture, sale, purchase, or use of intoxicating liquors, as a beverage. (2.) Require that we should do our utmost to influence all others to practice habits of strictest temperance. (3,) That, by forces, both moral and legal, we prevent all others from the worse than murderous traffic in liquors that can intoxicate. And while it is our most bounden duty to do thus personally, it is no less our duty, in all ways that are proper, to combine and co-act with others for the realization of these results. As we would drive the demon, alcohol, from the paradise of home, so should we banish it from the Eden of the neighborhood and community.

"The Churches have a duty to do in this regard, No pulpit can be innocently silent on this subject. The ministry may not imitate the example of the Priest and Levite and quietly pass by the poor drunkard who has fallen among thieves, and been stripped not only of money and clothing, but of reputation, reason and manhood as well, and left more than half-dead. To the limits of ability, they must be good Samaritans, and employ their utmost powers, personal and official, for the speedy overthrow of this monstrous iniquity. They should put themselves in personal contact with the miserable drunkard and his wretched family, and by ail means possible, seek their salvation. They should not only denounce drunkenness, but with rebukes doubly blasting, brand to blistering, the infamous traffic which causes it all; and with scourge, made of large or small cords, they should drive from the temple all engaged in the infernal commerce. It is a most disgraceful sight to see the poor victim of inebriety shut within the limits of gloomy prison walls, while his more guilty destroyer is welcomed to the highest and softest seat in the synagogue. The cry of the slave rent the heavens, and the popular Churches of the land were deaf to his cry. In the name of God and humanity let them not sin in like manner in relation to intemperance.

"Three things are necessary to the compassment of this reformation. (1) Public sentiment must be toned up to fully meet the demands of the hour. This must be done by the triple power of the pulpit, the platform and the press. (2) The enforcement of the laws already in existence against the rum-traffic: and (3) The enactment and enforcement of all such laws as are needed. Nothing short of this covers the whole ground.

"But all this means work. Forces must be organized, monies must be raised and appropriated. There must be work in the Churches — in pulpit and pew— in the Sabbath-schools, in the communities, in families and everywhere. Results as difficult as they are vast, are to be realized. And in this God-honoring, and man-saving work, let no Wesleyan minister or member be found in the rear of the foremost of God's embattled hosts. The forces of the enemy are organized and massed. Their attitude is insolently defiant. Hence, we must organize, mass forces, and "up and at them." Let us have "organized victory," and with the blessing of God, have it without delay."

In July, 1810, he wrote this editorial: —

ENTIRE CONSECRATION.

"Under this impressive caption we wish to answer two questions. First— What is it? Second — Why should we make it?

"What is entire Consecration? To Consecrate is to set apart; to dedicate to a holy purpose. Entire Consecration is the setting apart of all, without reservation or qualification, to the service of God.

"1. It implies an open, public committal to the service of God. Secret discipleship is excluded. No person can make entire Consecration to God and keep that fact in concealment. This light cannot be put under a bushel. If the act of Consecration is kept in concealment, that very fact proves that it is not entire. The cross of public avowal is not taken up.

"2. It implies the Consecration of the *whole being*. All the powers of affection, all of learning, of logic, of oratory, of social or civil position; all of friends and friendship — all that immediately appertains to the person, must be fully at the Divine disposal. No part of the price must be kept back. No separate interest— no antagonizing will is allowable. Its language is, without qualification or mental reservation, 'Lord, here am I; send me.' Send me to a hard place or an easy one, a high position or a low one, along a rough road or smooth one; give me many or few friends; let me be rich or poor, sick or well, at home with its quiet and plenty and comforts, or on desert wastes, or amid mountains of perpetual ice and snow; in hungerings or thirstings, in weariness and labor, in perils by land, in perils by sea, or in perils among false brethren; in prison or in palaces, in enthronement or martyrdom, in service or sacrifice, just as God shall order. The Divine will must be enthroned supreme in all that appertains to our person. Obedience must be unqualified and universal. Every duty faithfully performed; every suffering patiently endured; even life itself must not be withheld.

"3. Having said thus much, it is scarcely necessary to say that time, and property, and all property interests, must be wholly given to God, Every *day* and every *dollar* must be esteemed and used as belonging to Him, and in such manner as in our best judgment will most conduce to His highest glory. Of course this necessarily involves the life-calling and the bounds of our habitation. In settling these questions we must have primal reference to the Divine glory.

"4. All this is to be done, not mechanically or reluctantly, but cheerfully and heartily from a clear apprehension that it is our "reasonable service." Here is voluntary and perpetual self-abnegation — the deeding, signing, sealing, conveying and delivering, of all and singular, of self and appurtenances, forever, to God.

"This continuous act of Consecration finds faint illustration in the enlistment and vows of the soldier. Having enlisted and assumed his obligation, the soldier is the exclusive property of the Government — all his powers, all his interests, all his services, and even his life, are its property. But the services, sacrifices, and sufferings of the soldier are coersive; whereas all the Christian gives, does or endures in the cause of his Master through life, is voluntary, from the promptings of apprehended obligation and of supreme preference.

"But *why* this entire Consecration?

"1. Because it is right. We belong to God. He has made us. In Him we live, and move, and have our being. We live at His expense. And we are His purchased possession. He bought us with a price. And oh, what a price! Thus, all we are and all we have, belong, of right, to God. What can be more reasonable than that we render unto God that which is his due?

"2. It is our reasonable service because it is the best use we can make of our powers. It is not only *right*, but it is *wise*. To live with any other intent, to any other purpose, is to prostitute our powers to all that is calamitous to self and to others, with reference to both time and eternity. This is infinite madness. But entire consecration is the devotion of our powers to the highest and holiest of all purposes— is to make them productive of the greatest good possible to self and all others, both for this and the future state. The wisdom of this is equalled only by the folly and utter madness of its opposite. Here holiest duty and highest interest are coalescent.

"3. But God requires nothing more *of* us than he has done and proposes to do *for* us. He gave His Son to service, to suffering, and to death, for us. He kept back no part of the price. He drank the cup to its utmost dregs. With his expiring breath, he declared that the work of our redemption l is finished.' And for the future, he offers all that is possible for Heaven to bestow. If we will but become his people, he will become our God; Father, Son, and Holy Ghost, and 'all things' become ours. What an enriching contract is this! How little we give! How much we receive! Human thought cannot conceive. Angel-tongue cannot tell.

"4. But entire Consecration is an unalterable condition of salvation. This lesson is not sufficiently taught; and surely it is not sufficiently apprehended. It is usually conceded that a few eminent Christians and ministers of the Gospel should be thus wholly consecrated, but not so with ordinary Christians. It is to be feared that so-called ordinary Christians are not Christians at all. Is not the evidence but too conclusive, that too many professed Christians and Christian ministers live to themselves? 'By their fruits ye shall know them.' True, for the most part, young converts have but limited views of entire Consecration; but the consecration is fully up to the conception. This must be true in all after life. As the conception of Consecration, in import and duty, develops, the act of Consecration must become proportionately more complete.

"5, Consecration is the precise point of union between the human and the Divine. When all is placed on the altar, then comes down the Baptism of power. Are not this Consecration and attendant baptism the great want of the Church? Is not this the key to its want of general efficiency?

"This matter is eminently personal. Reader; How is this with you? Are you consecrated saved — unqualifiedly obedient; or is the work but partial and superficial? Have you the baptism of power? Will you now make the Consecration complete? Until this is done there is a controversy between God and thee. Oh, terminate this controversy at once; and become the material of which martyrs are made, which is a blessing to earth, and for which await the awards of an endless heaven!"

Conversion of Children

He was very much interested in the conversion of children. He was earnest in his teachings on this subject. "Bring the children early to Jesus" was his plea. I give a few extracts from his writings on *Early Piety.*

"There is nothing more beautiful, more important, nor that should be promoted with greater assiduity than early piety. With what pleasurable interest we read of Joseph, and Samuel, and David, and Josiah, and of Timothy who knew the holy Scriptures from a child. No marvel that David said, l Come ye children, hearken unto me, I will teach you the fear of the Lord;' nor that Solomon counselled remembrance of the Creator in the days of youth; nor that Jesus said to the coming generations, 'Suffer little children to come unto me, and forbid them not.'

"For years we have been deeply impressed with the conviction, that neglect of the children has been a most fruitful source of the weakness and inefficiency of the Church. Baptized children should sustain a relation to the Church similar to that sustained by the Catechumen to the Primitive Church. They should be esteemed and treated as candidates for its full fellowship and immunities. It is not to be doubted that childhood is the fulcrum, and early religious instruction and discipline, the more than Archimedean lever with which the moral world is to be turned over. — Persia educated her children to temperance, industry, and a prudent economy, and thereby gave strength, greatness and perpetuity to the State. Let the Church but educate her children to an intelligent and vigorous piety, and she will soon overthrow the great Babylon of sin. And the sooner the Church comes to fully understand this concealed magazine of power, the better.

"But we wish to speak more immediately of the great advantages of early piety. And,

"1. It is always *genuine.* Children know but little of those sinister motives which may induce to a mercenary, and hence, hypocritical piety. Their eye is single; and hence, the whole body is full of light. This is of primal consideration.

"2. Children do not have to overcome the force of evil habits early formed, nor unlearn what they have learned amiss. The soil of their hearts has not been pre-occupied with those noxious weeds. When once permitted to spring up, the roots strike deep, and adhere with most troublesome tenacity. Those who early become pious are at once saved immense labor and annoyance. And this is a most happy economy.

"3. Early piety is the only safeguard against the adverse influences of a world which is no friend to grace. Dangers stand thick through all the ground. They throng man's pathway from the cradle to the grave. The human heart naturally gravitates to earth and to sin. The heart of the young is most prolific, susceptible and unsuspecting. Nothing but positive piety can render the child proof against the joint action of unfriendly, internal and external forces. If you would not have the souls of the dear children polluted by sin, their characters stained by crime, and would have their eternal interests secure from most imminent peril, early sow the seeds and vigilantly cultivate the plants of piety in their young and tender hearts.

"4. Principles first imbibed and habits first formed are at once the most powerful and the most lasting. Hence, the nervous language of the Wise Man: — "Train up a child in the way he should go; and when he is *old* he will not depart from it." 'But a child left to himself bringeth his mother to shame.' How immensely important that Satan should not, and that God and the soul should have the benefit of this fundamental law of our being.

"5. If persons do not become pious while young, there is danger they never will; and this danger increases with each successive day and hour of sin. Nothing is more true than that continuance in sin hardens men in it. Conscience becomes callous, passion inflamed, sensibilities corrupted and perverted, and the will more and more perverse, until the case becomes appalling — hopeless. Sin is fearfully self-perpetuating.

"6. In addition to all this, there is but a step between every human personality and death — young as well as old.

> 'Great God! on what a slender thread
>   Hang everlasting things!
>   The eternal state of all the dead
>   Upon life's feeble strings!'

"7. Early piety alone can promise time in which to develop to maturity the Christian graces, and hence to furnish the world with the most admirable specimens of Christian character.

"If the harvest is either rich or abundant, the sowing must be seasonable. All agree that childhood and youth are life's seed-time. Those who do not become pious until mature in life, must needs contend against a double disadvantage. First, they have but little time in which to grow up to the 'fullness of the stature of men and women in Christ Jesus;' and second, they have the stubborn force of long continued habit against which to contend. Much more to do, and less time for the work.

"8. Time and opportunity to labor in the vineyard of the Lord — to bless the world, and to make life a grand practical success, make their plea for early piety. How deep and painful the regrets of those who worse than throw away a large portion of a life so brief. How blessed to give all of time and strength and life, to cheerful co-operative effort with God and all the good in the great work of human salvation. An *entire* offering on this holy altar, how good and acceptable to God.

"9. Early piety affords the best foundation for a substantial character. It makes strong in knowledge, in faith, in deep and varied experience, in purified affections, in husbanded energies, high purposes, holy habits, and joyful anticipations! Strong to resist evil. There was divine wisdom displayed in permitting those who had grown up amid the idolatrous practices of the Egyptians to die in the Wilderness, and in leading their children who knew not these practices, into the land of Promise. So does early piety give strength to grapple with the great crimes of any age — to exterminate moss-covered errors, and raze to their foundations the temples of time-honored crimes.

If Christian parents and the Church would respond to this urgent call, then must they do as commanded in Deut. xi: 18 — 21. 'Lay up the words of the law in their hearts and their souls, and bind them for a sign upon their hands, and let them be as frontlets between their eyes; and teach them to the children, speaking of them when they sit in the house, when they walk by the way, when they lie down and when they rise up, and write them upon the door-posts of the house and upon the gates.' Also xxxi: 11 — 13. When they come to appear before the Lord in the place which he shall choose, (in their religious assemblages,) they shall gather the people together, men, women and children, and the strangers within the gate, that they may hear, and learn, and fear the Lord, and observe to do all the words of the law."

Christian Patience

From an editorial upon this subject, I clip the following: —

"The man of tranquil, patient perseverance is in himself a moral host; whereas, without patience, although in intellect a giant, yet in moral force he can be but a pigmy. So, if we would be God-like, we must be patient. How through the heavy tramp of the ages, God works and waits. How during four thousand years he laid the foundation for redemption. In this great work there is no haste. Christ did not come till the fullness of time. And how he yet works and waits for the consummation of the redemptive scheme. He is in no haste; nor need he be. The ages to come are his in which to work. Sitting on the circle of the heavens, he surveys the thousand millions, of earth, "witnesses their deadly quarrels, brethren cheating brethren, the wildness and greed for gold, the thankless ingratitude which never sees the hand that feeds them, the oppression and enslavement of millions, the madness and slaughter of red-visaged war, the world lying in the wicked one, yet there comes no outcry from the heavens to still all this unrest; but gently, and patiently, the ministry of nature and of Providence proceeds from year to year; as gently, patiently, and unremittingly as if universally greeted with gratitude and praise. Then, Reformer, Lover of Mankind, Christian Minister, take for your model the Great God, and work and wait. — But finally — Patient continuance in well doing alone, is crowned with glory, honor, immortality and eternal life. Then, let patience have her perfect work."

From an editorial upon "Does God Work by Great or Small Means?" —

"These enumerated examples of Divine interposition indicate with unerring accuracy, the place of the power by which the achievements of the Christian Church, in her entire history, have been accomplished. Accordingly, we read: 'Not by might, nor by power, but by my Spirit, saith the Lord' — of enduement with power from on high — of earthen vessels being chosen, that the 'excellence of the power' may be of God, and not of men — and of 'weak things,' and l things that are not' bringing to naught 'things that are mighty.'

The disciples were weak, and yet they triumphed. Primitive Christians were weak, and yet they triumphed. Luther was weak, and yet he triumphed. Wesley and coadjutors were weak, and yet they triumphed. Early Abolitionists were weak, and yet they triumphed. So, numerically, we "Wesleyans are weak, and the things to be confounded are mighty, but if we know the place of the hiding of God's power, we shall triumph. Union with God alone, is the place op power. If in any case, this union is not complete, let it be MADE SO WITHOUT DELAY."

In 1871 the General Conference convened in Syracuse. Mr. Crooks was chosen President. At this Conference Rev. L. N. Stratton was elected associate editor with Mr. Crooks, who was also reappointed Agent. This Conference recommended that as soon as possible arrangements should be made to build a new and more commodious publishing house. They authorized the Agent to open a subscription immediately for the purpose of raising the needed funds. This work was commenced at once. "The people had a mind to work," and rallied nobly. A few months after, among his editorials, I find the following, aimed at the "love of money": —

Folly's Carnival

"Folly's Carnival! What is it? Is it spending the long, long nights in the frenzied whirl of the giddy dance? Without dispute, this is bad enough, and quite too much savors of the senseless pleasures of the night or savage life to find place or favor in the noon-day of Christian civilization. But this is not what is meant. Then, is it the uncompensated surrender of 'life, liberty and the pursuit of intelligent and virtuous happiness' at the debasing shrine of fashion, heartless as it is fickle? While it must be admitted that this is bad beyond the possibility of proper characterization, yet it is not the thing intended. Nor yet is it the desperate madness which impels an immortal being in pursuit of substantial good amid the dehumanizing slums of beastly sensuosity; nor firey floods of intemperance; nor yet the desolating waves of red-visaged war, after which this earnest mission is sent. The thing of which we write, is none other than that almost universally dominant love of money which an inspired Apostle so fitly styles 'the root of all evil.' For who does not know that pre-eminently, money is the Moloch of America? The name of its worshipers is 'Legion;' for they are many. In the nervous language of Pollock, never more true than now: —

'Gold many hunted — sweat and bled for gold;
Waked all the night, and labored all the day.
And what was this allurement, dost thou ask?
A dust dug from the bowels of the earth,
Which, being cast into the fire, came out
A shining thing that fools admired, and called
A god; and in devout and humble plight
Before it kneeled, the greater to the less;
And on its altar sacrificed ease, peace,
Truth, faith, integrity, good conscience, friends,
Love, charity, benevolence, and all
The sweet and tender sympathies of life;
And to complete the horrid murderous rite
And signalize their folly, offered up
Their souls, and an eternity of bliss,
To gain them — what? an hour of dreaming joy,
A feverish hour that hasted to be done,
And ended in the bitterness of woe.'

          *   *   *   *

              'Of all God made upright,
And in their nostrils breathed a living soul,
Most fallen, most prone, most earthly, most debased,
Of all that sold Eternity for Time,
None bargained on so easy terms with death.
Illustrious fool! Nay, most inhuman wretch!
He sat among his bags, and with a look
Of which hell might be ashamed, drove the poor
Away unalmsed; and 'midst abundance died —
Sorest of evils! died of utter want.'

"The 'root of all evil.' The infernal fountain, which feeds every form of vice and crime. The accursed rock on which countless thousands make shipwreck of immortal wealth. The debasing altar before which demonizing worship is offered at the expense of an 'eternity of bliss.' Alas, that unnumbered thousands bearing the name of a sinless Christ crowd the broad aisles of this temple accursed and abandoned of God, and whose open doors are the gilded gates to perdition.

"How this insatiable greed for gold congeals the liquid streams of mercy for the poor. How it paralyzes the arm of Christian enterprise, whether home or foreign. How it withholds tithes from the Lord's house, dooms to penury his ministry, and impoverishes to beggary the coffers of Christian charity. How it repels from all place in God's sanctuary the wretched children of poverty, but welcomes to highest seat the man with gold ring or woman in costly apparel. How un-Christ-like it renders all things bearing his name. How it feasts the flesh, but dooms the soul to endless Lent—Starvation! How its hoarded heaps blight the blooming hopes of fond parents, by withholding from the children the needed stimulants to healthful enterprise, and meanwhile dooming them the envied victims of the consuming vices of costly idleness,— thus entailing the double curse of dwarfing the beautiful and good, and developing to horrid proportions the sordid and selfish. Hence, the all prevalent lameness and blasting throughout the borders of the Zion of this money-worshiping age. Heaven pity us! This is indeed Folly's dreadful Carnival.

"Dear reader: Introvert your attention; and answer to your conscience and your God! Does the fatal virus of this fiery serpent circulate death through all the parts and powers of your soul? By all that is hallowed in eternal interests, let not this be so."

Once More in North Carolina

"Here I am, safe and sound in old North Carolina, after an absence of twenty-one years. I have not been to visit old familiar scenes, but matters have greatly changed, I assure you. The man at whose hotel I stop was foreman of a United States Grand Jury which indicted six hundred Ku-Klux, all under bonds., to be tried in September. Some of these, ministers of the M. E. Church, South. Am feeling quite like an American citizen here, where slavery once ruled as with a rod of iron and a knife of steel.

"Twenty-five years ago the coming September, we came to North Carolina. Then Slavery, both in fact and spirit, was dominant. The Southern wing of the Methodist Episcopal Church had seceded, because the North was unwilling to have a slave-holding Bishop. Hearing that the Wesleyan Methodists were anti-slavery, forty citizens of Guilford county met in convention and adopted the Wesleyan Methodist discipline, and applied to the Allegheny Conference for a man to feed them on the bread of life. To this call we responded, knowing well that it was at the peril of life. Although an entire stranger and threatened with every violence, yet God gave us prosperity.

* * * * *

"Jesse McBride was called to cultivate the ground already occupied in Carolina, and we gave ourself to the work of extending our borders into fields beyond. Another year of peril and prosperity throughout the whole work. Several camp-meetings were held, and with excellent results. Brother Bacon entered upon his third year in Virginia, McBride upon his second and we our fourth, in Carolina. But increased prosperity was attended with increased danger. All the time violence had been threatened; but now threats were more frequent and more fierce. The enemy saw clearly that they must dig up the sapling quickly or otherwise they would be unable to cut down the tree.

* * * * *

"Just as we knew they would be, flushed by this victory in driving McBride, with ten-fold determination they turned their batteries upon us; and by threats, and mobbings, and a reward offered for our arrest, they waged war upon us from May until August, the close of the Conference year, when with sadness, we turned our face to home and friends, leaving in this slavery-ruled land six Wesleyan Meeting-houses, and some five hundred members. Very many sold out and moved into States not cursed with the withering blight of Slavery.

"Yielding to successive calls, four years later, Daniel Worth returned to his native State, preached extensively for several months, was arrested for circulating Helper's Impending Crisis, and after some months imprisonment, returned to the free North and West. But Bacon and McBride and Worth are all dead. Died doubtless as the results of labors performed and hardships experienced in the South. Of these four, the writer alone survives.

* * * * *

"The war came on and freed the slaves. The seeds of truth sown in other years still live in many hearts. Hence, repeated calls again for Wesleyan preachers. Last autumn, the Missionary Board of the Indiana Conference and the Connectional Board jointly, responded by sending brethren E. Brookshire and R. L. Fisher to rebuild the walls of our spiritual Jerusalem.

"Immediately upon arrival they engaged in a revival at Shady Grove, resulting in nearly one hundred conversions and seventy-two accessions. At this place, Sabbath, the 21st July, we had the pleasure of dedicating to the worship of Almighty God a neat and well-proportioned frame structure? fourteen feet from floor to ceiling, and twenty-four by thirty-four; when all painted and furnished, to be the best Methodist rural meeting-house in three counties. And better still, notwithstanding the sore pressure of the times, when all completed, is to be free from debt. No one not knowing the circumstances, can appreciate how great this achievement is. The membership is composed of excellent material, substantial heads of families, and godly, zealous young men and women. A. revival in progress this week; and up to this Thursday, a number of conversions and twenty-five accessions. In all, they have three meeting-houses, and deeds covering thirteen acres, including a four-acre-lot on which a fourth meeting-house is to be erected. The entire membership is about one hundred and twenty-five; and new and inviting fields are still opening; so that at the close of the first year, prospects are good for a bright future.

"Although we have been worked pretty hard, averaging a sermon for each day, our visit has been a real pleasure."

High Point, N. C, July, 1872.

Mr. Crooks was absent from the office fourteen days, and in that time preached fourteen sermons. More than one-half of that time, day and night, was spent traveling, and in July, too. He was not well when he returned and did not fully recover from the journey before he commenced the round of Fall Conferences. He was soon taken sick, and for a number of weeks was a great sufferer; yet he attended all the Conferences and with the help of kind brethren sold his books and transacted the usual amount of Conference business, beside pressing the claims of the fund for the new Publishing House. He had nearly recovered from the effect of his illness when he returned and was ready for the work waiting for him at the office.

The following article was written in August, 1873. Mr. Crooks felt more and more the importance of our continued existence as a denomination. He could see a vast field of labor, which we might occupy if we would only step forward in the line of duty. He saw those fields "already white for the harvest," but the "laborers were few." It seemed to him that there was a great work to be done by us especially. As in the past we had to stand almost single-handed in opposing the popular sins of the day, so in the present we were in the front ranks of the battle between Christ and Belial, — because other denominations are not willing to boldly confront sin in high places, and follow the "meek and lowly Jesus," whithersoever he goeth.

Our Work Not Finished

In connection with, and immediately subsequent to the recent "reunion" held by a few ex-Wesleyans in Cleveland, Ohio, very strong asseverations are being made that our distinctive work as a denomination is finished, and that therefore our continued existence involves *schism*, and hence, sin against God and his Church. — A grave allegation indeed! We repel it. Hear us patiently.

"At this reunion Rev. John McEldowney is reported as saying— 'To me, it is *dishonoring* to God for brethren remaining, not to recognize the work as finished. I cannot see how it is possible that a fraction can maintain a *schism* by remaining separate.' The New York *Christian Advocate* takes up the above *pronunciamento* in the words following: 'We fail to see any good reason for the maintenance of the separate existence of the 'Wesleyan' body, now that they have gained every point upon which they originally dissented and separated.' And Dr. Crooks of *The Methodist*, also of New York, prolongs the refrain in the following lusty language: 'Of all our separatists, the Wesleyans would seem to have the least reason to remain out of the old family. In a case like theirs, it becomes a grave question whether continued disunion is a mere matter of expediency or whether it is not *sin!* — The conscience of the Church needs to be appealed to on this subject— not merely its prejudices or its interests. Charity, fellowship, brotherhood, co-operation — are these not virtues in the kingdom of Christ on earth? Many a banner-bearer of sectarian division will find himself recognized, at the last day, as only a traitor to the common cause of the common Master.'

"There, we like that close-jointed way of putting this great subject — this appeal to conscience, and the judgment. Doctor Crooks is right in placing our Church relationship just where the Bible places it, and just where we have held it for many years and *still* hold it — upon the firm basis of eternal right. And we add; this is exactly what has kept us out of the 'old family' of the Methodist Episcopal Church, and *still* keeps us out.

"But these good Doctors will please make note that their sword is double-edged— cutting both ways. While it is conceded to be duty to hold fellowship with true Christians, on the other hand it is equally duty to refuse fellowship to those who are not. And while we may not innocently split the Church — the body of Christ — neither may we innocently wed that body to sin, and thus commit high sacrilege. 'Charity, fellowship, brotherhood, co-operation,' are beautiful — all of them beautiful — but they must not find ultimate foundation in compromise with sin, nor in truce with the devil. Hence the pungent language of the Apostle — 'What fellowship hath righteousness with unrighteousness? What communion hath light with darkness? And What concord has Christ with Belial? — Wherefore come out from among them, and *be ye separate*, saith the Lord, and touch not the unclean thing; and I will receive you, and will be a Father unto you, and ye shall be my sons and daughters, saith the Lord Almighty.' Thus plainly, our being the children of God is *conditioned* upon our being separate from the unclean. Again: the Spirit through the Revelator says — 'And I heard another voice from heaven saying, Come out of her my people, that ye be not partakers of her sins, and that ye receive not her plagues.' And with solemn emphasis the Apostle says— 'I command you in the name of our Lord Jesus Christ that you withdraw yourselves from every brother who walketh disorderly.' Moral lepers have no more place in the fellowship of the saints than physical lepers had in the camp of Israel. To affiliate religiously with evil doers is to become partner both in their sins and their plagues. Hence, we may 'dishonor God' and become 'traitors to the common cause of the common Master' *by seeking to promote unity at the expense of purity.*

"And mark well, this trinity of Doctors teach the duty to return, but only upon the hypothesis that our distinctive work is finished — that every point of original dissent has been gained. The plain implication of their language is, that if our work is not finished, our continued existence is all right. We think exactly so, and are glad to agree with these learned Doctors on this central principle, But are their assumed facts well founded? Is our work finished? Has every point of original dissent been gained? These are the questions pertinent. But before answering, we wish to premise, —

"(1.) No marvel that Doctors Crooks and Curry, and such as they, see no cause for our continued existence; for years ago they were denouncing as schismatics, the very men whom they now laud as 'the greatest of moral heroes.' Such laudation is of questionable commendation.

"(2.) If even all the points of original dissent have been gained, it does not therefore follow that there are now no valid reasons for our separate existence. Other causes may have arisen during the past thirty years; or other good reasons may have existed then, not incorporated into the original platform. This is self-manifest.

"(3.) Every one of these Doctors know that 'Schism,' as originally used, had no allusion to denominational unity — that denominational lines do not bound the area of Christian fellowship; and that this talk about schism in such connection, is unworthy their learning. And as to the talk about our return to the bosom of the 'old family,' it is a family with which the majority of us never found domicile.

"But we now come to the facts. What are they? Is our work finished? Has every point of original dissent been gained? The facts are substantially these:

"1. It is true that chattle slavery no longer exists in this Country. But it is equally true that while it did exist, it found sanctuary in the Methodist Episcopal Church. True, also, that when at last it was abolished by the war-power of the nation, instead of sackcloth and penitent confession of complicity with the monstrous iniquity, we hear boastful thanks to God for long continued position in the front ranks of anti-slavery Churches. Such vaunting sacrilege might well appal heaven! This is the manner in which that point was gained.

"2. Great credit is claimed for having adopted lay delegation in General Conference. But what *kind* of lay delegation is it? Is it *equal* representation, as is ours? It is not. No more than two laymen can be elected from within the bounds of any one Annual Conference; whereas no such restriction obtains in relation to the ministry. But even these lay delegates are not elected *by* nor representatives *of* the unofficial laity. They are elected by Electoral Colleges; and the members of these Colleges are elected by the Quarterly Conferences, as the representatives of the Quarterly Conferences, which are the creatures and agents of preachers rather than of the people. In the Government of the Methodist Episcopal Church the unofficial laity have no voice — are a *nullity.* Only think of a million of members totally disfranchised! This is all that has been gained. Just this; and nothing more. And is not this lay representation with a vengeance? Something over which to vociferate, 'The work finished! The work finished!' In great haste truly, to have the work finished.

"This article is long enough; but we must be heard further. These Doctors accuse us denominationally, of high crime against the Church of Christ. We have given credit for what has been done. Now let us see what has not been done.

"Well, (1.) The Episcopacy has been neither abolished nor modified. The Board ol Bishops is larger now than ever before. And they still possess the same unlimited power over the time, labors and place of habitation of all the thousands of their ministers, as in the past. (2.) There still exists the three orders in their ministry, of Deacon, Elder and Bishop; while with us it is fundamental that there is but one order — that of Elder — and that all Elders are equal. (3.) With us the local Churches are independent in all questions of merely local interest. Our Churches receive and discipline their own members — choose their own pastors and each Class elects its own leader. But net one of these rights is known in the Methodist Episcopal Church. (4.) With us the pastoral relation is matter of mutual agreement between pastor and people. And even the congregations of the Old Catholics in Germany have this free right of choice of the men who minister to them in things holy; But in the Methodist Episcopal Church here in Republican America, no such right is allowed! In this Church neither of the parties most directly interested has any voice. With her, twelve men called Bishops absorb this sacred right of all the pastors and congregations of this Church of more than a million. (5.) With us is secured by disciplinary provision, the rights of all our ministers and members irrespective of complexion or race; and while by Constitutional amendment a similar equality of rights is secured to citizens of the United States, yet up to this date, the Methodist Episcopal Church has no such provision. (6.) In our Yearly Conferences the laity have an equal voice with the ministry. But lay representation is not known in the Annual Conferences of the Methodist Episcopal Church. (7.) So also in our General Conference is equal lay representation. But as shown above, in the General Conference of the Methodist Episcopal Church there is only a kind of *quasi* Quarterly Conference representation. In affairs of Government in the Methodist Episcopal Church, the non-official laity are a *nonentity*. They have only the right to *pay* and to *pray.*

"But an anti-scriptural and anti-Republican polity is not all. All through this and other countries savage and civilized, is a Secret Fraternity laying high claims to antiquity, morality and religion. In all its degrees every obligation is taken with an oath. In its first seven degrees, with the Holy Book, which says 'swear not at all,' before him on the altar at which he kneels, blindfolded and cable" towed, each candidate takes over half a hundred distinct oaths — this going on each week in thousands of lodges — no marvel that profanity abounds, and that l because of *swearing*, the land mourneth.' Monstrous obligations are taken, alike inconsistent with the duties of the citizen and the precepts of morality; horrid and murderous penalties are invoked; such as having the throat cut across— the tongue torn out by the roots — the left breast torn open and the heart and vitals taken thence — the body severed in the midst and the bowels burned to ashes — tongue split from tip to root— the skull smote off, and-so-forth; thus familiarizing the mind with murder, and mutilation horrible to con template. And what, if possible, is worse than all, this motley mixture of fact and fiction, mummery and murder, profanity and prayer, while ignoring the mediation of the Blessed Lord and Savior in its very prayers, yet holds out a false light; promising its votaries deliverance from sin and a home in the 'house not made with hands, eternal in the heavens.' And dreadful to contemplate, while these terrible practices are prevalent throughout the land, and thousands being decoyed into these mystic meshes, not only are the pulpits and presses of the Methodist Episcopal Church silent as the grave on the subject, but still more awful, thousands of her ministers and members statedly worship at these Christ-rejecting altars! A thousand times no; the work of the Wesleyan Methodist Connection of America is *not finished.* It is not '*dishonoring* to God' to be inflexibly loyal to Jesus Christ; and the arbitraments of eternity will so decide. Let others do as they will, to be holy, we must warn men against false lights, antagonize all sin, and be loyal to Jesus Christ, We cannot do otherwise. God help us."

Character and Characteristics of Rev. A. Crooks.

By Rev. L. N. Stratton.

The image of Minerva, towering above the Parthenon in Athens, and the Sphynx, which looks inquisitively over the unanswering sand plains of Egypt, were coarsely formed images. The distant observer deemed them cleanly cut and smooth. But it is said that close inspection revealed in them many a flaw and seam. Children at play with a pocket telescope are wont to place the large end of the instrument to the eye, in looking at coarse, uncomely objects. This, it is observed, gives them a fineness of form and finish which nature itself has failed to furnish. So is it with some men; close observation is detrimental to appreciation. But turn the small end of the telescope towards them, and "Distance lends enchantment to the view."

Not so with Adam Crooks. He would bear close inspection. He appeared well at a distance, but much better on a near approach. And if to any he seemed distant, it was only in that seeming which the mind instinctively grants to manly dignity and true worth.

His nature was confiding, and bis judgment good; so that multitudes came to his side, both for counsel and consolation. He was a close observer of men and things. He read character as a man would read a book. And though he came to his more weighty opinions slowly, when he did reach them, they were usually correct. This Napoleonic habit of studying characters, methods, facts of current history and events, made him a man of the living present. It shaped his thought in instruction; it regulated his business policy; it aided his opinions, as to the turn which national and ecclesiastical affairs would take, and which opinions usually proved to be well founded. Although by nature he was a student, and read the best part of the best books, yet of him it might be said, as of Abraham Lincoln: "He read not many, but much." But of all his reading, aside from God's Word, with the utmost care he "read the signs of the times." This made him a wise counsellor and a careful adviser. He never leaped at conclusions. If mists were too thick to penetrate, and the course improbable, he always went slowly and with caution. Had he been a General, he would have been a hard one to defeat. He would not be drawn into ambush, nor strike a strong blow at a shadow. Careful and prudent to find the position of the enemy, then never underestimating his strength, those who knew him would look for a stroke of masterly power which would sweep everything before it. These faculties made him a wise and successful leader.

There was one more trait of character which wove the web of his career with sunshine. That was his hope. He was never disheartened at a seeming failure. His face never grew long and gloomy over a seemingly backward turn of the wheel of fortune. If an honest effort failed of its anticipated results, and covered other souls with clouds, they were not his. Both his faith and better judgment drove them away. His faith said: "This is God's work and none of my business, only I am to do my best to save the day." And his reason said:

"Who has ever undertaken any great and good enterprise and seen it flourish from the first."

"The noblest plan is, when we fail,
To rise and try again."

This formed the basis upon which rested that genial, hopeful trait of character which set every true heart at ease in his presence. No such man as he ever sat down in despair, or sold out at half price, or sought to shift his pain of heart to his stomach by a dose of stramonium or ratsbane. Such a man, with such a faith and such a hope can never be a coward, or commit suicide. Labor was nothing, pain was nothing, long midnight rides over rough roads and through drenching rains, were trifles scarcely worth mentioning the next day. To mortal fear he was a stranger; and a close analysis of his mental and well-developed physical constitutions, makes it appear as less a wonder why, Spartan-like, he had so little regard for physical suffering, and seemed fearless of death. His unwavering Christian hope, founded upon an abiding faith in Him who said: — "I will never leave thee nor forsake thee," and "All things work together for good to them that love God," were enough for him. He *knew* these were God's words, and he *depended* upon them. Current events and transactions in human society were only surface incidents, liable to many phases and changes, while God's word, on which his faith was founded, was more than the solid rock which girdles the globe. Heaven and earth shall pass away, but not that word.

His figure was straight, and stood about five feet eleven inches high; his weight was from two hundred and five to two hundred and twelve pounds. His eye was a bluish hazel, and his hair, by age and toil, was turned to an iron-grey. His long, full beard, his round, full face, his clear, intelligent countenance and his erect and manly form, left the impression upon the strangers of a crowd, or the passengers of a railway train, that a man of more than ordinary gifts and position was among them. His habits were steady, his methods were uniform, his course one day, or in one. case of business or advice, all things being equal, suggested what it would be on the next day and occasion. So he seldom turned up in unlooked for ways and places. He was not moody. He did not do things "just as it happened." People would not say of him, in a case which he was to decide: — "It will be just as it happens to strike him." He decided from the law and the testimony. In his position, it is wonderful how many questions of importance there were to decide. And on his "Yes" or "No," turned the fate of ministers and Churches. To him this was a great care. His course was that of a conciliator. His efforts "made for peace." One of the last things he did, was to write several letters to save a pastor and a Church. He was very anxious for both. And often he was called in to aid in matters which others should have done for themselves, without taxing his physical endurance to its utmost limit. But people found him a frank and genial friend, and sought his advice as naturally as they would that of an elder brother. And he made them feel so welcome and at ease, giving to all liberally and upbraiding not, that it ceases to be strange that so many sought his counsel.

He never sought to put himself ahead, or to push himself upon public attention. He did not need to. His natural modesty caused him to desire to be unnoticed. But men who found him seeking seclusion in the public congregation, called him forth to take a place and part at the front.

His voice was clear and deep. Few men could be so well heard and understood. He filled the remotest point of the most spacious halls with his clear and measured utterances. His thought usually was very methodical. His speeches and sermons were cumulative. His texts were his sermons in a nutshell^ and his sermons were only about their texts and their natural corollaries and adjuncts. His texts were always *revealed* to him. He did not reason them out from the apparent needs, as some of us do, but he had depended from the early times in his ministry upon receiving by some sudden impression, his text. He studied his sermons thoroughly, and usually noted their heads on slips of paper, which he placed in a long pocketbook in his side pocket, ready for use.

With care he wrote his articles for the press. As there has never been a skillful master of any of the fine arts who leaped from the bottom to the top round of the ladder at a single bound, but has toiled through patient and steady effort to climb round by round, so the most successful writers have gained their eminence by care and toil. His friends and readers know how closely and clearly everything he wrote was written. Lest all might not easily follow the long steps he found it so easy to make, I have seen him lay aside sheet after sheet of well written manuscript, and write it again and again. Oh, could his readers have known the cost to him of brawn and brain and life-forces, they would have read what he wrote with even more solicitude. Not that it was difficult for him to write, but in what he wrote he was so painstaking that when it was done, it was *finished*, and like Gray's "Elegy," few persons could suggest an improvement in any particular,

Perfection was his aim in all respects. It was seen in his neat dress; in his deportment at the fireside and the table; in his salutation of his friends; in short, in tongue and pen, in public and private, in moral position and spiritual life, his aim was perfection. And while he enjoyed the sweets of a Christian life, it expressed itself, as in many other cases, in his lively, pleasant countenance. He was not a sad, gloomy, sorrowful, long-faced Christian. He lived above the clouds, in the sunshine, and like the parent eagle he sought to lead and lure others there. At times his quiet humor, and cheerful, playful words, sent glintings of sunshine down through many a chasm of gloom and cloud, to light up many a heart.

He was a firm believer in the superintendence of a Divine Providence over the minutiae of life. His personal history was full of incidents which proved his faith, and exhibited his trust. He transferred this same confidence from himself to the denomination which he served so faithfully and well. He believed that God had an especial use yet for Wesleyan Methodists. And as an agent of the will of Heaven, he sought with an unfaltering faith and fortitude to perfect the workings of the denomination. And as his labors drew to a close, he was firmly of the opinion that the true power of the Church, and the agencies at its command were advancing. A few days before his death he said: —

"Brother Stratton, I feel greatly encouraged by our denominational prospects. The Conferences which I attended last Fall manifested such faith and zeal; and gave such evidences of a love of hard work as I never saw before among them. Ministers are better supported, both in finances and influence in the communities where they are located. Then, there are so many able, efficient *young* men coming on, who within five years will be capable of filling any position in the gift of the Connection, that I feel more encouraged than at any other time for the past ten years. While lying sick in Iowa, I looked over the ground carefully, and I thought and said to my attendants, that *never in my entire life had I seen a time, when, if it pleased God to take me, that I could be so well spared as now.*"

An incident transpired while on his way from his sick bed in Iowa to Wasioja, the seat of the Minnesota Conference, He had been sick at the Michigan, Illinois and Iowa Conferences, with a run of Typhoid Fever, At the seat of the latter he remained, confined in his sick room, and a part of the time delirious, while Bro. D. F. Shepardson attended for him the Kansas Conference. This over and he arose from his sick bed, and unattended, cheerfully and hopefully started for Minnesota. The cross-roads are usually unsteady and irregular, At one point he found that the regular train had gone, and he must wait twelve or fifteen hours for the next run, and then ride through the cheerless hours of a chilly night: There was a freight train, with a wretched "caboose" in the rear, going out in a few minutes. He could scarcely think it prudent to expose himself to the constant draft of such a car. *He prayed God to help him.* The conductor came around. He told this official who he was, and the importance of his business, and that he scarcely felt able to ride in that car, else he cheerfully would. The Conductor reported the matter to the General Superintendent, who was at hand. A special car, with a neat state-room, was immediately attached, and a beautiful bed made up of high-piled hair cushions and ample coverings. He was aided into it, and said he slept like an infant for one hundred and fifty miles. He believed it to be a special providence of his ever-loving Father in Heaven, who notes the fall of a sparrow and hears the young raven's cry.

His health never appeared better than during the Summer prior to the last visits he made to the Fall Conferences. How clearly do I seem to see him, with a clear and somewhat florid countenance, sitting at his accustomed desk! How intelligent his countenance, how kind his expressions, how promising his prospects, how bright his hopes! After he had departed from his accustomed place, which it seemed that he might yet fill for years, in our issue of the *American Wesleyan*, August 19th, 1874, we published the following: —

PERSONAL.

"Rev. A. Crooks, whose cheerful face and friendly words we miss, has left his busy financial desk for a tour of the Western Conferences, to be gone about three months, Although he is to spend but a little time in each place, so extended will be his tour, it will require many oppressive days and cheerless night-rides to accomplish the journey. Though mid summer is decorating our valleys now, the sere and yellow leaf' will rustle to the tread, and from murky skies may form and fall the snow ere his return. These columns need not commend him and the important enterprises he represents to the favorable consideration of the brethren to whom he as God's servant once more comes. Soon agent and actors will take their last journey, do their last duty, and pass up to the auditing rooms of the Eternal Judge. For the golden bowl at last is broken, and the pitcher carried often to the fountain at length returns no more. We believe the lesson these facts teach will be heeded by us all."

It seemed almost prophetic. The feeling which prompted the expression was perhaps the outgrowth of that sad uncertainty which lies just behind the dim veil of futurity. Then, too, the dangers and exposures intensified the thought, and that this like other earthly things must end. Well, so it proved. He attended two dedications after the Conferences, and then, amid the chill and gloom of late October's dripping, he returned. A carriage brought him from the depot, first to the office and then to his home. Home had always been secondary to the office, and so was it still. In the next issue of the American Wesley an we gave him mention in the following personal: —

PERSONAL.

"Rev. A. Crooks, whose labors, successes, sickness and return have been duly noticed by our city papers and a multitude of his friends, has been at home since Tuesday, October 27th. He claims to be much better, and no doubt is; but he is coming up very slowly. He has been on the street a few times, and appeared, the ghost of his former self, at the office perhaps thrice since his return. He has lost thirty pounds from his two hundred and ten, and his physical strength has turned to the weakness of a child. His eyes seem large, his voice hollow, and his step unsteady. But his mind is clear, his thoughts active, and his soul growing brighter and more serene as he arises from the clouds and smoke of the battle toward the bliss of the everlasting gates. We do not believe that the Lord is about to take him home now, but only intends to show him both worlds from a point between; a point where the true value of the two appears more nearly correct than is usually manifest. May prayers still go up in clouds to Heaven's windows for him.

We have attempted to show why he thought himself in no danger. I seemed to see him on the verge of a chasm, invisible to himself, and over which it appeared to me there was great danger of his falling. But so Spartan-like and heroic, so dead to pain and careless of toil was he, that he had no fear of death. And when at length I wrote, "Adam Crooks is Dead," this hand never penned so sad a sentence, nor this heart felt so deep a pang. Not only was it for our own sakes who were here, and would feel his loss the most, but everywhere among our people, from the Atlantic to the Pacific, we knew a sad wail would go up to the gates of Heaven. Blinding tears fell upon the blackened columns of the *American Wesleyan*, in mourning, and many laid it aside for a time, not daring to risk their fluttering, almost murmuring hearts, to open it. From twenty to thirty thousand people knew him well and loved him much. He Was humanity's well-tried friend.

His faithful and devoted wife bears with patience and Christian resignation her loss. She seems to see him, not in the silent grave, but in a Christian's Paradise. She cannot, does not wish him back. And why should she? His battle is fought, his crown is gained, and he has entered into rest. From the clangor of arms and the rush of battle, he entered an open sesame at the side of the way, and stepped through into glory. Among the last sane words he spoke to me, he said: — *"My soul has been riding all night in a chariot of fire."* Yes, for but a little time the angel charioteer let him step out again. Then, when the Master wanted him, he did not let him suffer long — dragging slowly through the valley of the shadow of death — but he sent his swift coursers again. Our brother seemed to see them coming, and exclaimed to his wife: — "Quick! Be quick!" He kissed her hastily, spoke of the "rest beyond the skies," and before there was time to realize the danger, the angel whipped back through "the dark valley," and entered, with his prize, into the eternal morning.

We gladly let him rest. No winds can chill him there. No fevers fret his flesh. No earth-born hopes inspire new activities, and no earthly morning will call him to the front again.

> "Servant of God I well done!
>   Rest from thy loved employ;
> The battle fought, the victory won,—
>   Enter thy Master's joy.
>
> "In condescending love,
>   Thy ceaseless prayer he heard,
> And bade thee *suddenly* remove
>   To thy complete reward.
>
> "The pains of death are past,—
>   Labor and sorrow cease;
> And life's long warfare closed at last,
>   Thy soul was found in peace.
>
> "Redeemed from earth and pain,
>   Oh, may we all ascend!
> And there in Jesus' presence reign,
>   With our translated friend."

Home Life

For nearly twenty-two years the Lord permitted me to walk beside one of his own faithful servants. He was my all of earthly home, and my heart safely trusted in him. He was firm as the "everlasting hills" where right or wrong was concerned; yet kind always — careful of the comfort — tender of the feelings — and reciprocal in his affections. He often said, "Home is the dearest spot on earth to me;" yet where duty called him away, he was quick to obey, and while duty held him, he was content. At times I seem to hear him saying now, as so often in the past he has said, "We'll make our home a little heaven, where we can be quiet and rest after the battles of the day are all over; but we must be sure and not make unto us any idols. I believe God and His cause are first in my heart, and you are next to those" For years I tried conscientiously to submit patiently to his long and oft repeated absences, knowing that he went from his home because duty led him, yet all the time feeling that it was a hardship — that I had to sacrifice so much, for my home was very lonely without him. He was so rejoiced when I could say, I will, and do, let you go for Jesus' sake— I will stay alone, when the cause of God requires you, and do it cheerfully, as unto the Lord. His eye was surely "single" to the glory of God. When any measure was proposed, his first thought was, how will it affect the work, and no difference how hard the requirement, he always forgot self, and self-interests. He was always cheerful, and hopeful. If any clouds arose he always said "let us get into the sunshine."   With all his cares, and while pressed down with such a weight of anxieties, he never gave place to fretfulness, for his mind was stayed on One of whom it is said "Thou wilt keep him in perfect peace whose mind is stayed on thee, because he trusted in thee."

In looking back over all those years in which I have been so securely sheltered by his love, and through which we have tried hand in hand to walk in the way the Lord has led us, I can say, "surely goodness and mercy have followed us," and although our trials and conflicts at the time "seemed grievous," yet I now count it all joy that, I was privileged to labor and suffer with him for the Master here, and that through Christ I hope to share the Christian's rest with him in heaven.

I will give extracts from some of his letters to myself. Several of these were written before our marriage, and the remainder after the lapse of years.

Medina, Ohio, Nov. 10, 1852.

"**Dear Elizabeth:** —

This is my eighth year in the traveling ministry, four years of which were spent in the South. It is highly presumable I shall live and die a "preacher of the Gospel." My principal business will then be to save souls. The office is an awfully responsible one, and its duties are arduous. Nor is it desirable to be the wife of a minister. This position too, is a responsible and laborious one. Not the position for a pleasure -seeker, or the lover of honor, ease or fashion. For it, such have no taste; in it they can take no pleasure. But I will say on the other hand, if the heart is in the work, if the soul sympathizes with the Savior, notwithstanding all its responsibilities, labors, and pressing cares, it is a rich moral luxury to live and work in this glorious God-like cause — that of saving mankind."

Another time he said to me, "I expect always to be a Wesleyan Methodist minister. As long as I live, I intend to be in the active work. I cannot give you gold, nor promise you a permanent home. We shall be wayfarers — we must be ready to follow wherever duty leads us. But if we love God, and each other we may be very happy."

Medina, Ohio, March 8, 1853.

"**Dear Elizabeth:** —

Yesterday, after riding thirty miles through mud and mortar, over hill and dale, I had the exquisite satisfaction of finding your excellent epistle awaiting my arrival. And as I have many other things to write, I shall leave you to conjecture how well I was pleased with its contents. Yes: and ere my heart had ceased to throb with joy, and as I was thinking of an answer to-day, behold! another swift winged angel of good, dropped another sheet well filled with words of comfort — words which warm the heart, fire the soul, swell the bosom, light up the eye, radiate the countenance with sentiments of delight. I am satisfied, that as hunger prepares to enjoy food — sickness to appreciate health — fatigue to enjoy repose — so do the frowns and threats of foes prepare the heart to gladden and glow at the smiles and warm words of true friends. I leave you to make the application.

I thank God on your behalf, that Our Father, how sweet the name, vouchsafes his rich blessings to cheer your heart, and inspire the still firmer resolve to be his and always his. Sometimes I fear I have an idol, and that if required to give thee up for Christ's sake, I would be slow to make the sacrifice. I want to, aye, I do love you most dearly, but I would not love you more than I as a Christian ought. You beautifully express the feelings of my heart "that we should first live for God and then for each other." If we do this, we shall be happy. I hope I may ever prove worthy the confidence you have reposed in, and affection lavished upon me. Could I be so base as to win a heart as pure as thine, and take it from its girlhood home out upon the rough sea of life — the tempest-tossed ocean of time — and then prove unfaithful, I surely would most richly merit the righteous retributions of God;— I should expect them. Well do I know, and glad I am it is so, that I cannot make you unhappy without rendering myself miserable. The reverse is no less true. To make you happy is to bless myself. God knows it is my purpose to live so as to enjoy his approving smile."

Medina, Ohio, April 6, 1853.

"**Dear Elizabeth:**—

Your birthday favor came to hand yesterday. Language is too weak to tell with how much interest and pleasure I perused its rich lines. I incline to the opinion however that your feelings were very varied — not unmingled with sadness. But how could it be otherwise? — and, indeed, there are times when I love to ho a little sad. It seems to mend the heart. You are about to bid adieu to scenes Around which the tendrils of your generous affections have twisted and tied — to leave friends tried and true, and aa occupation in which your heart has been

111

enlisted for years, a calling of which good angels might be proud — carving ineffaceable hieroglyphics upon the imperishable granite of the eternity expanding intellect! Writing epitaphs which will be read by the light of the judgment' As an artist taking likenesses, which I trust will shine in the beauty of unfading youth, and glory of undying day! Who would envy a heart which unmoved could leave such a work! Not I. Your school days over! Nay verily. They have scarce begun. Life is a university of experience. And here we are only in the primary department. In the vestibule taking some preparatory lessons, previous to entering upon the enrapturing investigation of the science of Universal Being. What boundless fields of glorious discovery are before us; what limitless regions of knowledge are urging the eager mind onward — onward still, and ever onward! Cease to learn — cease to do— cease to be happy — *never.* That change will come — disappointment and discouragement to be met, without doubt; but they too are teachers, good teachers in this great school of experience."

West Chazy, May 1, 1873.

"**Dear Wife: —**

"It is too bad, but this is the very best I can do. I had no thought of any such tiring until it was too late; mail went out this morning at six o'clock and I cannot send a letter until to-morrow the same hour, so that you will not get this until Saturday; yet this is atoned for to some extent from the fact that you will get it the anniversary of our marriage.

Twenty years will have passed: O, how time flies! But thank God, our marriage is not the 'grave of love' as some modern *de*formers would style it — The sun of love shines much more brightly on us to-day than twenty years ago. How much better thus to 'wear in than wear out.' So may it ever be. Young folks think they know something of love, and so they do; but there is large margin for it to grow and ripen. Where shall we be twenty years from this? If living we shall be among the old folks. I sixty-nine, and you sixty-one or two; but mayhap one or both of us may be in Heaven. In all this, the will of the Lord be done. Yet it is a fact, that the longer I live the more Hove to live; not that I hold on to the thing of living here with greater tenacity, but more and more I love to labor for God and the good of others. For this, I should be willing to live a thousand years; aside from this, life to me would lose the lustre of its grandest significance. It amounts to this. The more we ripen up into the spirit of Jesus, the more we love to work for Him.

But I must stop writing, or I shall not get this into the mail for to-morrow morning, and that I must do without fail. Well, I shall think of thee often Saturday. We will not be separated in thought, and in our consecrations, incur hearts; we can be rewed though thus remote. 'Having many things to write unto you, I would not write with pen and ink; but I trust to come unto you, and speak face to face, that our joy may be full.' Peace be to thee. Greet the friends by name.' Ever lovingly yours."

1873.

"**Dear Wife: —**

We are having an excellent meeting. I wish you were here. I trust the good Lord is preciously near with you at home —that every meal is a sacrament — that you have momentary communion with God. Hope you are well and happy. I

112

fancy I see you in your cosy home, while I am a pilgrim." 'Rejoice evermore.' 'Pray without ceasing." 'In all things give thanks."

1873.

"**Dear Wife: —**

This is a real bright morning. Hope it is with thee, both external and internal. Well, there is not much in this letter, but from it you may learn that I think of you right early in the morning. Be sure and keep the 'City in view,' and 'keep step with the Captain.' Love to all. Pray for me. A few days and I will be at home, the Lord willing. I will keep him in perfect peace whose mind is stayed on me."

Aug. 29, 1873.

"**Dear Wife:—**

Both of your good letters are received. I read with tearful joy the victory you have gained, to endure hardness cheerfully for Jesus' sake. What a blessed victory. God be praised, I am trying to live on the mountain top of communion with God, and often feel that I am prayed for at home. The Lord give us glorious victory. Surely He will. 'All things work together for good to those who love God.' 'Christ in you the hope of glory' — What a wonderful blessing to have 'Christ in us.' His pure loving spirit. Fare thee well till we meet again. Ever faithfully and lovingly."

Sept. 11, 1873.

"**Dear Wife: —**

I have just come up out of Indiana— struck the M. S. R. R. here at Jonesville, fifteen miles from Coldwater, Have to wait for the train, so I write you. I shall expect to get a letter from you at Coldwater; then I will finish up this. I had to travel on a cross track yesterday up out of Indiana — an inferior affair; so about eleven o'clock last eve it stopped and put up for the night. This was a new experience since I came from the South. There I was a whole day traveling some sixty miles, and then put up for« the night; that was twenty-five years ago. Last night I improved the time. I wrote till a late hour— retired— had a refreshing sleep — woke up feeling quite wakeful—arose and wrote two or three hours, finishing up my account of the Conference. Thank God thus far, my health has been very good. Oh, how different from last year! Yours of the 7th received. So glad you are contented to suffer for Jesus. It makes you so much dearer to me. All well. Fare thee well. Love and blessing to you and all. Faithfully thine husband."

Oct. 4, 1873.

"**Dear Wife: —**

Yours of the 29th ult is received. Oh, it don't seem so far to Kansas when you once get there! It requires only four days for a letter to come. I like the Kansas brethren very much. They seem like a noble band of self-sacrificing moral heroes. Six have joined the Conference this session. This Conference is alive and wide awake. I little thought of meeting persons I had met before; yet here are a brother and sister Foster who lived a few miles from my native town and a brother Hosford, whom I knew twenty-eight years ago. Three weeks will soon speed by. You must, not allow yourself to feel lonely. Especially you must not repine. When you feel so inclined, go to Jesus. He is the best of company. I write on this paper because the other is all used up. I write by lamplight, and the family is not up yet; will get this mailed to-day if possible. Best love and blessing to you and all. God is love. Love one another.' 'Love fulfills the law.' Forever yours in love."

Kansas, Oct. 7, 1873.

"**Dear Wife:**—

Here I am among my relations — at a cousin's — Was at Bro. Henry's to-day — assisted him in raising his house. We all go to Robert's in Kansas City this eve. Henry and wife, Robert and wife, cousin Thomas and wife will all be there, but near fifteen hundred miles intervene between us. If you were only here! I have thought much of thee to-day— especially because I have been visiting. If I only had wings, or could take cars drawn by lightning, would I not see you this very night? But time is on the wing; only a few days more and then I can go to stay sometime worthwhile. Hope you are well and ever so happy. Let me see! You will get this about Saturday. Then only two weeks more. Bless me! Busy thought can bring us side by side, and we can have many a visit between this and then. My health continues as usual. God be praised. I shall hope to hear from you at Wasi-oja. I have a long ride night and day before me. The weather is beautiful here. Fare thee well. "Keep your heart in the love of God."

Oct. 17, 1873.

"**Dear Wife: —**

Your good letter of the 9th not received until yesterday—I began to feel hungry to hear from you. Your letters have so much better ring to them, than of yore. You have gotten into a better land than that in which you used to live; I know not how sufficiently to praise God. With you, I hope you may be kept there forever. How did you come to say you hoped there would be but one Sabbath more for you to be alone, if it is the Lord's will? How did you come to put that in? Well, it so happens that I have to turn about at Pittsford, Michigan, and go away back to Oshkosh, Wisconsin, and dedicate a church. They had posters printed and all the arrangements made and I knew nothing of it until I come here. Letters had been written, but I did not get them. It is a great thing to pray from the heart the Lord's prayer — 'Thy will be done.' And it is a blessed thing to realize 'My grace is sufficient.' — This is a possible experience and one we all need. Still beautiful weather. A *good* session of Conference thus far. I have to dedicate the church in which Conference is held, on Sabbath — then three more that week, making four churches in eight days — Then in a month or so come back to Iowa to dedicate another. This looks some like prosperity; God be praised — Glad God is reviving his work in Syracuse. May the time of captivity there be ended speedily. I am sure God is hearing prayer. 'Great peace have they that love thy law, and nothing shall offend them. 'In the world ye shall have tribulation, hut in me ye have peace.' 'Peace be unto you. My peace I give unto you. Not as the world giveth, give I unto you Peace like a river, and righteousness like the waves of the sea.' How blessed to daily and hourly commune with our Saviour *consciously*. But remember still there are heights beyond. Let us, 'Forgetting the things behind and reaching to those before, press toward the mark for the prize of our high calling of God in Christ Jesus.'

Letter Writing

His letter writing while at home was no small tax upon his time and sympathies. Many of his hours were spent in writing the absent. Encouraging those who needed encouragement. Sympathizing with those in sorrow, reproving in love, those who needed reproof, and in even so small a denomination as ours, there is often need of a peace-maker. Jesus will surely say to him. "Blessed are the peace-makers, for they shall be called the children of God," Many times he has come from the office weary in body and mind, yet no rest until some plan of action was arranged to help those in difficulty. Many times in the small hours of the night have I listened to the advice he thought he should give the parties concerned. It seemed a relief to tell some one of his cares. Perhaps the difficulty was concerning trifling matters, yet, there was danger that the cause of God would suffer, if oil were not poured upon the troubled waters. He seemed to have the faculty of gaining the confidence of all; for every one felt a freedom in confiding their interests into his keeping. They expected sympathy in joy or sorrow. Standing as he did at the centre of our denominational interests — visiting as he did for so many years our annual Conferences, he became well acquainted with our work all through the Connection. Almost knew individual churches. He was personally acquainted with nearly all the ministers— knew their successes and their failures — knew all they had to contend against — their self-denial for the Master — their zeal, their devotion and consecration. He often wrote, "We do have a band of noble brethren." His letters from the Conferences almost invariably testified to the presence of the Lord in their annual gatherings, and the faithful work done by the brethren. In looking over his letters I find often such expressions as these — "We have had a glorious session of Conference; for the Lord has been with us in mighty power." Souls were converted, and believers were strengthened." "The brethren go to their work with a renewed consecration. I expect great results, because of the baptism of power received." Also, "This has been a good year for this Conference. Thanks be unto God who giveth us such victories. It's all of the Lord — or Brother is on the mountain top. This has been his best year — over one hundred conversions. Prospects good, but our hope is in God. May He use us to His glory. I preached last night— a good time. The good Lord blesses me in His work. How much I need His grace. I am sure many are praying for me. Let us be more and more given to God. I think I know something of what Paul wrote of the 'care of all the Churches.' Seek daily communion with God. Be as busy as may be about His work and time will speed quickly. God bless you."

The Last Year

The last year of Mr. Crook's life was if possible crowded with more than usual labor. He returned from his visit to the Conferences in the Fall of 1873 feeling well in body and mind. The people had responded to his calls for sub-scriptions to the new Publishing House with great liberality. The work throughout the Connection was in a growing, prosperous condition. The Lord was with them at each session of Conference, to bless and strengthen. The brethren went to their respective fields of labor with fresh courage and re-newed consecration. New fields were opening, and new laborers were com-ing up to the work. He thanked God and took courage. He almost immediate-ly, in connection with his office work, took charge of a Mission Church about one mile and a half from his home, preaching twice on each Sabbath. A few weeks after his return, Bro. Stratton was taken sick, and for weeks was so feeble that we were all greatly alarmed about his recovery. Mr. Crooks took charge of the editorial work, and while all this was upon his hands, the clerk was also taken sick, which made additional labor. Before either was able to do full duty, he commenced a series of meetings at the Mission Chapel. Work-ing hard at the office all day, he would walk to the meeting, preach, exhort, conduct altar services, and late in evening would walk home, take a few hours rest, and then commence the labors of another day. This continued until time for the Spring Conferences. He attended the last of those in May, and in June, Bro. Stratton and family went West on a visit, and were absent four weeks. Mr. Crooks took entire charge of papers and office again. He at-tended the dedication of a church in Vermont, in July, and in August went to Michigan for the same purpose.

Immediately upon his return from the last dedication, he commenced his preparations for his usual Fall journeyings. His hands were full of business until the last moment. At dinner, on the last day, he said: — "I am going to try to get through with my work in time to have a half hour to rest and visit with you before I leave for the train." But there are always so many arrangements to make, so much to attend to, before leaving for such a length of time, that he could spare but a few moments for supper and the last il God bless you!" We expected to meet again in Michigan after a few weeks. He left home on the evening train, for East Orange, Delaware Co., Ohio, where the session of the Central Ohio Conference was to be held. Three years of our life had been spent happily in the cosy little parsonage at that place, He arrived in safety and good health, and wrote me a long letter, telling of old friends and his pleasant visit with them. He left there for the Miami Conference, and the week following he was in Richmond, Ind., attending the Indiana Conference. I will give an extract from one of his letters written while there: —

Sept. 3, 1874.

"Dear Wife:—

My health is still good, for me, at this season of the year. Some catarrh, but I think I am over the worst. The attendance is large — some say the largest ever known in this Conference. Six came to unite with the Conference. How thankful to God we should be for the success he is giving us. I am very thankful. Soon as possible I will let, you know whether you may look for me Monday or Tuesday. Good-bye till evening. Mail is in now, and no letter from you. Hope now for to-morrow morning, but I send you this. I am much better to-day. The Lord, be praised. Take good care of yourself; I know you will of mother. Don't too strongly look for me next week. Case is looking doubtful. Best love and blessings. Thine own loving husband.

He found that by riding all night he could come to my mother's on his way to the Michigan Conference, and spend a day with us. He was very weary, but enjoyed his visit very much. He had a long talk with mother. She did not think she should see him again, for she expected to be called soon to her "Heavenly home."

While making preparations for his departure, I could not entirely control my feelings. Seeing this, he came to me and said: — "It's hard, but we'll do this for Jesus' sake." We went to the depot; bade each other farewell. That was the last time I saw my husband when he looked like himself.

Ionia, Mich., Sept. 14, 1874.

"Dear Wife: —
I had expected to communicate with you again last week, but was away five miles from the post office; hence, I write this morning, immediately. We have had an excellent Conference session. Good attendance, a "blessed spirit of harmony and zeal. Six were ordained. My health is now about perfect. I have recovered from my annual attack of catarrh, and this morning, after the labors of yesterday, am feeling splendidly. O, how I thank God for good health! I hope you are well by this time. You must take good care of yourself for my sake. To look forward, it seems a long time until November; yet we know how fast time flies. You will be content taking care of mother. Bro. Curtis sends love to you all; he is quite feeble. Time is manifestly making its mark upon him. So it does and is upon us all. Now, be good, and do good. Let me hear from you often. Love and blessing to you and all. Thine own in love."

While going from the Michigan to the Illinois Conference, he had a severe chill, It lasted hours. In speaking of it after he came home, he said, "I thought I never could get warm again. The very marrow in my bones seemed frozen." He sent me a card from Sycamore, saying he was sick, and he would write me again soon.

Sycamore, Ill., Sept. 23.

"Dear Wife:—
No doubt you have been anxious to hear from me. Thursday eve I sent a card to you, reporting my sickness, then started to ride five miles to the Conference; or rather to my stopping place, which was two miles from the place of Conference. This was too bad for a sick man, to ride four miles each day. I would go in the morning and stay till evening, remaining indoors at night. I eat almost nothing. This wretched Hay-fever. I preached Sabbath, and came to this place Monday, too late to get a letter to you. I write this before breakfast. I am feeling better, but not well. Pray for me; I do for you. Write me often. Love to you, mother, and all. Ever thine own."

Sycamore, Ill., Sept. 24.

"Dear Wife:—

I write you by the hand of another, not being able to write now. I have been stopping here at Bro. Clark's, pastor of the Church at Sycamore, trying to rest up and doctor up. The Doctor says I am better, and thinks I will not have a run of fever. I am very weak. I start for Iowa to-day. Bro. Clark is going with me to take care of me and do the work. I shall do my very best to take care of myself, and will write you again when I get to Iowa. I know you will not cease to pray for me; I will not for thee. Hope in G-od. Don't be discouraged. All will come out right. Very best love and blessing to you and all. This is written by the hand of our excellent Sister Shepardson, for your loving husband."

Iowa Conference, Sept. 28, 1874.

"Dear Wife: —

I wrote you by the hand of Sister Shepardson, in Illinois, and by the hand of Bro. Clark, in Iowa, on oar way to the seat of Conference, and would now write you by the hand of Bro. Shepardson, who is to accompany me to Kansas. It required nearly a superhuman effort to reach this place. Having started Thursday noon, from Sycamore, Ill., we arrived at midnight at State Line, Iowa. There stretched out before us some fifteen miles of rough road, and it was raining furiously. This was rather a gloomy prospect for a sick man, but our good Heavenly Father brought us safely through it all. To his Holy name be rendered grateful praise. I left almost the entire business to Brothers Shepardson and Clark, simply settling with our Missionaries, and making my official report to the Conference. I only attended services Sabbath morning. The good brethren and sisters having kindly furnished me a couch on which to lie, and now having done all this, Mon day morning, I find myself vastly better than when we left Sycamore. It is truly wonderful how our good Heavenly Father can sustain amid suffering, toil and sickness. He shall have all the glory. And now, dear wife, be patient, trustful, and ever praise the Lord. This letter is quite extended. I had better rest. Give love to mother and all the family, and accept without measure, from your pilgrim, yet faithful and loving husband.

"P. S. Your two good letters addressed me here, were received Saturday evening.

"P. S. Sept. 29th. Programme changed. I have concluded to stop here a week and rest, and let Bro. Shepard do the business in Kansas. This will give me opportunity to rest and rally for the remainder of the tour. Young Bro. McGilvra consents to stay and care for me. Ever "loving, &c."

Oct. 5, 1874.

"Dear Wife: —

I promised to write the next letter with my own hands, but I find it much easier to employ the hand of another. I came here last Monday, and have been stopping here until this Monday morning, to rest up and get well. Have had excellent care taken of me, God appointing a Sister Riley and Bro. McGilvra to this work. Now the fever seems to be gone, but it leaves me quite weak. It will require some days to recruit, before I can renew my journey. I mean first, by the blessing of God, to take care of self, and they do my utmost for His cause. It may be I will remain here until Wednesday, before trying to start out on my tour. Only two more Conferences to attend, and two more churches to dedicate. I expect to return to Syracuse by the way of Leesville; but I do not expect to remain there very long. I wish the Estate affairs were all settled up. God will bring it about after a while. Take good care of yourself. Let me hear from you as often as possible. Give love to mother and all. Please accept a boundless share for yourself. Be sure and live very near to the dear Lord, and do all the good you can. From your ever-loving husband."

I received a number of postals written for him, all full of hope for a speedy recovery, and thankfulness for blessings given. After ten days rest, he started alone for the Minnesota Conference. He was not fit to make the journey, especially alone, but he said, "God took care of me." The next is written in a trembling hand, by himself.

Wasioja, Minn., Oct.;3, 1874.

"**Dear Wife:** —

Your two letters were brought from Kansas, also the one to this place received. I am improving slowly. Appetite does not seem to come. I think the attack was bilious. I start to Wisconsin to-day. A long visit with Professor Hand. He looks about as of yore. He is absent from his family nearly all the time. He sends kindest regards to Libbie. Well, not long now, if God please, till we meet at home. Won't it seem good. Dear wife, let us live near God. Love and blessing to all. Your ever loving husband."

Wisconsin Conference, Oct. 17, 1874.

"**Dear Wife:**—

Your good letter was received all right. I am still on the up grade. Have not preached since in Illinois, May next Sabbath, if the Lord helps. Yes, in about three weeks, God permitting, I hope to get home — about the first of November."

The next is an almost entire copy of his last letter to me, written in weakness and weariness, with a trembling hand.

Trempeleau, Wis., Oct. 21, 1874,

"**Very Dear Wife:** — Your postal was received last evening. Hope you are well as usual. lam here to dedicate a church at 2 o'clock to-day. Hope God may help me. I am still improving slowly, but it almost seems by the half inch, yet coming up. Glad to know you are trying to live near God. O, how important this! You wish to know on what day of next week I expect to get home. If God will, on Tuesday, if I do not go to Leesville; if I do go there, then Thursday. If you get home first, give love to all the friends. Blessings. Thine own loving husband.

(*"Soon face to face."*   A. Crooks.

After leaving Trempeleau, he had to attend a dedication at Xenia, Ohio. On the way, while in the cars, he made the acquaintance of two Friends; and as they were conversing about the reforms of the day, and the life work of the Christian, he noticed a gentleman seated nearby, who seemed very much interested in the conversation. As they neared Xenia, he approached Mr.

Crooks, asking "To what part of the city do you intend going? I live here, and can aid you." He told him where. Then the stranger said, "It is but a short distance. I am going the same way, and will carry your satchel for you. I have been listening to your talk, and I like the ring of it." They stepped to the door and found it raining. Then the gentleman said, "Let me call a carriage for you." He did so, and after helping him in, bade him a good day. Mr. Crooks rested very well that night, and the next day attended the dedication. After preaching, there were twelve hundred dollars to raise, in order to clear the church from indebtedness. They succeeded in raising the greater portion of it, and thinking they would not be able to finish it entirely, dismissed the congregation. He went to his resting place, lay down a few hours, thought of another plan, arose, went to the evening service and completed the work. He was too feeble to go to Leesville, as he had purposed doing, so he came directly home.

He was so thankful to get home once more. He was very grateful for the kindness and care bestowed upon him by others. Several times he said "I could not have had better care if you had been at my side; but it is so pleasant to be in my own little home again." He had every attention possible while traveling. At one time, the Superintendent of the road was at the depot when the train was being made up, and seeing Mr. Crooks' condition, he ordered a more comfortable car to be added to the train. Another time, the Conductor of a train had a lounge put into the baggage car; so that he could lie down while traveling. The hands employed on the trains seemed to vie with each other in kindness to him. The accommodations in the far West, upon those cross roads, especially, are not very good. He has journeyed many, many miles, upon freight trains, and even upon open gravel cars, seated upon his trunk, with his umbrella to shield him from the sun and rain. Several times he has written me of riding with the engineer and in one letter, written several years ago, he says: — "I am getting used to the rough and tumble of travel. You would think so, if you had seen me riding all night, last night, in a freight car, lying on a board for a bed, and my satchel for my pillow."

He came home the 27th of October. He was very feeble, and had changed so in his appearance, that he scarcely looked like himself. We all felt that he must have been very much worse than we realized at the time. That evening, while talking of his sickness, I told him of the desolation that would come over me at times, while at mother's — a fear that I should never see him again, and I said, "Oh, Mr. Crooks what should I have done if you had not come home?" Laying his hands upon my head, he said, "God would have helped you borne it." He also said "he believed that he was permitted to come home in answer to prayer." I feel assured, by some remarks he made as we further conversed, that night, that there had been times when he had felt his recovery doubtful. He traced the hand of a kind and loving Father all through his sickness, especially in raising up such friends, who were so tireless in their attentions to his comfort. He said farther, that "God had so prospered us as a denomination, that there would not be so much anxiety for the future as there had been in the past. He should not have so much care, and he was not going to let all his attention be given to outside work, for he intended to spare a little to his home. For years the Connection had claimed his whole time and absorbed his every thought; now, God was raising up others, who were working so zealously and faithfully that there was not that necessity for him to labor as he had been doing. He was going to rest and recruit."

Nearly every day he spent an hour or more at the office, having his accounts of business done at the Conferences properly recorded on the office books, and in answering letters which were awaiting his return. Some of these were for advice and counsel, and he wrote as the case seemed to need; sometimes planning the work for others, sometimes encouraging, and again giving counsel. When at home, he lay on the couch nearly all the time. He did not suffer much, but seemed so weary.

The first Sabbath morning after his return, he wanted to go to Church, but as it was stormy, he concluded to stay at home and rest. I left him with that understanding. Shortly after I had gone, he changed his mind, arose, protected himself as best he could, and came to the house of God. He sat by the stove during service, but before the benediction was pronounced, he asked permission to say a few words. He said he wished to thank the friends for their kind sympathy and prayers. He said it was in answer to prayer that he stood before them to-day. He spoke of the good dealings of God with him, and his perfect submission to the will divine. He encouraged them to continue to pray; for God did hear and answer prayer.

There were several times in which, for a few days, he seemed to gain strength; then he would have chills or a return of fever, and he would lose all he had gained. At one time he gained several pounds in weight; but it could not have been good flesh. There was not a perfect circulation of blood through his system; for one foot and limb were cold nearly all the time. His appetite was" very fickle; sometimes craving very little, and then almost ravenous in its demands.

The Mission Church had been without a supply for the pulpit for several Sabbaths, and he was so anxious for that little flock for which he had labored so earnestly, that he walked to the place of worship, and preached from these words: — "Keep yourselves in the love of God, looking for the mercy of our Lord Jesus Christ unto eternal life." Jude, i: 21. He preached about forty minutes. His voice, at first, was weak and tremulous; but he became so engaged in urging his hearers to faithfulness, that it became as strong and powerful as it ever was. He rested a while, and walked home, and that night he had another chill, from which, in a few days, he seemed to rally. He afterwards rode to the place of meeting, and preached his farewell sermon to them, as they had succeeded in securing the services of another pastor. This proved to be the last time he gave the "bread of life" to others. His text was:— "And when he Was gone, a lion met him by the way and slew him." 1

Kings, xiii: 24, The leading thought he tried to impress upon their minds was a carefulness in obeying the commands of God. He did not remain to Class-meeting, but took each one of them by the hand, asking God to bless them, he bade them farewell. They never saw him again, until they looked upon his shrouded form.

When expostulated with for working when so feeble, he said, "I am doing my duty; God will take care of my body." His mind rested calmly, trusting in God. He said several times, that he never felt he could be spared from the work as well as now; there were so many brave, zealous, earnest workers coming into our ranks. The young and old were so baptized with the spirit of labor and sacrifice for Jesus, that the work would still go on; 'but,' he always added, "it is just as the Lord wills; I am in his hands, to do his will."

About this time, letters came, asking advice concerning a Church difficulty on a certain part of the work. It seemed to press heavily upon him. He ex-claimed, "Why cannot brethren bear with each other!" He was advised to send postal cards to the parties, stating his feebleness, and that he would write them more fully, as soon as he was better. This he did; but a few days later he wrote several long letters, trying to calm the strife among brethren.

The year was drawing to a close. He felt there ought to be some earnest words said to our subscribers, urging renewals and the enlarging of our list. He arose one Monday morning, and as soon as breakfast and morning devotions were over, he drew a stand near the stove, and began to write. Nearly the whole forenoon was spent in preparing the Prospectus for 1875. Then, there were callers who occupied his time for an hour or more. When at last alone, he laid his weary body upon the couch; and as I sat beside him, taking my hand in his, he said: — "I know you are feeling anxious because I have worked so hard this forenoon. I had to do it. The subject was in my mind and on my heart. I could not lay it aside. It was time for the Prospectus to appear in the paper, and there was no one who had the facts as I had. I had to do it. This morning, as I knelt beside my bed, I said, O, Lord, living or dying, I will do my duty.' It was my duty, and God will take care of the results. It has always been, my experience, that God has given me strength to do the work he has for me to do. While attending the Conferences and Dedications, as feeble as I was, many times I felt that I could not hold up my head; yet, when the time came for me to speak, to preach or to present the interests of our cause, God was by me, to support and strengthen. Now, do not feel worried, for I am in the Lord's hands, to do his will."

He was "exceedingly interested in the women's temperance work in our city, and was anxious that I should attend every meeting. One day, he had lain upon the couch nearly all the forenoon; not in much pain, yet suffering from prostration. It seemed to require an effort to lift even his hand; yet he urged me to go to the meeting that afternoon. He said, "you cannot do any-thing for me; I will lie here and rest while you are gone." He seemed to feel sorry when I told him I could not leave him. I did go to a number of meetings, partly to please him, when my heart was divided between the interests of the cause and my poor feeble husband at home. We had many calm, quiet talks, during those last weeks, upon personal experience. He was so restful, and trustful, and hopeful, expecting to get well, because he had such confidence in the strength of his constitution to throw off disease, and there was so much work to be done for the Master, and he had such a love for that work, that his mind was almost entirely occupied in arranging work for himself and others. Self was so thoroughly crucified; he had no anxiety for the present or future. All was well with him, and he lay passive in the hands of the Lord, awaiting his guiding, ready to go or stay, just as the Lord willed.

He said, at one time, "I hope to have more time to write now, than I have had for the past few years. There are several subjects upon which I think I shall write more fully. I think good can be done. I want our people established, settled, and grounded on these subjects." One was our perpetuity as a denomination. If we will, with "patient continuance," labor on, success is before us. Another one he mentioned, was u the great importance of heart and life consecration to God." This was a subject of vital importance to him. Personally, he drew very near to God; seemed to talk with him, as with a dear friend. His earnest prayers for the cause he loved, and was willing to labor for, shall never be forgotten.

Those last weeks were blessed, precious weeks. He seemed in spirit so like himself. His cares were laid upon One strong to help. He was so thankful to get home, he fully entered into the enjoyment of our quiet, peaceful home. He was tender, loving, cheerful, hopeful and trustful. It was quiet rest for body and soul.

He went to the office nearly every day, until the last week. Tuesday, one week before his death, he went twice. About eleven o'clock he came home, very weary, and laid on the couch. He did not wish any dinner, but wanted to rest. He seemed comfortable as he lay there, and having to go out to meet an engagement, at two o'clock, I left him for an hour or two. When I returned, he was feeling badly, but was trying to transact some business appertaining to the printing office, with a stranger who had called to see him. When we were alone, he complained of a pain in his stomach, somewhat similar to his old complaint, (Bilious Cholic). But as it was not very severe, he said he would drink some peppermint tea, and be covered up warm, and get into a perspiration. He thought that would relieve him. He suffered all night, but he did not feel anxious. In the morning, we thought we ought to be more thorough, and commenced giving him medicine which was prepared for him, and had always given relief. About noon he was better of the pain, but had a high fever, which increased as night approached.

Bro. Stratton called during the afternoon, to make arrangements for the missionary meeting, which was to be held the next day. I asked him if he thought he should be able to attend the meeting. He answered, "If I cannot go to the meeting the brethren can come here." He felt that the meeting must be held then, for our missionaries were needy. During the night his fever was very high. His mind was wandering. He was traveling — working — had so much to attend to. In the morning early he was better. I wanted him to have a doctor, but he said, "Wait, I think I shall be better now." After a time I left him sleeping, and went into another part of the house to attend to other duties. In a little while hearing him up, I went to his room and found him trying to dress himself and could not. I asked, "Had you better get up now? he said "O yes," and indistinctly referred to the missionary meeting.   I gave him the aid he needed, and leaving him a moment I heard his voice and went to him immediately. He tried to tell me something, but could not articulate clearly. Then he laid back upon the bed and motioned me to cover him up. I sent immediately for the doctor. He was conscious when he came, yet did not talk coherently. He lay all day in a stupor; when roused he seemed to know what was said to him. Several times during the day he would get up and out of bed as though he must go somewhere. I would quietly arrange his pillows or bed, and say, now your bed is nice, he would lie down without any resistance and be covered again. This continued until about midnight. His fever left him then, and he slept sweetly until four o'clock, when he called me by name. He was perfectly rational, and could converse easily. He remembered some things that transpired during the previous day, but for the most part it was a lost day to him. He now seemed more natural than he had for several days past. He was his own bright self again. After he had eaten a little breakfast he said, "I was so sick yesterday morning that I was not conscious of the time for morning devotion; we must not forget our family altar; you will bring the Bible here beside my bed and read it to me and we will pray together." This was done until the last morning, when he was again unconscious. When the doctor came, he found him so much better that he encouraged us to hope that he would soon be well.

About eleven o'clock that day he had a slight chill, but he did not appear any the worse for it, as it lasted but a few moments. Saturday morning we moved his bed into the sitting room. He seemed strong — walked quite easily. In the afternoon he sat up in the arm chair and said, "he felt better." He did not suffer except a soreness across his stomach. He had some fever nearly all the time. He slept quietly that night, awoke refreshed and still seemed better. The doctor came about ten o'clock and was pleased with the improvement in his condition. He said he saw nothing in the way of his recovery if we used care. The doctor sat and conversed some time with us — and among other things he said, "I have been hearing something of your hard labors." Mr. Crook's said, "his labors in the past had been very severe, but he now felt there was no further need for him to carry such a weight of responsibility. In the future he was intending to take better care of his health. There had no one been wronged but his wife. She had been called upon to sacrifice very much for the cause for which he was laboring; had in fact given up her husband for ten years, but he meant to do better by his own home in the future."

He continued, "I cannot of course tell how it will be, but I feel as though there were twenty years of service for Christ before me yet." The doctor said he would not be surprised if there were. He sat up twice during the day — had very little or no appetite, but was free from pain. We spent a calm, bright, joyous Sabbath day. One or two of the friends saw him for a moment. The doctor's order was that he should be kept perfectly quiet, for his fever still clung to him. He sat up in his arm chair twice during the day, but that night he was very restless. He was not in pain, but his mind was so full of work. He was planning important work. He said in the morning he had prepared several tracts and he thought when he got well he should write them out and publish them. He thought they would do good.

When Bro. Stratton called, he told him of one or two little matters which had escaped his mind when he saw him. After he had finished, he said: "There, they are off my mind now." He told him of his restless night, — the work he had been doing during the night. I give Bro. Stratton's account of his visit: —

"On Monday morning, he said, in answer to inquiries: — 'No, I was not nervous, but I could not sleep. My mind was in a chariot of flame. I was blocking out tracts, and one article especially. One tract on *Why be Wesleyan Methodists?* He mentioned other enterprises by name, and the joy of his soul. He expressed the desire to see the great work of holiness of heart and life more and more developed among our people; and it seemed to us that his countenance glowed like the face of Moses, just down from the Mount of God. He then spoke with great tenderness of the unwearied attentions of his wife, introducing it by saying: "Brother Stratton, I have the best wife in the world.'"

He fully appreciated every little attention. During the morning, he called me to his bedside, saying, "I think we will write a 'certain' letter to-day." I told him he was not well enough. He answered, "I have all that I am going to say arranged in my mind, and if you will write it, then it will be off my mind." I promised to do it for him in the afternoon; it was not remembered again. He slept some during the day. He was perfectly rational, and sat up a short time. We had several conversations about what he intended to do, as soon as he was able. One thing, he had promised, as soon as he was well enough, to visit a Church where there was some misunderstanding among some of the members. He spoke of his promise as he lay there on his bed. There was such an earnestness in his eye, as he said:— "I shall talk plainly with them. I read, years ago, an allegory, which is to the point in this case. When the Devil wishes to get the control of men, he holds up to them his end of the great magnifying glass, through which men look at the things of this life, and they see everything just as he wants them to see it; so he controls them; when, if they would only turn the glass around, look through the other lens, they would see just as the Lord wanted them to see. They would learn his will in the matter. I shall tell them they must be very sure which lens they are looking through." The doctor called in the afternoon, with another physician. As he was not well, and feared he was going to be sick, he brought this one with him for counsel, and to attend to his case if he were not able to come in the morning himself. They both encouraged us to hope for recovery. An old friend saw him a moment. He was glad to see her, and sent love to all the friends, and expressed a hope that he should see them soon, A short time after this, he was taken with a chill, which lasted about twenty minutes, and during this time he was perfectly wild. I never saw him so much so before. After using restoratives, the chill left him, and he was perfectly rational again. He said the chill had not hurt him; his fever was not increased any, and he thought he was weak, and perhaps he had not kept covered as well as he should. He relished a light supper, and after having his head and feet bathed, he fell asleep, and had refreshing slumber all night; yet, every time I went to his bedside, he would awake. About midnight, he awoke and said: — "We have been having such a glorious work. We have organized a splendid Sabbath school." Then looking at me closely, he said, "Why, I am at home! Really, I do not realize half the time whether I am at home or not, I am so very busy." He wanted some snow to eat; and while eating it, told again of his joy at being with me. He was his own loving self once more.

Those last days are beautiful days to remember. He was so patient. Not one complaint was heard from him. Everything was just as it should be. He so often said, "Thank you," or "You are so kind." It was a pleasure to do for him. For years we had not enjoyed such uninterrupted communion with each other. He was so quiet, and rested so calmly in the arms of the loving Savior. There was a halo about him. As I think of those days, I remember his face shone with a loving light, not of this world. As the day dawned, he said, "Dearest, it is daylight." I asked, "Do you wish me to get up?" He answered, "On my own account, I do; but on yours, I rather you would lie longer.' As I arose, he wished to change from the bed to the couch. After arrangements were made to make him comfortable, he arose, partly dressed himself, and walked to the couch. I asked, "How do you walk this morning?" He answered, "Quite like myself." I covered him warmly, as we supposed; but after a little while, he asked for more covering and again, after a short time, asked for more, saying he thought he was going to have a chill. I gave him warm drinks, and put hot applications to his feet and hands. He was not wild, as he was the night before; but sank into a stupor from which it was hard to arouse him, and when aroused, he did not talk connectedly.

Soon, the doctor came; but he was better, and conversed with him rationally. I commenced to tell the doctor about his chills, and my fears about them; and he looked up at me, saying: "Those chills have not hurt me. My fever is not increased. I am weak, and easily affected by any change. The doctor coincided with him, and said we must be very careful about the temperature of the room, when we made changes. He also said he did not see anything in the way of his recovery, if we used care. Soon after this, Bro. Stratton called; but he must have had another chill, and could not tell of it; for he was in a stupor again, and did not talk connectedly. He spoke of a beautiful picture, beautiful doors, and beautiful colors. When Bro, Stratton left, I went with him into another room, for a few moments. I told him of my fears; but that the doctor did not seem alarmed.

When I returned, Mr. Crooks had evidently tried to arise from the couch, for his feet were on the floor. I asked, "Do you want to go to the bed?" He answered, "Yes." I helped him to sit up. In a moment he fell back, apparently lifeless. I aroused him, by rubbing his hands and face; and said to him, "Now, I will help you get up." I did so; but he fell back a second time. Then I called in friends. We used every means to arouse action we could devise; but without success. After carrying him back to the bed, we sent to the Wesleyan Office and for the doctor. While the messenger was gone, we still kept doing all we could for him, and finally gave him some wine. After a little, he opened his eyes, and tried to speak; but for a while did not articulate a word distinctly, except, "Come! Come!" I said to a friend, who stood nearby: "It is so hard that I cannot understand what he says." He heard what I said, and looking at me earnestly, he said, distinctly: "Why, I said it three times." He had tried three times to tell me something; but failed to speak so as to be understood. In a moment there came a great earnestness into his eyes, as he grasped my hands, saying, "Be quick!" and drew me to him, and kissed me, looking into my eyes as though there was something he wanted to make me understand. In a moment, he drew me to him again, saying, "Be quick!" and kissed me. After he did this, he said, "There is rest beyond the skies," or "There is rest in the skies." Three or four times he said, "Be quick!" as though he had but a moment in which to say "farewell." He held my hands with a close grasp, and continued trying to speak; his head and lips were moving, and a faint sound could be heard; a murmuring of inarticulate words, until he sank, to speak no more.

The doctor came, gave him medicine, and went to see the physician who had attended him during his sickness, and who had been sent for; but he was not able to leave his room, and returned in time to see him

"Breathe his life out sweetly there"

Thus, he quietly, peacefully, "fell asleep in Jesus," about thirty minutes after twelve o'clock, Tuesday, December 15th, 1874.

Obsequies and Memorial Services in Honor of Rev. Adam Crooks

"The services at the residence were conducted by Rev. Elijah Gaylord, late President of the Syracuse Conference. He spoke as follows:

"Dearly beloved friends, we have met at this house of mourning, and would call upon our hearts and all that is within us to magnify His grace which has distinguished us as the monuments of God's amazing mercy. We all mourn and feel deeply afflicted, and yet we feel that God doeth all things well. We know there is one heart that bleeds at this providence. There are many who sympathize. Deeply afflicted, we shall remember with sadness this event for many days, but we hope and trust that God will bless this affliction, deep as it is, to all who were connected with our beloved brother who has departed. We feel that we had, all of us, an interest in him. He has been, in a certain sense, public property. We feel, deeply feel the loss of our departed brother, and while we mourn we can but realize that our loss is his infinite and eternal gain. We can say in the language of one of old, "The Lord gave and the Lord hath taken away; blessed be the name of the Lord." May the spirit of the Lord, the consolation of his grace, and the power of the Holy Ghost, rain down upon this dear sister, and all the friends of our departed brother, and may we all share in the same grace and mercy. We bless the name of God that He has spared our deceased brother so long, to the Connection, and has made him so useful. May his mantle fall upon some, yea, upon many devoted servants of the cause of Christ, and fit them for the important duties that he has so ably conducted, and may the dear Lord enable us still to live and triumph in his grace.

"He then closed the services by prayer.

"SERVICES AT THE CHURCH.

"Memorial services at the Wesleyan church.

"The church was hung with black and white, arranged in festoons around the entire interior; with the pulpit heavily draped with black cloth adorned with vines. Within the chancel rail, on the communion table, both also draped, stood a large and elegant cross composed of calla lilies and white flowers. Another cross of white flowers, and an elaborate crown and cross of the same pure material, camellias, japonicas, double white primroses, daphne odare, with white fringe chrysanthemums, the cross sprinkled over with smilax? and the crown with white rosebuds, adorned the coffin.

"The remains, enclosed in an elegant rosewood casket, were borne by the following named gentlemen as pall-bearers:—

"Rev. S. H. Foster, pastor of the First Wesleyan Church of Syracuse.

"Rev. L. N. Stratton, assistant editor of the *American Wesleyan.*

"Rev. D. S. Kinney, President of the Allegheny Conference.

"Rev; J. P. Betker, President of New York Conference.

"Rev. A. S. Wightman, President of Syracuse Conference.

"Rev. N. Wardner, President of Champlain Conference.

"Rev. G. L. Paine, Mexico, N. Y.

"Rev. A. P. Dempsey, Seneca Falls, N. Y,

"Rev. E. Barnetson, Groton, N. Y.

"Rev. S. Burgess, Blodgetts, Mills.

"Rev. E. Gaylord, Syracuse, N. Y.

"The relatives and friends of the deceased followed, Mrs. Crooks being supported by her brother, Edwin Willits, Esq., of Monroe, Michigan, while sympathizing friends and neighbors filled the house to its utmost capacity.

"The services, which were under the direction of the pastor, Rev. S. H. Foster, were opened with reading of the hymn, "Unveil thy bosom, faithful tomb," by the Rev. Seth Burgess, followed with prayer by the Rev. A. F. Dempsey, the attending clergy kneeling around the chancel.

"Selections from the xxiii Psalm, "The Lord is my shepherd," and from 1 Corinthians, xv, "As we have borne the image of the earthly, so also we shall bear the image of the heavenly," were read by the Rev. J. P. Betker, of New York.

"The hymn, "How blest the righteous when he dies," was then sung.

"Rev. S. H. Foster announced that short addresses would be made by several friends and co-laborers of the deceased, many of whom had come from a distance to attend these memorial services.

"As for myself, little did I think, when last I shook hands with our departed brother, that he was so soon to be taken from us. On that occasion, as I took him by the hand to say good-bye, a smile played upon his face and he said to me, "All is right, brother, all is right." We are here, as a Church and congregation, as mourners to-day. But we mourn not as those without hope. There are many outside of our own Church and congregation, who are in deep sympathy with us in our affliction. Our departed brother was to us a leader, and in the relations he sustained to us he was our head. When in our exodus, we came to the Red Sea, the voice of his words, as he essayed to speak on God's behalf, were, 'Go Forward!' He was our Moses? who was 'faithful in all his house,' like as ancient Moses, in all the relations he sustained to us as a denomination, bearing testimony as did Moses of old. He will no more be seen by us 'in the tabernacle of our congregation.' No more will he come forth from the revealed glory of God's approbation and presence, to cheer us on. But our hope is, that God will raise up unto us a Joshua in his stead.

"Two verses of the 837th hymn were then sung.

"When floating on life's troubled sea,
    By storms and tempests driven,
Hope with her radiant finger points
    To brighter scenes in heaven.

"She bids the storms of life to cease
    The troubled breast be calm;
And in the wounded heart she pours
    Religion's healing balm."

REV. J. P. BETKER, OF NEW YORK.

"None, perhaps, who are present on this occasion are in any condition to speak. We are mourners around the coffin of our best friend, and we cannot speak as in calmer moments we might. I came nearly three hundred miles to attend this funeral. In my experience as a man, I have found very few real friendships in the world. I can count on my fingers' ends the true and genuine friends of my heart. One, is in that coffin to-day. I feel ill-qualified to speak here. But in thinking of my brother I can think of one thing as true of him — his great soul; his great mind. He possessed the true elements of greatness; and if I were to attempt to impress anything upon the brethren here, it would be the imitation of that greatness of soul that distinguished him. All true greatness has its beginning in piety. I knew him when he was almost a beardless boy. He and I started in the ministry at the same period, belonged to the same Conference.

I remember the first place that I ever preached as a Wesleyan minister; the next one who follow ed me was brother Adam Crooks.

I say true greatness begins in real piety; and I never knew one truly great the genuineness of whose piety there could be any suspicion. The foundational basis of true greatness is integrity. And if there was one among us distinguished for truth; for integrity; for solidity in this respect, it was Adam Crooks; a man of truth in all the developments of his character; in all the manifestations of his spirit. Wherever Adam Crooks was, there was a true man. True greatness too is characterized by a boundlessness of benevolence. A great soul cannot nurse itself in selfishness. His spirit was a broad catholic spirit, that took in all mankind. There was not a child who was beneath his notice. The last time that we put up together at our Annual Conference, we slept, ate, and talked together; and all the little children about the house had a sweet word from him. I never knew him to be otherwise than kindly disposed in every respect. And because he was thus disposed he made himself what he was — great.

True greatness, too, is estimated by its depths of principles and its breadth of measures. I never met a man that I thought was so perfectly settled in what he believed to be true as this dear brother.

* * * * *

"True greatness is distinguished by a moral courage that takes no account of the odds that are against it; makes no arrangement for defeat, and assures itself of victory because its cause is just.

"I do not think I could say anything more true of our brother than this; that he took no odds of the mighty forces that were against him. He went down to North Carolina in the days when it was as much as man's life was worth to call himself an Abolitionist; and he' passed through fearful prison scenes there, and all through the history of the great war against the fearful system of slavery, he went right into the very heat of the battle, not asking whether we should be defeated, but having the most firm confidence in the justice of our cause — a cause which he lived to see so gloriously triumph.

"True greatness knows no fraudulent concealments of its principles or aims, and whatever you and I may think of this brother, especially those who differ with him on the question of Secret Societies, we must give him credit for this statement, and it grew out of the very nature of his character that 'True greatness knows no fraudulent concealment of its principles or aims.' He was a day-light man. His works were done in the light, and not in the darkness, and so he stood broadly and firmly fixed in his relation to truth.

"True greatness may not always convert its opposers to its own standard, but it will command respect. And I venture to say that although our brother was firmly seated in his views, and challenged all combat as to the truth of his position, there is not a man in this city whose opinion is worthy of respect who would not say, "Adam Crooks has deserved my regard and respect."

* * * * *

Rev. G, L. Paine, of Mexico, N. Y.

"As has been said, we are mourners here to-day. We cannot talk as we would under other circumstances. But I would say, I have been associated in Conference capacity with this dear brother in the Rochester Conference, ever since he has been here as Editor and Agent, up to this last Spring. Our first meeting was a happy one. Favorable opinions were formed on the first look I had of him, and as we met from time to time in Conference relation, every word seemed to add to the respect and the regard I had for him. Often in our Conference relations knotty questions came up; something that appeared personal, whereby feelings might be touched, and I have seen the dear brother start across the Conference floor to some person, and it seemed as if the magic touch of his hand, and the words dropped from his lips, would quiet everything down, and calm all heated feeling. And then standing anywhere on the Conference floor, when a difficult question would come up, and it seemed that there might be a break, he would unravel and point out the course, and the Conference, seemingly, would take the course, and all would be harmony. These things as they fell from his lips brought that brother to my heart.

"I stand here to-day as a second mourner with these brethren that have stood by him; and my trust is that by and by we shall meet this loved one where parting scenes will never come.

"Two verses of the 852nd hymn were then sung.

> "I would not live alway; I ask not to stay,
> Where storm after storm rises dark o'er the way;
> The few lurid mornings that dawn on us here
> Are enough for life's woes, full enough for its cheer."

"Rev. Seth Burgess of Blodgett's Mills, N. Y.,

Spoke as follows.— 'There is very much that might be said in regard to our brother who is gone; much that to our mind is interesting; but there is one trait of his character to which I wish to call your attention just a few moments; and that is as an honest man and as a successful financier. At the time that brother Crooks was elected Agent, if my memory is correct, I was elected as one of the members of the Book Committee; and that, as a matter of course, brought us into an association that we otherwise should never have had; and I can say in truth, that with all brother Crook's other good qualities, he was an honest man; honest I believe to the very letter. It is one of the prominent principles of the Christian religion to be strictly honest. Brother

131

Crooks has. always sought to have his doings examined and investigated; and when I proposed a little less than four years ago, to have the books of the agent audited, brother Crooks favored it at once; coveted it; wished to have it done. We appointed a committee who examined the books and everything was found satisfactory.

"Brother Crooks was not only an honest man, but he has been a very successful business man in our employment. It would require more time than I have to give you much of an idea of brother Crooks' business transactions. But it is enough to say that when he became our servant in this department, we were excessively poor; we were so poor that the retiring agent discouraged us from trying to carry forward the enterprise. Brother Crooks has done well. We are not rich to-day? but we are by several thousand dollars better off financially than we were when brother Crooks came in here as our Agent. Time, as I said, fails to tell you what he has done; but his life with us, or so far as we knew of, has not only been a life of humble, devoted piety, but it has been a life of successful business. And he succeeded, perhaps, beyond what any other man we have would have done. As to this we do not know; but we trust that God in His providence will raise up another man to take brother Crooks' place and carry forward that enterprise in which brother Crooks' whole soul and body was enlisted. I felt more, when I came here, like taking a seat down there with those mourners, than I did like standing here; and I did not expect to stand here. But I am glad to say this much, and I believe that we who knew him can bear testimony to the same truth, that brother Crooks was an honest man.

Rev. A. S. Wightman of Syracuse Conference.

"My relations with our departed brother, as many in this congregation know, were very intimate. I was his pastor for some years, and I can see now just the pew where he used to sit, with his open, loving, manly face fixed upon me, as I would endeavor to preach the Gospel. It is a pleasant thing to remember to-day that he always treated me with the most profound respect, and never allowed an opportunity to pass without giving me words of marked encouragement. Often when I have felt despondent and discouraged, I have gained new courage from his hearty and cheerful words, which always seemed to be appropriate to the very time. There is a kind of friendship that might be called sunshine friendship. It is easy to be friendly to everybody when it costs us nothing; but it is quite another thing to be a friend in need — when there requires to be some little outlay on the part of the one showing that friendship, in order that the benefit designed may be imparted,

"In my experience with this dear brother, I have seen it verified many times that he was truly a friend in need. Often in times of trouble and sorrow he has taken me by the hand with the generous tear quivering in his eye, and has said, 'Brother, do not be discouraged; trust in God and look higher.' Oh! as such reminiscences as these come to my memory, I feel indeed like a mourner on this occasion.

"An incident occurred previous to the election of our present editor, Rev. L. N. Stratton. Brother Crooks found it necessary to leave the office a part of the time to attend to business in distant parts. He was in the habit of leaving the editorial work in my hands. On one occasion — perhaps the first occasion of his absence — I said, 'Brother Crooks, what instructions will you give me now in reference to the management of the paper during your absence.' 'Nothing, my brother,' said he, 'But the exercise of your own judgment; only remember this one thing— strike hard and high for the truth. And there was an expression of nobility, of Christian strength of character, that he made at that time, and has left upon my mind a marked impression, I seem to have adopted it as a sort of rule of life.

"I feel that I have lost a friend and a brother. Such a one perhaps I shall not meet again. But this thought is an especial comfort to me. I have seen enough of the world's trials and sorrows. I feel very often now a longing for quiet rest; and I know that I shall find rest in that home to which our dear brother has gone, where there are no tears and where sorrows never come."

Rev. D. S.. Kinney, President of Allegheny Conference.

"Receiving at the midnight hour, over three hundred miles distant, the announcement of the sad bereavement that convenes us to-day, I stepped across the way to one of our "fathers in Israel;" one whose name is well known as a minister among us, in advanced life, walking closely with God, and broke to him the sad intelligence, said, "Father Lamb, why could not God have taken me and left brother Crooks a few years longer?" We both knelt before God, and I know that our hearts were so moved, that cheerfully, had it been God's will, we would have died that he might have lived. I knew nothing about the circumstances of the case, but I thought perhaps my dear brother Willits here, was so circumstanced in the far West that he could not be here and sympathize with his sister, and the wife of the dear departed might perhaps desire me as among the mourners, and I therefore decided to come, and to willingly sit, if it might be, by her side, she having been my teacher when a boy, and being my teacher at the time of her engagement and marriage with brother Crooks. I can say that I heartily endorse — having been most intimate for over twenty years with our departed brother, all that has been said of his traits of character. But I wish just here to say that brother Crooks was a growingly pious man. He knew the worth of prayer, as perhaps many of us do not. I have personally, in those fearful conflicts of the recent years of his official relationship here among you, and with us as a Christian family; I have known him, like the dear Master in the days of his incarnation, *to spend the whole night in prayer*. And the last years, and months, and weeks of his life, marked a growth in intense personal piety and devotion to God. The last work that he has dictated, that is in our hands, that he sent to me in pamphlet form a few days only ago, — "Processes of Salvation," — in which the distinctive Wesleyanic and Methodistic view of entire consecration to God and sanctification, is so clearly defined and scripturally enforced, has not been with him a simple theory, but has been an experimental reality.

"We frequently have corresponded, as well as had personal conversation, these recent months, upon this subject. And while brother Crooks was a thoroughgoing reformer, (all that has been said with reference to that, I can say amen to) yet after all, he did not desire the continuance of our organization simply on account of our reforms. He wanted us to maintain the truth and the right, and to be a distinctively holy people. The last letter I got from him before he started upon his Western tour — which proved in my estimation the fatal tour of his earthly career — he sat down and wrote to me a short note. He evidently had been in the office, engaged in earnest wrestling prayer; said he, "Brother Kinney, join me in praying that our Churches may be set on fire of God." Oh, how my heart responded, and how I have endeavored to keep that request. And as I learn in the departing moments of our brother; getting a glimpse of the glory that was being revealed, and uttering, perhaps, in not the clearest articulation, but yet the sentiment that, "There is rest in the skies." I feel that there is rest in the glory of God's grace, or rather, taking the language of a letter not long since received, that there is, 'room in God's golden, spiritual chariot for us all to ride.' By his help and grace I mean to ride there, and I expect to greet our dear departed brother in the skies where 'there is rest.' "

Rev. D. D. Lore, D. D., Editor of the *Northern Christian Advocate.*

"Dearly beloved Christian brethren; my friends and myself, are here this afternoon to express to you our deep sympathy in your affliction, and our Christian love. We are not here for the purpose of eulogizing the brother which you have lost, You knew his worth, well. I have been impressed by the remarks made, and am satisfied, and indeed was satisfied before this, that he was a great and good man. You have lost from your branch of the Church of Christ, a leader; a strong and courageous leader; one who never feared to do the right. I loved brother Crooks personally.

"Similarity of profession brought us into contact. I met him frequently. I never met him without pleasure. I never met him without discovering real manhood. We differed with regard to some things, and why should we not differ. We agreed to differ. Yet I loved him as a Christian brother, and his name and memory in our Church, so far as he is known, I am sure is respected. He *commanded* respect as has been said by one of his brethren here.

"But we are not here to occupy time so precious, and it belongs to others who stood in closer relations to this dear man than we stand; — closer in many respects, but not closer in others. We are one in spirit. We are all brethren in Christ Jesus. We look forward together through the blinding tears of earth, to that happy day when we shall meet with our Savior in yonder brighter clime, and there greet each other as one common band of brothers. "May God bless the afflicted Church," is the prayer of those I am permitted to represent here. May God bless you, dear brethren, and may you be a light in the world, set for holiness of heart and of life, pushing forward the victories of the Cross."

Rev. L. N. Stratton of the *American Wesleyan.*

"It is almost useless for me to attempt to say anything to-day. No words I might use could express the feeling of my heart. Language is lame; it goes limping after thought. The intimate relationship that I sustained to brother Crooks as co-editor, was such as to place us in constant communion with each other. We saw each other by day and by night; at all hours and all seasons. I loved him much. The death of no one outside my own family relations could have caused me such deep sorrow as his own departure. But he is gone. In my dreams he comes back. He gives me counsel again as he did while here. He came to my office, as it seemed to me, night before last, to tell me something, as he has often done in the past.

"He had peculiarities that fitted him, especially for the leadership that he had. He turned back for no storms. He was courageous. There was no night so dark as to keep him at home when duty called him away; no train going so late at night, or so early in the morning that he could not take it. The miles were not too many, nor the roads too bad, nor he too weary, to fill his engagements at the hour. If the railroad station were twenty miles from where he might labor on the Sabbath, and he should take a train at six o'clock on Monday morning, he would be there, even if he had to travel the distance through rain und darkness, in an open wagon. There was no effort that it was too hard for him to make, and make cheerfully. He dared everything. He rode over everything. He *made* events, as it seemed, if they did not occur. He bent all his energies with a will that was ruthless, to push forward the enterprises m which his soul was enlisted. We never, it seems to me now, shall see his like again. But God knows. He can raise up such agencies as he wants, and can do his work without any of us if he wishes us removed. Oh, how gladly would I be there in that coffin, if that would place him here! But God knows best. He is our leader. Jesus is our friend; and more than ever I feel like putting my head on his breast and saying, 'Thy will be done.'

"In our prayer-meetings our dear brother has especially been remembered. I suppose a few nights since, when there were so many engaged in prayer for his recovery, that victory would turn for us. For at first it seemed to us that we could not, must not have it so; but at length all said, 'Thy will, God, be done,' I then looked for victory, but God knew best, and it is done.

"A great load rests upon our hearts, upon our lives, upon our Connection. We who are brethren in this work, must lift the harder now, that the weight rests upon us the more heavily.

"Our brother was a man who had a kind word for everyone. He was kind in his affections for all denominations of the Christian Church. I see around me here brethren of whom I have heard him speak so highly — brethren in the ministry. Could I speak his words again, how gladly would I give them to these brethren of other Churches, who mourn with us his sad loss. His voice we shall no more hear; but his words of admonition and encouragement rest in our hearts and in our memories. We shall cherish them. We pray that God may fit us for all he is fitting for us r and help us to bear the burdens that are resting upon us.

"My dear friends, let us be just what the Lord would have us to be, that we may meet our dear brother in the Paradise of God."

Rev. N. Wardner, President of Champlain Conference.

"Sad— deeply, solemnly sad is this funeral hour. Soul's fondest ties are riven, and the falling tears of sable widowhood, in silent, speechless grief give evidence that the soul's full fountain of sorrow is broken up. Friends from near and far gather, and their mingled sighs and tears say, 'See how they loved him.' For a prince and a great man is fallen in Israel to-day; but thank God, fallen with his well girt armor bright with use, and his face toward the foe. For, our dear brother, in whatever moral conflicts he was engaged, dared to do right and to suffer for that right doing if need be. Early in life he laid his heart, his body, his all at the foot of the Cross, and Heaven sanctified the offering. And he went forth to labor in his Master's vineyard clothed with power, and when — I remember with gratitude — when freedom and oppression grappled in mortal conflict in our land, down in the Carolinas, his voice echoed the notes of a freedom-loving Gospel. In the very teeth of oppression, our brother spoke words of liberty. He dared to beard the lion in his lair, and though a ruthless mob thrust him into a loathsome, Southern prison, yet he lived to bless his own liberty and to see the soul of a nation's martyred President go up to God with the broken manacles of four millions of freed men in his hands. And on those blood-rusted manacles there were scars methinks, made by the burnished steel of our brother as he wielded the sword of eternal truth for liberty and the right. Who wonders that a man who dared to stand and defend the right in the face of any and every oppression; who wonders that to day — a leader as he was, and revered and loved as we learned to revere and love him— that we gather about his bier and shed tears of affection; pearly drops of love; for we loved him, and the Church bows with speechless grief, and through eyes suffused with tears, looks up and struggles to say, — Heaven help us to say — 'Thy will be done.' The cause of reform with which he was identified in every phase, bows and weeps; for a friend is gone. That heart, that hand, that voice which is still to-day was identified with every good word and work. Every holy enterprise found a place in his heart, in his sympathies, in his prayers. May his falling mantle wrap some spirit with the same devotion: the same consecration; yea, wrap many."

"Mysterious are the ways of Providence; a busy Providence does not stop to explain all its whys and wherefores, and yet, I suppose, dear sister Crooks and afflicted friends, the light of Heaven will dispel all the darkness and mystery that may be gathered around this affliction from the hands of Providence. Look up to the light. For just beyond these heavy clouds blazes the sunlight of eternal glory. Our brother Kinney has told us, that our departed brother with his dying lips sought to speak what methinks his vision saw of life, bliss and heaven — 'There is rest beyond the skies. There is rest beyond

136

the skies.' Ah! — it is labor *here*, it *was* labor with him; he coveted it; he threw his giant arms around it and prayed Heaven to sustain him in it. It is rest *now* for him; let it be labor for us. Though he was our leader we mourn, and it is right we should mourn; we can but mourn. Yet yonder, on a throne, high and lifted up, sits One who will lead us; and methinks, amidst the storm which has gathered around us, though the vessel heaves and rocks beneath the tempest's power, I hear a voice above the sound of the waves, 'It is I: be not afraid; trust thou in Me and all shall be well.'"

The choir and congregation then united in singing the first two verses of the 808th hymn.

Rev. E. Gaylord, of Syracuse, dismissed the congregation with the benediction.

The choir sang,

"Asleep in Jesus!— blessed sleep!"

as the large audience moved around to view the remains. Finally the coffin was closed and the remains were borne away to the hearse and the charnel house in Oakwood. There the coffin was reopened, and the relatives took the final leave; the affectionate wife placing tenderly a rich bouquet of white flowers beside the cheek of her precious one, as the last kind act of affection before the final adieu. This done, the coffin was closed and lowered into the outer case, and left in the house of the dead to await the choice of a burial-place. The carriages were refilled, and we all mournfully passed away through the chilly evening air, leaving the mortal part of our beloved brother in its cheerless bed. Let him rest — he has often wearied; let him be quiet now, for often has he borne the weight of the charge on the battlements of sin. Revered, honored, loved; the memory of his name is fragrant with affection, and its mention will be a battle-cry to all our Churches.

Expressions of Sympathy and Appreciation

Letter from Rev. L E, Royce.

And so my dear brother Crooks sleeps. Fifty years on earth, and then away to the cloudless land. I saw him first Sept. 2nd, 1851, then twenty-seven years of age. As members of the same Conferences, we were intimate for seventeen years, and for twenty-three we have met every year save one. In August I saw him for the last time. For three days we occupied the same room and the same bed. Our last night together we talked late and lovingly, all the years of our past were gone over. Much that he said was spoken in confidence and must not be repeated. He impressed me in that night's talk with his singular honesty, and manly affection. I have thought that leadership had made him a little forgetful of old friends. The thought perished in the warm words of that midnight hour. Indeed I found his love as green as a maiden's and as steady as the star. I have loved him so much, I want, with a trembling hand, to drop one little flower on his grave. With a figure so commanding, a voice so full and rich, an experience so Christian, a mind so well stored with practical truths, he could have stood in the first pulpits, with an executive and financial skill possessed by but few; he could have made for himself a grand record in connection with any of the great boards. He chose to stay with a people who, in the eyes of the world, were feeble, and with a small human prospect of a permanent future. In this he proved his loyalty to heart-convictions and shamed others, who for place and pelf put these convictions under their feet. I know not that he leaves his wife stocks or money — he leaves her what is better,— "a good name." I weep for him as for the kindred of my Father's house, and extend to her whose soul is now filled with sorrow my prayerful sympathies. I have seen his birth-place. I write within a few miles of where he entered wedded life. I hope after a little to see him on the shining shore." Till then I pray for his courage and endurance.

Memorial Meeting.

The sad news of the death of Rev. Adam Crooks, editor and publisher of the *American Wesleyan*, of Syracuse, N. Y., formerly for many years pastor of the Wesleyan Church of this city, was received by his many friends and personal acquaintances with extreme sorrow and universal regret. An impromptu memorial service was held at the church Sunday morning, December 27th, when appropriate remarks were made by the pastor, Rev. J. E. Carroll, Rev. Mr, Sturtevant, M. B. Clark, James Christian and others, all breathing the most intense sorrow at the death of Mr. Crooks, and expressive of their admiration of him as a Christian minister and friend.

Memorial Resolutions.

At the regular meeting of the Syracuse Ministerial Association, held at the parlors of the Fourth Presbyterian Church, December 2 1st, 1874, the committee reported the following resolutions, which were unanimously adopted.

Whereas, Since the last meeting of the Syracuse Ministerial Association its circle has been broken by the death of one of its most respected and honored members, Re V, Adam Crooks, D. D., therefore

Resolved, That this association has received the sad tidings of the death of our brother Crooks with most sincere and heart-felt sorrow.

Resolved, That his firmer and decided Christian character, his eminent Christian zeal and courage, his untiring energy in every good word and work, his spirit of quick and fraternal sympathy, his determined adhesion to his principles and his confessed abilities, have endeared him to his brethren of this association and given him a high place in their respect.

Resolved, That we tender the deep and sincere sympathy of this association to his bereaved wife and kindred.

Resolved, That we convey our heart-felt condolence to the denomination which in the death of Dr. Crooks has suffered the loss of an acknowledged leader.

(Committee:) Nelson Millard, J. L. Darsie, H. A. Sizer, M. L. Berger, A. F. Beard.;

From Religious Telescope.

A truly great man in Israel has fallen. Rev. Adam Crooks, of the *American Wesleyan* Connection, died the 15th of December, aged fifty years. For a number of years he had been the publishing agent and one of the editors — part of the time sole editor — of the *American Wesleyan*, and treasurer of most or all of the Connectional Boards. In these positions he displayed remarkable power, especially as a financier. He was almost the soul of these important departments of the Connection, and the last years of his life were, to a considerable extent, given to the raising of a fund for the building of a publishing house. At the time of his death, though the Wesleyans are not strong, numerically, twenty-two thousand dollars had been secured. As a servant of God and a leader of an heroic division of the army of Christ, he was an extraordinary man. Well may the Wesleyan people especially, and true Christians generally, regard with sincere grief the departure of this noble leader in Christ's Church militant.

During the years when the foolish attempt to unite the non-episcopal Churches into one Church gave so great an impetus to disintegration in the Wesleyan Church, Mr. Crooks stood as the chief standard-bearer of his Church, and exercised an influence which was blessed of God as the chief means of saving that denomination from dissolution, and in turning again in its favor the tide of prosperity. His labors, the past ten years, will give luster to some of the most important pages in the history of a Church which has been more useful in its influence on other Churches, perhaps, than in its own direct work, which has been evangelical and heroic. He had typhoid fever while visiting the Western Conferences last Fall, and, probably owing to an energy which denied him that absolute rest from cares and labors which his condition demanded, he at last yielded before continued disease, and fell asleep in Christ, at his home in Syracuse, New York. To his worth as a man, as a Christian minister and editor, the tears of his co-laborers and of his people, the tribute of the ministers and members of other Churches of Syracuse, especially the editorial fraternity there, bear strong testimony. The great leader fell when all eyes were turned to him as a trusted one, but fell when his people had reached a point where others could, better than ever before, move forward, leading the Church which he loved so well and for which he had toiled so hard, in the pathway of safety, and to still greater victory and prosperity.

As a preacher, editor, and financier, Mr. Crooks was no ordinary man. In him were combined, in a remarkable degree, gentleness and energy, discretion and courage, tolerance and radicalism.

Twice have we heard brother Crooks preach before a Conference, and we have enjoyed his company in our home. He was a genial, pious, whole-souled man. And his person and bearing contributed not a little to his influence as a preacher and leader. In the language of Dr. Lore, he was "the very personification of mature manhood; large and powerful in physique, active and energetic, calm and dignified in mien, he seemed to be the man of the multitude, formed to bear burdens, made to live." He was the very embodiment of caution and boldness, courtesy and firmness. As a preacher, he was clear and able, spiritual and inspiring, ever faithful to truth and to the right His eloquence possessed strength rather than polish, grandeur rather than the flowers of rhetoric and elocution. There was, however, in his ser mons, a surpassing moral and spiritual beauty combined with other essential elements, which, in the estimation of either the learned or the unlearn ed, constitute the God-chosen teacher or leader Both times we heard him, his sermons were worthy of the body of intelligent ministers present and still "the common people heard him gladly." To our departed friend and Christian brother, to our fellow-worker in the gospel vineyard, to our co-laborer in the great cause of moral reform, to the patient sufferer and successful toiler, to the great leader and now crowned hero, we pay this feeble tribute, and answer back, Farewell! But our farewell is not forever. With thousands that have revered and loved him, we hope to greet him among the glorified when the voice of Him whose throne is ever on the side of truth, purity, and holiness, and against deception, sin, and iniquity, shall call his servants from labor to reward, from bearing the cross to wearing the crown.

From Methodist Recorder.

"The last *American Wesleyan* comes draped in mourning at the loss of its editor, brother Adam Crooks. It seems that his over work at the Fall Conferences, and in the office and pulpit since, has prematurely removed this busy man from the ranks of Christian laborers. He was a devoted servant of the Church of his choice. He was not only the editor of the weekly paper, but the treasurer of several Boards, and the adviser and friend whom pastors sought from all parts of the Connection. He was a strong man, physically, intellectually and spiritually; a true reformer, upright, honest, straightforward, and full of faith and hope. The Wesleyan Church will miss her valiant leader. He was true to his paper, true to his people, and true to God. We join in sincere lamentation with our sister household of faith, and mingle our tears with hers at the grave of a good and an eminently useful man. He loved liberty more than position, truth more than fame, his little, earnest, united, and zealous Church more than the popular sects with all their emoluments and honors. Peace to the ashes of our dear, dead brother. We hope to overtake him in the land of rest."

From Northern Christian" Advocate Published at Syracuse.

"The death of this Christian brother shocked our citizens by its suddenness on Tuesday, the 15th inst. We had been accustomed to see him in our streets, the very personification of mature manhood, large and powerful in physique, active and energetic, calm and dignified in mien, he seemed to be the man of the multitude formed to bear burdens, made to live, but he has fallen in the day of his strength, amidst a multiplicity of cares, and apparently when most useful and most needed. Brother Crooks stood as the head and representative of the American Wesleyan Church. He was Editor and Agent of the publication department, and Treasurer of the various Connectional funds, and benevolent institutions. In these respects, the Church, humanly speaking, depended entirely upon his ability and energy. He took this position when Dr. Prindle resigned and many others, leading men of the Wesleyan Church, judging it better to abandon their organization and return to the Methodist Episcopal Church. Many of their prominent men did so. A crisis had come in their Church affairs, and dissolution seemed imminent. At this juncture brother Crooks threw himself into the breach, and as one of the speakers at the funeral said, became their Moses, and cried "Go forward." It is not, perhaps, too much to say, that if there had been no Adam Crooks at that crisis, there would have been no American Wesleyan Church now; certainly it would not have been what it now is. His loss to the Church as far as human foresight can see is irreparable.

"Brother Crooks was a devoted Christian minister, moulded after the strictest New Testament pattern. He was a man who never chaffered with duty, he knew only to do right and was ready to meet the consequences. He was religious in his emotions as well as in his principles. His Christian experience was mature, rich, and mellow and bright. We were brought into communication with him frequently as a brother-editor, and always found him genial and manly. At the time of his death he was but fifty years of age and had been in the ministry about thirty years. Although he had been sick for some weeks, up and down with fever, contracted during a western tour of Conference visiting as agent of the Church, neither he nor his friends supposed his end was so near. Death came unexpectedly to all. Only a few moments before he died, he seemed to catch a glimpse of the open door through which he was to pass out from this to the other world. He said in haste to his wife, "Quick, quick," and drew her to him and kissed her, and murmured indistinctly that there was rest — and soon after ceased to breathe. "He rests from his labors and his works do follow him."

From the Christian Cynosure.

Our beloved brother Crooks is gone over the silent river before us. We shall not attempt his biography.

Mr. Crooks took the helm. As was said of Gen. Hamilton, "He touched the dead carcass of the public credit and it stood up." He restored the dilapidated business of the Book Room at Syracuse. The paper *American Wesleyan* became self-sustaining. Without a particle of sectarian feeling, he aided in saving his denomination. H a true New Testament bishop without either the human prerogative or the name. He was almost ready to commence the erection of a new National Publishing House at Syracuse; and there stood around him godly and good men who are opposed to the world's evils, and who, it is hoped and believed will carry to completion his designs.

> "Thou hast fallen in thy armor
>   Thou beloved of the Lord;

141

With thy last breath crying 'Onward,'
  And thy hand upon the sword;
And we'll think of thee, O brother,
  In the trials yet to come,
In the shadow of the prison
  Or in cruel martyrdom."

Expression of the Connectional Boards on the Death of Rev. A. Crooks

In the course of temporal events, the afflictive portion of which we could not control, we the various Connectional Boards and Associations of the Wesleyan Methodist Connection of America are assembled. Under a deep sense of our obligation to, and dependence upon the infinite wisdom of Almighty God we would bow ourselves before the dealings of his hand, and ask his divine strength to be our portion through the severe trial which is now upon us. By the painfully sad circumstance of death, we miss to-day the presence, counsel and encouragement of our dearly beloved Agent and Treasurer, Rev. A. Crooks, and we cannot refrain from expressing, by these few words, some slight sense of our great bereavement.

Taking charge of the Connectional finances as he did at a time when there was scarce a dollar in the treasury, and the means for further conducting the publishing interests were alone in the hands of a people who had everything to dishearten and discourage them, there seemed little to hope for, save the deliverance of that God, who is able to subdue his enemies, and bring strength out of weakness. As the years passed on, the people learned that it was safe to trust their new Agent. None feared any alienation of their funds, or that their confidence would in any way be misplaced.

Since that time, many times ten thousand dollars have been paid to him for the various Connectional enterprises of our people, and twenty-two thousand dollars pledged toward a new Publishing House. With the faithful, trustful spirit which was characteristic of himself, the people have rallied to the support of the great principles of our denomination, and beneath his financial and Christian leadership, unexpected successes have been attained.

His large experience and close observation, his cool judgment and undaunted faith, made him a valuable adviser, a true friend, and a safe and prudent manager of the Connectional finances entrusted to his care. Thousands of persons had submitted their individual cases to his careful advice, and not less than thirty thousand people, within and outside of his denomination had known, loved and trusted him.

But he is gone. His voice is hushed at the head of the hosts of God's moral army. His toils are passed, his work is done, and he has passed within the sweet and hallowed quiet of his eternal rest. He has left the companionship of his old friends and associates, and left them to work on, without the advantage of his experience, observation and advice.

But we cannot believe that any who are grounded Jn. the faith of the gospel of our Lord Jesus Christ, and who cling to the distinctive principles of *American Wesleyan*ism, but have such faith and principles, not simply because our brother had faith in them, but because they believe those principles to be founded on justice and the eternal rock of truth. And now that he has fallen in the harness of the battle, at the head of the fearless band he led, no true soldier of the Master will, we believe, feel like falling back, or "bating one jot of heart or hope." The Grand Captain of our salvation still lives, and we believe will lead us on to victory. Perhaps we were trusting too much in our dear brother, and now the God of the armies of Heaven and earth wishes to show us that He who can thresh a mountain with a worm, can lead us to success without any distinguished human agency.

When we have suffered the loss of leaders in other times, our brethren remaining have rallied to duty as never before; and now, perhaps, it remains that all our "Churches shall be set on fire of God" in seeking to work up to the high point of the personal Christian experience which was lived and taught by our devoted brother.

We can but pause in sorrow to drop our tears of grief above the dust of our departed leader. But for the sake of the perishing souls for whom he labored, and Christ died, we will arise, and with hearts undismayed, press forward to duty to the end of our days. And we would exhort brethren everywhere to rally to the high responsibilities resting upon them. Let there be no sluggards now. And if every one will "look beyond the watchman" to the God of the armies of Israel, we may see such a forward movement as never occurred even in his own day. And it may come to pass that he who slew his thousands in his lifetime, may slay his tens of thousands by the influence of his own death. God is our leader, in him will we trust, -- **Published by Order of the Boards.**

The following tracts are among the last of Mr, Crooks' writings. It is thought advisable to give them this form, in order that their circulation may be extended, and their influence widened; and that they may be preserved to bless those who read, for years to come.

Counsel to Converts

The most memorable epoch in 'the soul's history is the time of its espousals to Christ. From that moment there is a vitalizing and felicitating union between it and the Father, Son and Holy Ghost, to find its high and holy complement amid the measureless ages of immortality. But in spiritual laws and habits it is but an infant almost without experience and without knowledge. To begin right and to grow and develop in the spiritual — in eternal life, is of unspeakable importance. Hence please read, with fervent prayer, these earnest words of counsel.

1. Be certain beyond the possibility of mistake as to the fact of conversion. Do not rest in the judgments of others. Know for yourself. Do not settle down satis-

fied while there is a lingering shadow of doubt. The matter is too important to allow of doubts. Be sure your experience is scriptural. Here are some scriptural evidences. — Peace with God. The Apostle says, "Therefore being justified by faith, we have peace with God." This peace consists in a sweet tranquillity of soul arising from pardon and conscious reconciliation. God has pardoned us, and we are reconciled to him — are at-one with him — all antagonism has ceased. Love of Christians, is another evidence. "By this we know we have passed from death unto life, because we love the brethren." This is much more than a mere respect for Christians. Most persons have this. But it is a knitting of soul with soul — an instinctive drawing to Christians, as a part of ourselves, or as belonging to the same -family — a secret, but strong spiritual affinity. New interest in, and better understanding of the Bible, resulting from having the eyes of the understanding opened, is another evidence. — Love of enemies — conscious communion with God — minding spiritual things — having keen spiritual appetite and relish — are all evidences of conversion. But though scriptural and valid, yet these are all inferential. We have peace with God; love the brethren; love our enemies, &c. &c, therefore we are converted. But there is a higher evidence, — There is the direct witness of the Spirit. We may argue that because we see, and hear, and love and hate, and enjoy, and suffer &c, that therefore we exist; that it is conclusive. But aside from all this, there is a consciousness of existence, So too, aside from all inferential evidence, there may be a direct consciousness of spiritual life. This is the witness of the Holy Spirit. Let no convert stop short of this highest evidence. It is of infinite importance to begin right — that the conversion is both genuine and thorough.

2. Bear every cross. This is a fundamental condition of discipleship. At the very outset of your Christian career settle it well to shun no cross, however heavy. Every time the cross is borne there will be an increase of strength' with con-scious Divine approval. Every time you bear the cross you will learn more and more, that at least one half of it is borne by the Savior. When lifted, it is not so ponderous as it had seemed; and every successive time it is lighter than the pre-ceding. On the other hand, when shunned, the cross grows heavier and heavier, until there is neither strength nor fortitude to take it up. As one has beautifully said, "The cross is like the wings of a bird. The bird must bear its wings, and then the wings bear the bird." You will find this to be eminently true. Then, from the first, be cross-bearing Christians. There are none others.

> "Bold to take up, and firm to sustain
> The consecrated cross."

3. Be zealous workers. The Churches have too many drones already. You are wanted for no such purpose. Just in proportion as you are a blessing to the Church will the Church be a blessing to you. The Church and world are filled with backsliders, because filled with idlers. By all means find something to do for Je-sus. Seek to be useful. Be *earnest* workers. Your alternative is *work or die!* By all means let these words characterize you truly — "Zealous of good work." The command of the Master to each and to all is, "Go work to-day in my vineyard." Be strict in your obedience to this Divine command; and "ready to every good word

and work." Do something for Jesus each day, and not only will you not backslide, but you will be a healthy, happy, useful, growing Christian.

We repeat it — The one alternative is — *Work or die.* Action is a law of spiritual, no less than of natural life and development. It is palpable that in the absence of life there can be no intelligent, well-directed, effective and remunerative action. And it is equally true that in the absence of such action there can be no healthful, growing, happy, vigorous, spiritual life. In such case, there may be the form without the power— the body without the soul; the shadow without the substance, the corpse without the shroud and coffin; but little more is possible. You do not wish to belong to an army of corpses, an assemblage of skeletons, a "valley of dry bones;" or even disciplined infants, invalids, dyspeptics and dwarfs. What miserable substitutes these, for spiritual athletes and giants! Not enough that a mere tithe of the professed soldiers of Christ, are pressing the battle with the vigor of desperation. 'Twere madness to even hope for brilliant achievement until the whole army comes into such determined action. — "The kingdom of heaven suffereth violence, and the violent take it by force." Among the Lacaedemonians, every citizen was a soldier. So let it be with you. Let every man, woman and child professing to love the Lord Jesus, "come up to the help of the Lord, to the help of the Lord against the mighty."

4. Be scrupulously conscientious. "Shun all appearance of evil." Never give the devil the benefit of your doubt. Never allow large margin between sin and holiness. Draw the lines sharply and distinctly. Never be found in proximity with Satan's territory. Make the distance between you and it as great as possible. For every temptation have a *prompt* and *emphatic* No! Thoughts of evil, when indulged, instantly become evil thoughts. These are the only doors through which the devil can gain entrance into the heart, As you regard the life and liberty of your souls, keep these doors well bolted, and you are comparatively safe. But without this there absolutely can be no safety. "Lust, when it hath conceived, bringeth forth sin;" and "the wages of sin is death." Avoid every wrong. Practice every right. Do every duty. Be strictly, scrupulously, uniformly conscientious. Keep your conscience as the apple of the eye of your soul. *Prefer death to sin.*

> "What conscience dictates to be done
>   Or warns me not to do;
> This teaches more than hell to shun,
>   That more than heaven to pursue."

5. Too much account cannot be made of prayer. "Pray without ceasing." "Instant in prayer," — ready for it at all times. "Praying ail prayer and supplication in the Spirit." — For everything we need. "Pray everywhere"— in secret — in family — in social and business walks — in the great congregation. "Lifting up holy hands without wrath and doubting." — no sin in the hand — no wrath in the mind — no doubting in the heart. Emphatically, the Christian life is one of prayer.

> "Prayer is the Christian's vital breath;
>   The Christian's native air, —
> His watch-word at the grates of death,—
>   He enters heaven with prayer."
> "But pray with faith in Jesus' name."

145

Just as well hope to live physically without breathing, as to live spiritually without praying. Prayer exhales sin, and inhales holiness — exhales the human, and inhales the divine — exhales self and inhales God! To cease to pray is to cease to live.

6. Study the Bible much, and make it your guide. Read good books; counsel with Christians; give good heed to preaching; but allow none of these, nor all of them together, the place of the Bible. Make the Bible alone, the ultimate rule of faith and practice. Young converts often select out eminent Christians as their patterns, thinking if only as good as these, that is all they could hope. But even a Paul could only say, "follow me as I follow Christ." Christ is the only perfect model, and the Bible the only sure guide. A neglected Bible — neglected closet, and a neglected Christ, is salvation neglected.

7. Seek to be useful. There are a thousand ways in which to do good. Reckon that day as lost which records no good accomplished — no word of caution, reproof, or comfort spoken— no deed of charity done— no look of pitying kindness given. So taught even Pythagoras, a heathen philosopher. Let the sun go down upon no such day of your life. Do not be mere absorbents — mere receptives of good; but give out good in return. "Freely ye have received; freely give." Let heart, and hand, and feet, and tongue, and eyes be avenues for the out-flow of good to others. Seek to be eminently wise and good, that you may be thus eminently useful. And be ready for any errand of mercy, any post of service that Heaven may appoint. Shine like the sun; not for *yourself,* but for *others*. But *shine!* Make mountain and valley lustrous with the light of intelligent Christian example. If others are indifferent, or walk in darkness, let not the fault lie at your door.

8. Be punctual in the observance of all the means of grace, private and public. These are your spiritual meals, and regularity is essential to spiritual health and growth. Never suffer business nor any earthly interest to encroach upon these.

9. Be select of your companions. Not that they must be of the *rich* and *cultured;* but they that belong to the *royal family of Heaven.—* And not merely nominal, worldly, unspiritual, and lukewarm formalists; but those who live nearest the summit of the mount of heavenly communion. And read none but the best of books. Select your companions from among the spiritual giants and Princes of the House of Israel.

10. Do not be too much the subject of mere emotions. Not evanescent emotions, but fixed principles; not delight but duty; not greatness, but goodness; not happiness, but holiness; not rapture, but running; not words, but wisdom; not lust, but love; not glory, but God? Too many mistake here. *Be sure you do not.* It leads either to sensuosity in religion, or otherwise to measuring our grace by the false rule of mere feeling. Shun this rock.

11. Studiously avoid spiritual pride. "Esteeming others better than yourselves." As above, *goodness,* not *greatness.* Rejoice in the successes of others. Let there be no bitter jealousies, envying, strife, or evil speaking. The largest corn and fattest pastures are found in the valleys. So do Christian graces grow best in the valley of true humility.

12. From the first, learn to be liberal. "The liberal soul shall be made fat." "The Lord loveth a cheerful giver." As Wesley taught— Get all you can — honestly of course; save all you can; give all you can. Get and save not to hoard; but that you

146

may have wherewith to give, Just as well talk of a sober sot, as of a stingy Christian.

13. Never rest satisfied in present attainments. But, taking the Apostle's rule, forgetting things behind, and reaching to those before, press toward the mark, for the prize of the high calling of God in Christ Jesus. Higher! — and still higher!!

Do these things, and thou shalt not only save thyself, but also many others.

PLEA FOR HOLINESS

Holiness is personal purity. It combines the two conditions of the absence of all that is wrong, and the presence of all that is right — complete death to sin and life to righteousness. It is pre-eminent personal. Separate from the individual, there can be no holiness. It does not consist in externalities, nor yet in mere emotions, but in a *fixed state of the heart.* Upon both of these points there has been vast confusion. Implanted in the heart, it finds certain development in the life. Its highest statement is loving God with all the heart, soul, mind and strength, and loving our neighbor, (friend or foe,) as ourselves. Not that we are to approve either the character or conduct of our foes. — God does not approbate his enemies. — But we must have for them no malignity — nothing contrary to good-will. But perforce of an eternal law of our being, to thus love God we must be like him. We must be "created anew after the image of God in righteousness and true holiness."" For "*like loves its like*" But the object of these lines is a *plea* for holiness.

1. God commands it. His language is plain, pointed, and positive. "Be ye holy; for I the Lord your God am holy." This of itself is sufficient. When God commands, let angels and men obey. Holiness is the supreme law of the Moral Universe. If we would not be in vital antagonism with this great law, let us be holy.

2. Sin is essentially hateful and wrong; is hateful because wrong. For this reason God hates it with a perfect hatreds If he did not hate it with all the powers of his being he would be a sinner. Then, as we would not give place in our heart to that which is thus hateful in the eyes of God and of all sinless beings, let us be holy.

3. Sin is essentially subversive of the Divine Government. But this government is an infinite good, and its overthrow would be an infinite calamity. Who can fully estimate the magnitude of the consequences of the destruction of God's government. Surely none but God himself. Then if we would not allow that which would be thus disastrous to God and his boundless universe to attach to our deathless nature, let us be holy. Let us antagonize sin as we ought.

4. But again: — Sin shuts us away from communion with God. Out of fellowship with God and all the good. — Aye more; —in desperate warfare with all these: — who can abide the thought! Yet sin imposes and eternalizes this dreadful necessity. Yet holiness is the only door of escape from this direful calamity. To the account of sin is to be put down unmeasured evil, and to the account of holiness unmeasured good. Then by all this double possibility of good and evil, are we called to an existence of ceaseless holiness. Shall we hold ourselves proof against such motives as these? If not, let us be holy.

5. If we would bear a resemblance of God and all the good of the universe, we must be holy.

6. If our relationship to God and the virtuous of all worlds would be friendly, we must be holy.

7. If we would not be in identification with all the abominable of all worlds, we must be holy.

8. Without holiness, all our prayers and acts of worship must be without avail. Holiness is a condition fundamental to acceptable worship. If we regard iniquity in our heart — any iniquity — the Lord will not hear us.

9. Holiness is the life-principle of every form of virtue. Hence, in its absence, even these forms will eventually decompose and disappear.

10. By a powerful law of our being, we assimilate to those whom we venerate and love. The loving child becomes like his parent, and the admiring pupil like his preceptor. Love and admiration of the Divine Being are essential elements of holiness. Hence, by virtue of this law, holy moral agents become more and more holy: or more and more like God. Hence, too, the language of the great Apostle "But we all with open face beholding as in a glass the glory of the Lord, are changed into the same image from glory to glory, even as by the Spirit of the Lord." Hence, also, the "Beloved Disciple" — "We know that when he shall appear, we shall be like him; for we shall see him as he is." How distinct and marked this resemblance shall become by virtue of the operations of this law during an endless eternity, may not be thought nor told; but if holy, it shall stamp our eternal experience. And is it unreasonable to suppose that perforce of a law of like potency, the unholy and unhappy lost will wax worse and worse during eternal ages? All these tremendous results concenter upon the single condition of being holy. Then, how shall it be? Shall we spend our eternity in rising higher and higher in every moral excellence; approximating nearer and nearer the exact image of the Divine; or shall it be spent in sinking deeper and still deeper into unmeasured depths of moral deformity and obloquy? Reader: This tremendous question confronts your soul at each successive moment for decision. Oh, let it be made *now* in such manner as all the facts of time and eternity shall approve!

11. As sin is the greatest possible evil to moral agents, so is holiness the greatest possible good. Holiness alone can adjust our being in self-harmony, as in harmony with God, his law, and plans, and purposes, and the administration of the affairs of his boundless empire. Holiness renders all the infinite resources of Jehovah, and all the mighty forces at his command, tributary to the highest good of its possessor. Sin sets all these infinite resources and mighty forces at war upon the interests of its guilty perpetrator. Every where, all over the Divine nature and administration, may be seen written in emblazoned characters — **"Without Holiness none shall see the Lord."**

And now, dear reader: What is your attitude to these over-mastering truths? Are the infinite resources of Jehovah, with all the mighty forces of the universe at work for your highest good; or are their concerted activities effectuating your utmost ruin for time and eternity? The answer depends upon your relation to holiness. What is that relation? What shall it be? Can the fleeting pleasures of sin compensate the soul's eternal undoing? Surely not. Then, by all its priceless interests determine to be holy from this very hour. Let the decision render the memory of the hour precious and hallowed amid the peerless glories of the palace of God!

12. But in its far-reaching influences this subject is not limited to the individual moral agent. For, as it is written, "No man liveth unto himself." In the immediate and sundry relations of husband, wife, parent, child, brother, sister, friend, &c, &c, our character must affect for weal or for woe, the character and destiny of many others. Nor is this tidal-wave of contagion, — holy or sinful— confined to the immediate circle of relatives, friends and contemporaries; but with the ceaseless flow of time sweeps on to bless or blast countless thousands: — may be millions! Thus has the guilty taint of the sinning pair in Eden infected their countless progeny. So, in like manner, the blessed influence of the good is unconfined and undying. Shall we commit sad havoc among immortal souls until God's angel shall strike the knell of time? The subject is unspeakably awful. And were it possible, the pleadings and protests of unborn millions might well be in favor of the holiness of all now living. But in this they are wholly defenseless. Then let us make their cause our own, and for *their sakes* as well as *our own;* and as we would not, in the form of our influence, be guilty of committing *soul-murder during all time*, let us be holy.

13. Our final plea is made in the name of our adorable Savior. His mission to earth finds final culmination in man's holiness and happiness. Therefore, by his incarnation, poverty, passion, illustrious example, betrayal and denial, cruel mockings and scourgings, boundless sufferings and agonizing cry upon the cross; by his death, burial, resurrection, ascension and intercessions; by the gift of the Spirit, establishment of his Church and institution of his ministry; by all of these, as in one united call, are we importuned to be holy. If we are holy, we come into the rightful possession of all the blessed benefits of the atonement, both for time and eternity. But if not holy, the blood of atonement will cry for vengeance, as the guilt of all other sins combined cannot cry. This is the pivotal point upon which all turns. If holy, the atonement becomes to us the source of peerless blessings; but if not holy, the blood of the Son of God shed for our redemption thunders for our eternal undoing. Reader: How shall it be? Shall God's munificent expenditures for our salvation, be so perverted *by our own act*, as to deepen our eternal damnation? Awful thought! Shall we thus at once abuse God's boundless love, dash beyond the limits of recovery, the bliss of heaven, and plunge our souls beneath the fiercest waves of endless woe? If not, *we must be holy.*

The foregoing considerations appeal alike to all; but super-added to these are others which apply exclusively to Christians. Here are some of them.

1. If you would have power with God and man for good, you must be holy.

2. If you would not mar and scar the beauty and symmetry of the Church of God, and blight the healthy growth in grace in those with whom you are in holiest fellowship, you must be holy.

3. If you would not hold out false lights, and guide an already perishing world against the ruinous rocks of sin; if for the saving salt of holiness you would not give the world the fatal virus of sin, you must be holy.

4. If you would not be a false witness against Christ, and bring his matchless cause into disrepute with mankind, you must be holy. To be intrusted with the honor and reputation of Jesus, involves a fearful responsibility. If you would not basely betray this holy trust confided, you must be holy.

5. The Church is the conservator of the nations, and of the world. It is the salt of the earth, and the light of the world. If it does not sufficiently possess the conserving and saving properties, the nations must relapse into barbarism, moral rottenness and ruin. Here again are involved fearful responsibilities; and to fully respond to these, you must be holy.

Finally: It you would not transmit to coming generations a type of Christianity that will blast, blacken, and ruin souls, instead of blessing and saving them, you must be holy.

Thus, if you would be true to your own interests, and the interests of God, and of all others for time and eternity, you must be holy.

What do you say? What is your answer? Decide this great question now. — This instant.— Upon your knees before God! Will you now make a perfect offering of time, talent, ease, pleasure, property, reputation, friends, and if need so require, life itself? Will you keep this offering upon the altar *forever*? And making this offering a perpetual act, do you now take Jesus Christ as a Savior *from all sin*? **Will you be holy?**

May the great God, Father, Son and Holy Ghost help you! Amen.

Processes of Salvation

Salvation, in a gospel sense, means complete deliverance from sin, and thereby deliverance from its consequences, and the eternal exaltation of the soul and body to all possible perfectability and blessedness in heaven. The theme of salvation is the greatest of all themes. And the work of salvation is the greatest of all works. And although the entire work is expressed by the one word — salvation; yet it has its processes. Concerning some of these processes, vast confusion exists even in the minds of many Christians. Well-defined views upon this subject are of very great importance. Hence we would dissipate this confusion, and make each point as plain as possible.

The first step we name is *conviction.* This is a complex state, implying a knowledge of God and his law, with a pungent sense of guilt or of ill-desert because of the violation of this law. Now conscience is thoroughly awake and at work. And although this state may be wholly involuntary and even against the will, and therefore possesses no moral character, it is yet indispensable to salvation; for without it no one will seek salvation.

The second preliminary step in this process is *penitence.* By this we mean sincere sorrow over our past sins. Now sin begins to be seen and regarded in its true light, as exceedingly offensive to God, and detrimental to every interest of man, both for time and eternity. Now we begin in earnest to deplore our sinful state. The direct tendency of this sorrow is to produce repentance. Hence says the Apostle, "Godly sorrow worketh repentance." Not enough that we are deeply convicted; not enough that the soul is sorrowful because of sins committed. All this may be, and yet we persistently refuse to cease our sinning.

Another step must be taken — viz: *repentance.* Genuine repentance consists in a present and complete abandonment of all known sin, together with a determined struggle for deliverance therefrom. Mark! — Not a purpose to abandon sin after-while — nor yet to abandon some sins and continue to cling to others;

neither to abandon them for any limited period. But this abandonment, in purpose at least, must be *present, complete,* and *perpetual,* The surrender must be unconditional. The purposed obedience must be ab*solute and unqualified*, at any and every cost, be it life itself, otherwise our repentance is a sham and a mockery. It is to be greatly feared that in these times of shams and superficialities, the repentance of too many is only in the seemings. Reader! Has yours been *genuine* and *thorough?* If you would have your conversion genuine, your repentance must be thorough.

Repentance prepares the way for *justification*, or pardon. The soul may now be said to be in moral attitude to be forgiven. Not that repentance is in the least degree meritorious. For while it is fitting and indispensable, it yet in no sense, nor to any extent, merits pardon. The meritorious cause of our justification inheres exclusively in the complete atonement made by the sufferings and death of our Lord Jesus Christ; he having "by the grace of God, tasted death for every man." As the poet sings:

> "Jesus paid it all —
> All the debt I owe."

Hence, "God can be just and the justifier of him that believeth in Jesus." And hence again, the moment we cease our agonizing efforts to make ourselves better, or to free ourselves from guilt, and trust for salvation simply and confidingly in "the redemption which is in Christ Jesus," that very moment all our sins will be freely forgiven, and we shall stand justified before God as really and as fully as if we had never sinned. This act of pardon is at once instantaneous and complete. And now becomes *apropos* the simple and beautifully expressive language of the great Apostle, "Therefore being justified by faith, we have peace with God, through our Lord Jesus Christ." And with speechless rapture we can sing

> "My God is reconciled;
> His pard'ning voice I hear;
> He owns me for his child,
> I can no longer fear."

Coetaneous with pardon, and its invariable attendant, is *regeneration.* When freely pardoned by the Father, through the Son, we are, the same instant, regenerated by the Holy Ghost, adopted into the heavenly family, and receive the Spirit of adoption, "crying Father, Father." This work is instantaneous; done in a moment, in the twinkling of an eye. As regeneration is the unvarying concomitant or accompaniment of justification or pardon, theologians frequently employ the terms, justification and regeneration interchangeably, as designating the same state. The Scriptures characterize it — being born again — created anew in Christ Jesus — the love of God shed abroad in the heart by the Holy Ghost, and like forceful language. In all these processes the Holy Ghost has been active. — In producing conviction, contrition, repentance, inspiring the faith which trusts only in Christ for pardon; for "no man can say that Jesus is the Lord, but by the Holy Ghost" — active also in creating the heart anew, and then in witnessing to its own blessed work.

We would award to the justified or regenerate state all that the Scriptures authorize. In this state there exist all the Christian graces. The current of our being is reversed. Love is the soul's ruling impulse, and obedience is not only possible, but also delightful. A growth in the Christian graces is also possible; and indeed if justification is retained there must be this growth. At the moment the soul is regenerated it is conscious of nothing averse to love. It bears the image of Christ. In some sense, God is loved with all the heart — the heart is pure — sanctified — free from sin, in the sense of voluntary transgression — communes with God, and has an assurance of a title to heaven.

These things being conceded, many erroneously teach that beyond what is known as justification and regeneration, nothing is either necessary or possible. Then what are the facts? What is truth concerning this most important subject? We conceive it to be as follows:

1. Although at the time of regeneration the soul is unconscious of anything averse to the reign of love, yet in after experience and while enjoying a sense of the Divine favor, it becomes clearly conscious of the presence of appetites, passions, propensities, impulses, dispositions and tempers, unfriendly to the unqualified reign of our only Lord and Savior, and to yield to which is sin. Not that these are sin; but if allowed to become active or ruling, they develop into sin.

2. These propensities, impulses, &c., are traceable to and consequent upon the fall. But for the fall they would, with us, have no existence.

3. These adverse impulsions are not produced by volitions, but are back of and beneath the will, and ever and anon act upon it. They are interior fountains, deep within the citadel of the soul, ever ready to spring up and pour out their murky contents. And coming as they do within the field of consciousness, their presence cannot be denied. Hence they are distinctly noted by all trust-worthy theologians, as Wesley, Watson, Clarke, Cook, Fletcher, Finney, Buck, Dwight, Hill, Helffenstein, Lee, Foster, Dempster, &c. The Presbyterian Confession of Faith not only makes note of the presence of these tendencies to sin in the regenerate heart, but teaches also that they cannot be completely extirpated in this life. And all these authorities admit that when regenerated, the soul is, in a modified sense, pure and sanctified; but not that it is *wholly* pure and sanctified.

As Finney, Lee, and others clearly teach existing in the sensibilities as mere passive states, *they are not sin in the sense of transgression,*— -But (1.) To yield to them even in intention or by consent, in the absence of the opportunity to yield in the overt act, is sin. (2.) Being adverse of the Cross of Christ, and to his unqualified reign in and over the soul, it is his prerogative to cast them out. (3.) To make truce with them so far as to consent to their continued presence, while knowing that they may be cast out, is sin. In such case their very presence involves moral culpability. To make truce with the foes of Christ in any form, is criminally sinful. Hence relentless warfare upon those impulsions, is fundamentally necessary to continued justification. (4.) That these tendencies to sin are not cast out by regeneration is self-manifest, from the fact that usually, if not universally, they exist in the heart after it has been regenerated. (5.) Since mere regeneration, (being born again,) does not cast out these internal foes, their extirpation must, in this sense, and on this account, be a *distinct* work. This is as plain as that two and two equal four, or that a circle, square and triangle are not the same. And as sanctification begins with regeneration, the extirpation of those impulses and attendant baptism of the Holy Ghost, may on this account be called the continuance of the same work. It is the completion of a work begun in regeneration. Hence contention over the question whether it is a distinct work or only the same work continued to completion, is not wise; being more speculative than practical, and hence is styled by Mr. Wesley a "war of words;" and it may serve to divert attention from the *great* and *vital* work of having our internal foes extirpated, and the occupancy of the whole territory of the soul by the pure love of Christ. Being a distinct work, it very properly has a distinct designation. And being the completion of a work commenced in regeneration, it is very properly designated *entire* sanctification.

That this designation is in consonance with the teaching of Inspiration, as well as in accord with experience, is apparent in the light of the following with other passages of Holy Writ.

"Having therefore these promises, dearly beloved, let us cleanse ourselves from all filthiness of the flesh and spirit, perfecting holiness in the fear of God." 2 Cor. vii: 1. This passage clearly assumes (1.) That the Christians addressed may not have been cleansed from all filthiness of flesh and spirit. For why exhort to the doing of a work already completed? (2.) That there is such thing as an imperfect state of holiness; otherwise there could be no such process as "perfecting holiness."

"And the very God of peace sanctify you wholly; and I pray God that your whole spirit and soul and body be preserved blameless, unto the coming of our Lord Jesus Christ." 2 Thess. v: 23. As Dr. Lee well says— "This text supposes that sanctification in part without being entirely sanctified, is a possible condition; for it would be absurd to pray to be sanctified *wholly*, if there is no such thing as being sanctified in part without being wholly sanctified."

The foregoing truths furnish large margin for variety in the experience of Christians. Here is a soul regenerated; but on the one hand neglecting to cultivate the good, and on the other to suppress its tendencies to sin, hence apostatizes. A sad experience this, which fills the land with backsliders. Here is another with whom the warfare between the good infused, and the tendencies to sin not yet extirpated, is almost equal. He alternates between light and darkness, justification and condemnation, sinning and repenting. But little, if any, real progress is made. Alas, that this should be the exact experience of so many! Still another, not knowing his right to full gospel freedom, seeks no greater victory than to *control* his tendencies to sin — anger, pride, envy, jealously, love of the world, &c.; yet holding the evil in constant restraint it becomes less potent, while the good, carefully cultured, grows and strengthens. Here is steady progress; but not complete victory. Stoutly denying the possibility of complete deliverance in this life, the measure of experience, and the contest with its internal foes is ended only "down at the river." A fourth gains successive victories over these internal foes; and receives new baptisms of the Holy Ghost, just as those foes come conspicuously within the field of the soul's consciousness. Each successive victory is complete in *kind*, but limited in extent. Impulses adverse to spiritual life and growth, in ambush, still tenant the heart, until the last one is brought to view and cast out; each successive victory being attended with deeper and still deeper baptisms of the Holy Ghost, until the work of entire sanctification is completed. Dr. Lee styles this, *gradual* or *progressive* sanctification. But a fifth surveys the whole field of the soul's wants at one searching and appalling view. And oh, how appalling! He sees and feels the mighty work to be done; and is as *clearly* and *deeply* convicted of the necessity of a clean heart, as formerly of the necessity of pardon. In the strength of Divine grace the resolution if formed. The single sentiment of *"Victory or Death"* permeates every part and power of the deathless spirit, now stirred to its uttermost profound. The life-and-death struggle is terrible. For these internal foes die hard. Consecration of the entire being deeper, broader, higher than ever before reached, is now made; taking houses, lands, time, talent, reputation, friends, wife, children, life; *everything.* Faith in Christ as a *perfect* Savior and *all-conquering* Captain, measures up to the full demands of the occasion, and trusts him for complete deliverance from these tendencies to sin just as fully as it trusted him for pardon; and in a moment the mighty work is wrought-! — *Self dies,* that Christ may hold undisputed sway over the entire empire of the soul. Now ensue unutterable joy — the perfect Rest of Faith — a life of light and love — the sweet tranquillity of heaven.

Now, why admit the reality of the first four experiences above delineated, and deny the fifth, which is indefinitely the most glorious, and is attested by the open profession and holy lives of such shining names as Messrs. Fletcher, Bramwell, Carvosso, Nelson, Mrs. Hester Ann Rogers, Mrs. Fletcher, Lady Maxwell, and a host of others, God's noble men and women who testify that "the blood of Jesus Christ his Son, cleanseth from all sin?"

Reader! Does your name, of right, belong to this list? What does conscience answer? Shall it be there?

Between the extremes above indicated is margin for many shades of experience; and this variety in experience gives origin to variety in theories. We are now prepared to note some points of difference between the states of regeneration and entire sanctification. These are marked and well-defined.

1. The convictions preceding those states are different. Sinners are convicted of sin, guilt, and of the need of pardon and reconciliation. The regenerate are convicted of internal tendencies to sin, in the form of passions, propensities, tempers and dispositions, and are deeply conscious that continued justification and the favor of Heaven, are conditioned upon their extirpation. Of course this consciousness does not attach to those who do not apprehend the possibility of complete deliverance, in this life, from these impulsions to sin.

2. There is difference in the consecrations made. In the case of the repentant sinner, it is usually less or more confused, vague and limited; owing to abounding spiritual darkness. In the case of the soul intelligently seeking full redemption, the consecration is clear, well-defined, deep, broad, high, and all-comprehending.

3. There is a difference in the blessings sought. The repentant sinner seeks, believes for, and experiences pardon and reconciliation. Beyond this, the knowledge of his needs does not extend. The regenerate seek, believe for, and experience complete deliverance from the foes lurking within, with the attendant baptism of the Holy Ghost. One apprehends and trusts in Christ as a Savior from the guilt and dreadful consequences of sin. The other apprehends and trusts in

Christ as the complete deliverer from all indwelling tendencies to revolt and rebellion.

4. Hence there is a difference in those states themselves. With the regenerate, the tendencies to sin are only *controlled.* With the entirely sanctified they are extirpated. With the regenerate, there are deep undercurrents of the soul averse to a life of entire consecration — impulsions clamoring for both existence and indulgence. In the wholly sanctified, all those deep under-currents are friendly and helpful to a life of unqualified holiness. So that, so far as internal foes are concerned, the empire of the soul is left in peace.

5. Hence again: there is marked difference in the temptations of the two states. With the regenerate or partially sanctified, many of their temptations are from within, while with the wholly sanctified, they are from without. The regenerate are conscious of something within, in sympathy with suggested evil; while with the wholly sanctified, there is no such sympathy, but positive and intense antagonism to all known sin. The regenerate are often tempted *directly* to sin; whereas the wholly sanctified seldom are. With these, Satan, coming in the guise of an angel of light, operates upon and through something *in itself innocent,* or it may be *morally excellent;* to secure an illegitimate use of these. As in the case of Eve, her desire for food, or wish to be wise. Or in the case of Jesus — his hunger; or his perceived faith in Divine Providence, to cast himself from the pinnacle of the temple; or of his dread for terrible sufferings, as in the garden of "strong crying and tears." Sometimes he seeks to take advantage of the holiest sentiments of the soul, and mis-lead and mis-direct, — for example, our tender regard for the honor of God, and the success of his cause. On the one hand, he may seek to hold us back — we must have our faith to ourselves — must be *prudently* zealous — we must not be too forward, or we will be thought officious, and our power to do good thug be destroyed, — or on the other hand, he may urge us too fast and too far; and thus beguile into fanaticism; or as in the case of Paul, he may send a " messenger of Satan to buffet us" — a brother, or sister, or wife, or husband, or pastor, or private church-member, or sinners. But perhaps the master device of Satan in this regard, is to lead us, all undiscovered, to the excessive indulgence of that which, in itself, is innocent; such as love of husband, wife, children, reputation, or appetite, or native impulsions, in themselves entirely legitimate. At this point especially, there is necessity for eternal vigilance. Thus in a thousand ways Satan may buffet, annoy and embarrass those who are wholly sanctified. It is well to be wise, and know "The depths of Satan."

And just here it is in place to guard our readers against fatal mistakes. And,

1. Be slow to make your own experience the primal test of truth, respecting this great subject. Especially do not say — "When first converted, I was more happy, and loved more than at any period since; therefore there is no such thing as progress in the experience of salvation." Is not such an experience sadly defective? What meaneth the parable of the one, two, and five talents? The Scriptures and all nature, alike teach the doctrine of *progress.*

2. Do not mistake mere regeneration for entire sanctification. It may well be feared that there are those in the Church who are destitute of the grace of Canst; and, deeply conscious of the immense vacuum in their souls, come to Jesus humbly and devoutly, and being greatly blessed, assume that they are wholly sancti-

fied, while they have received nothing beyond justification; a blessing of which, up to this time, they were destitute.

3. Be particular not to mistake partial for complete sanctification. Be not deceived. Be *thorough.* Go to the very bottom in this experience. Leave no ground to doubt that either the consecration or the faith is complete.

4. With the utmost care guard against every species of fanaticism. Satan is just as well pleased to push us a little too far as to have us jail below privilege and duty. Hence, some believe themselves so much beyond where the Savior was, that they cannot be tempted. Others again think themselves so much in advance of the inspired Apostle, who said "we know but in part, and prophesy but in part," that they are away above mistake — have no need of the Scriptures; being in all things led by the Holy Ghost. And still others separate themselves from those dear children of God who have been only regenerated, and fellowship those only who are wholly sanctified; and thus produce schism in the body of Christ. By these and other devices, Satan succeeds in distracting the Church, and bringing the blessed doctrine of holiness into disrepute, and even ridicule. But of course it is no valid objection to a doctrine, that it can be *perverted.*

5. Too many, having professed entire sanctification cease their efforts for progress; forgetting that there is a fundamental difference between *purity* and *maturity.* By all means, and with all possible assiduity, avoid this error. The sanctified soul is only in good position for bolder flights into the measureless beyond. When fields are cleared of all wild-growth, we expect the grains to grow the faster, and the gathered harvests to be the richer. But in neglected fields, the enemy will sow tares. *Present grace can he retained only by getting more.* Neglected conformity to this fundamental principle in the economy of grace accounts for the sad fact that so few who profess entire sanctification succeed in retaining it. The honor of God and salvation of souls demand that this ruinous evil be remedied. When the demand of the age is spiritual athletes, shall we supply it with an army of infants? *This must not be.* But we proceed.

Distinct from the baptism of *purity*, is the baptism of *power.* The promises are distinct, and so are the blessings. How much the whole Church needs this mighty baptism! How her hallowed interests lie in waste from its want. How considerations weighty as the worth of souls and measureless as eternity, with voices, plaintive as the pleadings of Heaven's own pity, invoke the Church to a universal and perpetual Pentecost! Only this can make her "fair as the moon, clear as the sun, and terrible as an army with banners."

But still beyond, is *the sealing of the Holy Spirit.* As, in this life, the sinner can overleap the bounds of possible return to God, so this sealing "unto the day of redemption" make its possessor, quite as certain of the boundless bliss of heaven, as if already approved and crowned. Not that there is any absolute impossibility that they should sin, fall, and be lost; but only that all who know them are well persuaded that they will persevere and be eternally crowned. We do not unduly magnify the grace of God. Read the prayer of the inspired Apostle, Eph. iii: 16 — 21 — That they might be *rooted* and *grounded* in love — that they might know the love of Christ, which passeth knowledge — might be *filled with all the fullness of God* — and then, "unto Him that is able to do *exceeding abundantly above all that we ask or think.*" etc.

No, we do not exaggerate. Are we all "agonizing to enter in at the straight gate," and to come up to the full measure of privilege and duty? Reader, are *you* seeking to be thus *thorough?* Are you "forgetting things behind, and reaching to those before? Are you allowing those impulsions or tendencies, which if indulged, crystalize into sin, peaceable possession of a single inch of the territory of your soul; or is the entire being, with all and singular of appurtenances, consecrated to the undisputed reign of Jesus? Do you momentarily apprehend Christ your *complete* Savior? Do you live up to the highest point of Gospel privilege; or are you content to live below it? Can you live below privilege and be even justified? *But are you emptied of sin and filled with God?*

www.ingramcontent.com/pod-product-compliance
Lightning Source LLC
Chambersburg PA
CBHW051728040426
42447CB00008B/1030